The Transmission of Affect

Teresa Brennan

CORNELL UNIVERSITY PRESS

ITHACA AND LONDON

First published 2004 by Cornell University Press

First printing, Cornell Paperbacks, 2004

Printed in the United States of America

Library of Congress Cataloging-in-Publication Data

Brennan, Teresa, 1952–2003
The transmission of affect / Teresa Brennan.
p. cm.
Includes bibliographical references and index.
ISBN 0-8014-3998-1 (cloth : alk. paper) — ISBN 0-8014-8862-1 (pbk. : alk. paper)
1. Affect (Psychology)—Social aspects. I. Title.
BF531.B74 2003
152.4—dc22
2003019730

Cornell University Press strives to use environmentally responsible suppliers and materials to the fullest extent possible in the publishing of its books. Such materials include vegetable-based, low-VOC inks and acid-free papers that are recycled, totally chlorine-free, or partly composed of nonwood fibers. For further information, visit our website at www.cornellpress.cornell.edu.

Cloth printing   10 9 8 7 6 5 4 3 2 1

Paperback printing   10 9 8 7 6 5 4 3 2 1

Contents

TERESA BRENNAN was in the final stages of editing *The Transmission of Affect* in December 2002. On the night of December 9, she went out on an errand and was crossing the street when she was hit by an automobile. She never regained consciousness and died early in the morning of February 3, 2003. Dr. Brennan had been working on the finishing touches of her favorite chapter and reviewing the copyedited version of the manuscript on the night of the accident. The remaining review was completed by her long-time assistant and literary executrix, Woden Teachout, and her trusted researcher, Sandy Hart.

Foreword

Teresa Brennan

In Memoriam

I first encountered the inimitable Teresa Brennan ten years ago when I was a just-minted undergraduate, gone to England to seek my fortune, and wandering the vaulted halls of Cambridge University in search of gainful employment. On a bulletin board, which was evenly divided between job and housing notices, I spotted a small slip of paper with handwriting in blue ink. "Wanted," it read, "Amanuensis to help write a book." There was a telephone number, which I wrote down with a sense of rising good fortune. Next to it was another slip of paper with the same handwriting and the same blue ink. "Flat to Let," it advertised. The following description caught my eye. Instead of the usual phrases about sunny rooms, hardwood floors, or separate entrances—the type of details one might expect in a rental arrangement—the ad said simply, "Would suit feminist theorist." That settled it. Here was an intellectual, a feminist theorist, and (clearly!) an eccentric, and she wanted an assistant.

It was a mostly wonderful, sometimes difficult year. Teresa would pace her book-lined study, hair elegantly swept up, and speak her thoughts as they came to her. I sat at the keyboard and captured her words in text that glowed green-gold from the monitor. Often the telephone interrupted us, and Teresa would be off for hours as she wielded her persuasive powers and sultry voice on a colleague, an editor, or her bank manager. Sometimes she sent me off to the university library for sources; more often, she'd send me off for cigarettes. On those days when she got going, nothing would stop her. Her versatility amazed me. She'd move from third-world feminism to Marxist theory to Melanie Klein and somehow tie it all together in a coherent whole. "My critics say I have a nineteenth-century mind," she told me—but for her, such encompassing thinking was a point of pride. Teresa was not one to parse out small questions at the expense of her argument; she loved the reach and explanatory power of theory.

She was infinitely generous with her resources, with her friends, and with her time. For a research assistant, it was a dazzling honor to be invited to accompany her to her editor's offices in London, or to meet the editor of the *London Review of Books*, or to have dinner with one of the many eminent intellectuals with whom she was personal friends. Later, when I was in graduate school and she was teaching at the New School in New York City, she flew me there to work on a project and treated me to dinner every night. She was equally open-handed and open-hearted with all her students and assistants. She incited us to think boldly, she fostered our creativity, and she encouraged us in whatever field we had chosen. On more than one occasion she offered to coauthor an article or coteach a course. She hoped, at some point, to gather all her colleagues and mentees together in the Bahamas. She envisioned a community of friends and thinkers who would swim, write, and engage each other on the burning question of, in her favorite Lenin phrase, what is to be done.

Teresa surrounded herself with beauty. After she left Cambridge, England, she lived in a series of ever more enchanting places: Manhattan; Spy Pond in Arlington, Massachusetts; Ocean Ridge, Florida; and, finally, Spanish Wells in the Bahamas. She found gorgeous things immediately compelling. She would arrive home with an Egyptian bracelet, an elegant beach umbrella, or, on one memorable occasion, an entire carful of silk flowers. "Won't these be lovely over the pool in the Bahamas?" she asked, arranging them on the floor and over the doorways. Details, especially logistical and financial ones, were too prosaic to be heeded. She never once rushed out the door for an airplane or an appointment. They would wait for her, she reasoned. On occasion she was wrong, but more often than not, she would emerge with a first-class seat or a particularly serendipitous social engagement as a result. At one point, she spent her last twenty dollars on a steak for her cat, Ptolemy, and a bottle of champagne for us. The next day, somehow, there was more money. She didn't abide by the same earth-bound rules as other people did, and the world seemed to understand this and clear a path for her.

Teresa loved to write, a pleasure that seemed to intensify with time. I think of her especially as she was in Ocean Ridge. She would sit in front of the computer dreamily, light a cigarette, and read through what she had written. Where she came to a part she found particularly compelling, she would nod. "This is good. This is really, really good," she would say. I had to restrain her from deleting all the facts, which she found generally uninteresting once she knew them herself. She used her assistants as a kind of mirror, helping her reflect and refine her ideas as she wrote. I learned when to be quiet and when to offer suggestions. Every once in a while she would murmur, "Would you get me some tea, W?" and I'd bring her tea, steeped, as she liked it, for only the length of time it took to whisper "darling." The phone would ring, lunchtime would come and go, packages would arrive in the mail, the doorbell would sound, and Teresa typed on, oblivious to all such distractions. Finally, she would emerge from her working trance with an enormous stretch of her arms and a brilliant smile. "How about a swim?" and we'd go down to the beach where she luxuriated in the water. She loved floating out in the waves, surrounded by the blue-green warmth. One could always spot her in the sea, the only swimmer bobbing in the water with a brimmed hat and stylish sunglasses.

Teresa came to motherhood as a mature woman, adopting her daughter, Sangi, a year and a half before she died. She loved Sangi with a fierce, unguarded love that was different from anything I had seen in her. When Sangi was caught in Australia waiting for the proper immigration papers, Teresa went wild with anxiety. She would not do her scholarly work until she had exhausted every avenue of possibility for the day. She spoke to Australians, Americans, Nepalis, diplomats, senators, and minor officials of all kinds; she wooed, she cajoled, she threatened. She called Sangi every night, oblivious to the expense. She spoke eloquently of how interconnected the two of them were and of how much a part of herself she felt Sangi to be. "I feel like I'm missing a limb," she told me. Her sense of both the power and the piercing vulnerability of motherhood added emotive dimensions to her intellectual work.

I once called Teresa a walking Rorschach blot—a description that she loved. People responded in all sorts of ways to her powerful personality. More than most people, she embodied extraordinary contradictions. She believed in revolutionary politics and strict attention to grammar. She relished the pleasures of the senses, but occasionally launched on a strict dietary regime of boiled vegetables and water. A Catholic with a lover's quarrel with the Church, she felt off-kilter if she hadn't been to Mass. She called her assistants sweet, childish nicknames—"Charmin,'" "Petal," "Blossom"—and then urged them to go out and organize the workers. She demanded a great deal of those around her. She herself could be such an overwhelming figure that it was sometimes difficult to find one's own sense of self while with her. She was the most charming and captious of mistresses.

My favorite memory of Teresa is of one night when I had been working with her in Florida for two weeks, and I was supposed to leave for home the following day. We had been working to the point of exhaustion on *Globalization and Its Terrors*, writing, revising, editing, until all that remained was checking the footnotes. For days, she had been pleading with me to extend my stay—"Just one more day, to finish the book"—and finally, late that afternoon, I agreed. "Let's celebrate!" she said. She put on her royal blue-and-gold sarong and ambled off into the Florida evening, returning with sushi, a bottle of *Veuve Cliquot*, and several friends. She opened the champagne and filled four glasses. "To the book!" Her cat, Ptolemy, wandered outside and down to the beach, and we followed. The night was warm, the ocean was calm, and the sky was full of stars. Teresa began to sing old Gilbert and Sullivan tunes and chase Ptolemy over the sand. She was so playful, so full of release—so different from and yet so much the same as the serious-minded professor working diligently in front of the computer screen until 4 A.M.. She engaged us all on the destruction wrought by globalization; gave Ptolemy the gentle head-butts that he loved; then danced wildly and joyfully to Gloria Gaynor's "I Will Survive." After her friends left at midnight, she swam in the pool under the stars, then came back in, switched on the computer, and announced, "Now. To work."

The night Teresa was hit, she was working on the finishing touches of chapter four of this book: "The New Paradigm." Teresa considered this the keystone chapter, not only of *The Transmission of Affect* but also of her work as a whole. A few weeks earlier she had declared herself done with the chapter. As she pressed "save," she turned to me and said, "Now I've said what I've been trying to say for twenty-five years." This didn't stop her from tinkering: all her assistants knew that the only way to get her to release a book was to take it forcibly from her. But it does mean that just before she went out that night, she was perfecting a chapter of which she was incomparably proud. She was no doubt thinking about the transmission of affect as she stepped onto the street.

The final review of the copyediting of the book has been completed by Teresa's beloved assistant Sandy Hart and myself. It has been a bittersweet experience. Reviewing the copyeditor's queries has brought fresh memories of Teresa. Despite the fact that she hated such tasks, Teresa had forced herself through the first twenty-five pages. At times, she was cheeky and coy. In one passage, the manuscript described how one feels energized by some friends and loves, and bored and depleted by others. When the copyeditor asked if she meant "lovers" instead of "loves," she wrote in the margin, "I don't know about you, but no one boring gets near *my* bed." On another page where he asked a clarifying question, she wrote, "Tell you later!" We kept stumbling across phrases and ideas that she loved: the socially subordinate rodent, the wounding smell of sadness, the demons as negative affects. In one place, she had left intact a personal note that Sangi had typed into the text. I have loved finding these personal touches, indicating the ways in which Teresa's work and her life intersected. For me, they have underscored the fact that *The Transmission of Affect*, while offering an important new intellectual paradigm, is at the same time an intensely personal book. It, like Teresa herself, combines intellectual force and interpersonal insight in a work that is original, provocative, and life-affirming.

WODEN TEACHOUT
Middlesex, Vermont
June 2003

The Transmission of Affect

CHAPTER ONE

Introduction

Is there anyone who has not, at least once, walked into a room and "felt the atmosphere"? But if many have paused to wonder how they received this impression, and why it seemed both objective and certain, there is no record of their curiosity in the copious literature on group and crowd psychology, or in the psychological and psychoanalytic writing that claims that one person can feel another's feelings (and there is writing that does this, as we shall see). This is not especially surprising, as any inquiry into *how* one feels the others' affects, or the "atmosphere," has to take account of physiology as well as the social, psychological factors that generated the atmosphere in the first place.[1] The transmission of affect, whether it is grief, anxiety, or anger, is social or psychological in origin. But the transmission is also responsible for bodily changes; some are brief changes, as in a whiff of the room's atmosphere, some longer lasting. In other words, the transmission of affect, if only for an instant, alters the biochemistry and neurology of the subject. The "atmosphere" or the environment literally gets into the individual. Physically and biologically, something is present that was not there before, but it did not originate sui generis: it was not generated solely or sometimes even in part by the individual organism or its genes.

In a time when the popularity of genetic explanations for social behavior is increasing, the transmission of affect is a conceptual oddity. If transmission takes place and has effects on behavior, it is not genes that determine social life; it is the socially induced affect that changes our biology. The transmission of affect is not understood or studied because of the distance between the concept of transmission and the reigning modes of biological explanation. No one really knows how it happens, which may explain the reluctance to acknowledge its existence.[2] But this reluctance, historically, is only recent. The transmission of affect was once common knowledge; the concept faded from the history of scientific explanation as the individual, especially the biologically determined individual, came to the fore.

As the notion of the individual gained in strength, it was assumed more and more that emotions and energies are naturally contained, going no farther than the skin. But while it is recognized freely that individualism is a historical and cultural product, the idea that affective self-containment is also a production is resisted. It is all very well to think that the ideas or thoughts a given subject has are socially constructed, dependent on cultures, times, and social groups within them. Indeed, after Karl Marx, Karl Mannheim, Michel Foucault, and any social thinker worthy of the epithet "social," it is difficult to think anything else. But if we accept with comparatively ready acquiescence that our thoughts are not entirely independent, we are, nonetheless, peculiarly resistant to the idea that our emotions are not altogether our own. The fact is that the taken-for-grantedness of the emotionally contained subject is a residual bastion of Eurocentrism in critical thinking, the last outpost of the subject's belief in the superiority of its own worldview over that of other cultures. Critics who have no difficulty with, if they do not actively endorse, the idea that progress is a modernist and Western myth are nonetheless blind to the way that non-Western as well as premodern, preindustrial cultures assume that the person is *not* affectively contained. Here, multiculturalism comes up against a boundary its proponents do not wish to breach. Notions of the transmission of affect are suspect as nonwhite and colonial cultures are usually suspect.

But the suspicion is not reasonable. The denial of transmission leads to many inconsistencies in theories and therapies of the subject. For instance, all reputable schools of psychological theory assume that the subject is energetically and affectively self-contained. At the same time, psychologists working in clinics experience affective transmission. There are many psychological clinicians (especially among the followers of Melanie Klein) who believe that they experience the affects of their patients directly.[3] Transmission is also documented (with varying degrees of thoughtfulness) in the study of crowds and gatherings. The uneven literature on codependency bears witness to how the transmission of affect happens in relationships, but here, too, the theory is not rich. These areas, among others, are addressed here in *The Transmission of Affect*. The concept of transmission is relevant to supposedly psychogenic epidemics, among them chronic fatigue syndrome (CFS) or attention deficit hyperactivity disorder (ADHD). One explanation for these phenomena is that of hysterical identification, and this is partly true. But the problem with the designation "hysterical" is that people forget, no matter how often it is said, that hysteria, like psychosomatic illness in general, is biophysical in its effects. It really is in the flesh, not to be disposed of by a stiff upper lip or the power of positive thinking. Misapprehensions about hysteria are themselves instances of the tendency to split biological or physical inquiry (real things) from psychosocial explanation (not real things). Because of this split, the mechanism of hysterical identification has not yet been specified. Unlike the mechanisms involved in stable group phenomena, the transitory identification with a temporary group formation or the dynamics of a "psycho-epidemic" needs more explanation. It is all very well to say that people in crowds or social groups can identify with one another, can rapidly produce a group or mob consciousness that overrides their individual reason or leaves them ridden with symptoms; but the fact tells us nothing about the means. It does not tell us how a social and psychological affect buries itself within or rests on the skin of an utterly corporeal body.

Before outlining arguments on how the transmission of affect takes place and offering preliminary definitions of terms, I stress again that I am using the term "transmission of affect" to capture a process that is social in origin but biological and physical in effect. The origin of transmitted affects is social in that these affects do not only arise within a particular person but also come from without. They come via an interaction with other people and an environment. But they have a physiological impact. By the transmission of affect, I mean simply that the emotions or affects of one person, and the enhancing or depressing energies these affects entail, can enter into another. A definition of affect as such is more complicated.

The term "affect" is one translation of the Latin *affectus*, which can be translated as "passion" or "emotion." As Amélie Rorty has shown, there are historical changes in the taxonomies of the key emotions, affects, desires, and passions (terms that are used synonymously in varying translations from Greek and Latin up until the late nineteenth and twentieth centuries, when "passion" became reserved for sex and heartfelt commitment, and "desire" was separated from "affect").[4] But the same terms—love, lust, hate, anger, envy, shame (or guilt)— continue in evidence from ancient times to the present; they are found in ancient Greek taxonomies of the emotions, before that in Egyptian and Hebrew tabulations of demons, and continue through to Freud and after. The first philosophical text of the subject, Aristotle's *Rhetoric*, organized the affects in terms of "anger and mildness, love and hatred, fear and confidence, shame and esteem, kindness and un-kindness, pity and indignation, envy and emulation."[5]

Present definitions of the affects or emotions stem mainly from Darwin's physiological account of the emotions and something called the William James–Carl Lange theory. The James–Lange theory (miscalled in that there were real differences between James and Lange, especially concerning James's awareness of the external factors influencing the emotions) essentially dictates that bodily responses give rise to affective states. This view is popularly rendered by examples such as "crying make us sad," although for William James the issue was far more nuanced. Nonetheless, the primacy he gave to bodily changes was anticipated in Descartes's belief that emotions are passive perceptions of bodily motions. Descartes's belief inclines us toward isolating motions that can be verified by another observer, and this is reinforced by modern psychology.[6] Knowledge of this bodily motion, even internal bodily motion for the modern X-ray eye, is no longer gleaned by the path of bodily sensation but by that of visual and auditory observation. The predilection for the readily discernable physiological change is accompanied by reducing complex human motivation to the drives of hunger, love-sex, aggression, fear, and self-preservation. Bodily changes in fear, hunger, pain, rage, and affectionate or sexual arousal become the basic categories of endogenous drives, while drives in turn are identified as the source of the affects. The problem, as will be evident, is less in the emphasis on the bodily changes than in the reductionism in understanding them. These bodily changes are not viewed as "intelligent" or as intentional unconscious processes capable of being reconnected with conscious ones (although I believe they should be).

In sum, taxonomies of the emotions and affects have descended from three branches. One is ancient; another is identified with Darwin; and a third stems from James and Lange. Because of their observational basis, the lists descended from Darwin do not reckon with more complex affective states such as envy, guilt, jealousy, and love. In some taxonomies, these cognitive affects are termed desires. In the twentieth-century's cognitive psychology, a distinction between affect—as a present thing—and desire—as an imagined one—was elevated into theoretical significance, partly to reckon with the cognitive component in desires, which involves goals and thinking. Here I shall address both forms of affect. But critical in complex transmission, especially, is the moment of judgment. As we will see, the projection or introjection of a judgment is the moment transmission takes place. Moreover, the idea of judgment as intrinsic to the experience of affect is not foreign to the existing literature.

By an affect, I mean the physiological shift accompanying a judgment. The notion that passions and affects are themselves judgments is implicit in the frequent definition of affect as, to quote an example, "any evaluative (positive or negative) orientation toward an object."[7] The idea that affects are judgments, or, as a new vernacular has it, attitudes (as in, "lose the attitude") has less common currency than the notion of affects as surges of emotion or passion. But the evaluative or judgmental aspects of affects will be critical in distinguishing between these physiological phenomena and those deployed in feeling or discernment. In other words, feelings are not the same thing as affects. Putting it simply, when I feel angry, I feel the passage of anger through me. What I feel with and what I feel are distinct.[8]

At present, the literature treats feelings as a subset of affects, along with moods, sentiments, and emotions.[9] But "feelings," etymologically, refers to the proprioceptive capacities of any living organism—its own (*proprius*) system of reception. Standard definitions concentrate on how what is received by way of stimuli originates within an organism, although stimuli, of course, also originate from without. "Feelings" refers to the sensations that register these stimuli and thence to the senses, but feelings includes something more than sensory information insofar as they suppose a unified interpretation of that information. For our purposes here, I define feelings as sensations that have found the right match in words.

The distinction between affects and feelings comes into its own once the focus is on the transmission of affect. But there is no reason to challenge the idea that emotions are basically synonymous with affects (if more an evidently physiological subset), or that moods and sentiments are subsets referring to longer-lasting affective constellations. What does need to be borne in mind is that all affects, including even "flat affects," are material, physiological things. The more cognitive emotions—such as envy—may appear relatively bloodless, precisely because they are projected outward. Via a forceful projection, they may be felt and taken on board by the other, depending on circumstances. Further definitions of affects and feelings will follow more detailed discussion of transmission. The only other point that needs to be stressed at the outset is that affects have an energetic dimension.[10] This is why they can enhance or deplete. They enhance when they are projected outward, when one is relieved of them; in popular parlance, this is called "dumping." Frequently, affects deplete when they are introjected, when one carries the affective burden of another, either by a straightforward transfer or because the other's anger becomes your depression.[11] But the other's feelings can also enhance: affection does this, hence the expression "warmth." Simply put, you become energized when you are with some loves or some friends. With others you are bored or drained, tired or depressed. Chronic fatigue syndrome, for instance, may be a kind of leaching of a person, a draining off of energy by cumulative environmental stresses and by person or persons unknown.[12]

All this means, indeed the transmission of affect means, that we are not self-contained in terms of our energies. There is no secure distinction between the "individual" and the "environment." But transmission does not mean that a person's particular emotional experience is irrelevant. We may influence the registration of the transmitted affect in a variety of ways; affects are not received or registered in a vacuum. If I feel anxiety when I enter the room, then that will influence what I perceive or receive by way of an "impression" (a word that means what it says). On the other hand, if I am not aware that there are affects in the air, I may hold myself solely responsible for them and, in this case, ferret around for an explanation in my recent personal history. Thus, the content one person gives to the affect of anger or depression or anxiety may be very different from the content given to the same affect by another. If I pick up on your depression, my focus perhaps will be on my unfinished book. Yours, more seriously, may be on the loss of a loved person. I may be somewhat startled, if I reflect on it, to find such depression on my part in relation to my unfinished book, which may be a bit depressing to have undone but which should not feel like death. It should not demand such a strong affective response. The point is that, even if I am picking up on your affect, the linguistic and visual content, meaning the thoughts I attach to that affect, remain my own: they remain the product of the particular historical conjunction of words and experiences I represent. The thoughts are not necessarily tied to the affects they appear to evoke. One may as well say that the affects evoke the thoughts.

I have observed a phenomenon that suggests that the affects may, at least in some instances, find thoughts that suit them, not the other way around. This is suggested by the manner in which guilt and anxiety need not be attached to a crisis. A parent may have guilt and anxiety at the prospect of a child's tertiary education. When that problem is resolved, the same parent may have just as much guilt over failing to take out the garbage or anxiety over the nonappearance of the plumber. It is as if the relevant emotions attach themselves with equal intensity to various thoughts; whether the source of the anxiety is trivial or serious, the extent of the anxiety will remain the same.[13] The noncorrespondence between thought and feeling here is significant. As Freud observed, affects and thoughts follow separate paths, although he also believed that both affects and thoughts were derivatives of the same original "stuff." I will return to this question, arguing that thought and affect have become split over time. But, at this point, I want to stress only that it is affects, rather than any notion of the transmission of thoughts or telepathy, that we are discussing. Thoughts, indeed, appear more individual or personal than affects.

What is at stake now is how the idea of transmitted affects undermines the dichotomy between the individual and the environment and the related opposition between the biological and the social. That does not mean, I stress again, that there is no distinction between the individual and the environment. That is evidently absurd. We are all of us at least somewhat distinctive in persona and phenotypically unique, as well as proprioceptive, even when our thinking and emotional responses are resolutely similar.[14] Moreover, we are accustomed to judging and thinking of one another as affective types, or at least as having distinctive affective personas. The persistence of the affect in a given individual raises the question of endogenous affects, as distinct from transmitted and transitory affects.[15] The nature of the resistant and constant affect, as distinct from the transitory affect, is not in itself a distinction between the endogenous (in the sense of given or genetic) affect and the transmitted affect. In both its more stable interactive form and its transitory forms the transmission of affect may feature in or distort a person's affective makeup. One can have an enduring affective interaction with the other, which positions both parties in ongoing related affective personas. At the same time, there is a personal affective history made up of objects and fantasies, and this leads us to expect continuity in affective disposition.[16] I am not saying that transmission is the whole story of the affective persona, or even the half of it. But at this point I want to foreground people's transitory and persistent similarities, especially their affective similarities. After this, the question of the individuality of persons, and how it is achieved and maintained, comes into sharp focus.

One cannot grasp what is really distinctive about distinctiveness or individuality without first appreciating that it is not to be taken for granted. It is not to be taken for granted precisely because of the artificiality of the distinction between the individual and the environment at the level of physical and biological exchange.[17] At this level, the energetic affects of others enter the person, and the person's affects, in turn, are transmitted to the environment. Here lies the key to why it is that people in groups, crowds, and gatherings can often be "of one mind."[18] Moreover, once the physical and organic levels are taken into account, one can begin to appreciate that other environmental factors are at work in the transmission of energy and affect. Visitors to New York City or Delphi testify happily to the energy that comes out of the pavement in the one and the ancient peace of the other. But investigating environmental factors such as these falls outside the scope of this book.

This initial investigation is limited to the transmission of affect and energy between and among human subjects. It is limited to establishing the case for transmission by diverse means: deductive argument from clinical findings and biological facts, some history (theology and philosophy) of the affects, and a little modern neuroscience. Ranging thinly over so many fields is only warranted in an *initial* making of the case, and I do not pretend that the case is definitive, or the evidence for transmission remotely exhausted by what follows. The business of collecting that evidence and understanding transmission, in terms of theory, science, and practice, has barely begun. My aim is to make enough of a case to justify taking the investigation further.

Science and Transmission

In actuality, the scientific investigation has already started (and started again) under other names. Through it, two forms of the transmission of affect can be identified. There is transmission by which people become alike and transmission in which they take up opposing positions in relation to a common affective thread (the angry and the depressed; the loved and the lover). The form of transmission whereby people become alike is a process whereby one person's or one group's nervous and hormonal systems are brought into alignment with another's. Neurologists call the process "entrainment," either chemical entrainment or electrical entrainment. Chemical entrainment works mainly by smell; that is to say, unconscious olfaction. For example, pheromones—molecules that can be airborne and that communicate chemical information—signal and produce reactions by unnoticeable odor in many hormonal interactions, including aggression, as well as sex.[19] I suggest smell (in this case unconscious olfaction) is critical in how we "feel the atmosphere" or how we pick up on or react to another's depression when there is no conversation or visual signal through which that information might be conveyed. I also suggest that hormonal interactions account for how the hormonal process situates people in different as well as similar emotional places (the abuser and the abused, for instance).[20] The implications of the hormonal research in understanding affective dispositions are noted often, in that hormones are held responsible for sexual aberrations, irascibility in adolescence, and surprising conduct in middle age. Like such terms as "passion," "hormones" now connotes sex and reproduction, rather than a general class of affects or affect-related drives. But the discovery of hormones is a little like the discovery of genes: new ones are identified constantly, as are the biological activities they facilitate or impair.[21] Hormones direct human action and response in fields from reflection to stress, growth to aggression, as well as sex and reproduction; there is no field of human action that does not involve hormonal messages. They are by no means the only candidates to consider in understanding the mechanisms of transmission, but they are the obvious ones with which to begin, especially as there are so many discrepancies in hormonal research when considered from a neo-Darwinian or self-contained standpoint. It has been established now that the pheromonal odors of the one may change the mood of the other.[22] The release of these odors is governed by hormones, and the molecules involved are hypothetical pheromones. In this way social interaction changes our biology (as distinct from the notion that biology determines social behavior). Moreover, if we take affective transmission as a starting point, the resultant hypotheses can explain otherwise intractable hormonal and endocrinological evidence and are consistent with the findings on the course of endogenous drives. Smell emerges as critical in communicating responses ranging from the aggressive to the soothing; it is also a vehicle for effecting changes in another's hormonal (hence affective) composition.

We shall return to this issue, but first, let us deal with a familiar objection to the notion of affective transmission: it might exist, but it works by sight rather than smell. Does it not spread, say, by the visual observation of a depressed person's physiognomy and body language? On the answer to this question hinges much of the argument of this book. Because what is interesting about the question is the resistance it reveals to the idea that a foreign body—something from without—can enter into one's own. If entrainment is effected by sight, then on the face of it, our boundaries stay intact. We become *like* someone else by imitating that person, not by literally becoming or in some way merging with him or her. I think it is true that entrainment (whether it is nervous or chemical) can work mimetically, but not only by sight. That is to say, people can act alike and feel alike not only because they observe each other but also because they imbibe each other via smell. But repeatedly, we will find that sight is the preferred mechanism in explaining any form of transmission (when evidence for transmission is noted) because this sense appears to leave the boundaries of discrete individuals relatively intact. Smell and various forms of neuronal communication are not such respecters of persons.[23] In fact, sight is not altogether pure here, either, nor is there only one form of vision.[24] Visual images, like auditory traces, also have a direct physical impact; their reception involves the activation of neurological networks, stimulated by spectrum vibrations at various frequencies. These also constitute transmissions breaching the bounds between individual and environment. But for the main part, sight is perceived as the sense that separates, where the other senses do not. Given that olfactory and nervous entrainment exist, and add to them the effects of sight and hearing (which I do not mean to discount), then the mystery really is how a person maintains a distinct identity.

For, despite hormones, pheromones, and wavelengths affecting one's chemistry or nervous system directly, the fact is that people are different. The fact, too, is that even when a strong affect has most people in its collective grip, there are exceptions. A favorite theme of plays and screenplays is the lone resister, the one who holds out against a common affect, usually of persecution. Thus Ibsen's doctor in *Enemy of the People* and the old man who will not sing with the boys in *Cabaret*. How can someone do this? The question is complicated because the individual holding out against the group affect is not the only instance of resistance. In the psychoanalytic clinic, a practitioner who experiences the transmission of affect from a patient consciously discerns whom it belongs to. I shall explore the question of discernment in what follows, noting here only that the resister in the group and the clinician who discerns have in common an ability to distance or detach. But this mysterious ability, this aptly called "self-possession," may come into focus more clearly if we consider what it is not.

I argue that the capacity to resist or discern unwanted affects is *not* based on the boundaries that "healthy" persons are said to possess and "unhealthy" ones lack. It cannot be based on these boundaries if these boundaries are formed by unconscious projection—and some are, as we shall see. Projecting is the opposite of discernment because projection directs affects outward without consciously (as a rule) acknowledging that it is doing so; discernment consciously examines them. Boundaries may depend on projecting, but this is only one route to self-containment. There is another, based on discernment. In the course of psychoanalysis the extent of unconscious projecting is, or should be, reduced. But conscious discernment of the affects, to my knowledge, is not one of the formulated goals of the treatment. Nonetheless, there are reasons for believing that emotional discernment is valued in cultures and historical periods that are more inclined to take the transmission of affect for granted, that is to say, are more conscious of it.

To put this another way: In other cultures and other times, there are—or have been—different, more permeable, ways of being. Historically, these codes of manners and courtesy have stressed a series of virtues whose common denominator was a regard for the feelings of others one the one hand and self-restraint in the expression of the (negative) affects on the other. An identity based on forming "boundaries" by projection (for example, an identity based on angry retaliation for imaginary or real disrespect) is not the only identity one can have.[25] The way is open to further historical inquiry once we make an initial case for the idea that the self-contained Western identity has to be a construction and that this construction depends on projecting outside of ourselves unwanted affects such as anxiety and depression in a process commonly known as "othering." To be effective, the construction of self-containment also depends on another person (usually the mother, or in later life, a woman, or a pliable man, or a subjugated race) accepting those unwanted affects for us.[26] That projection in the strong sense goes on all the time is perfectly obvious once one knows to look for it.[27] It presupposes no more than the idea of the unconscious presupposes, namely, the idea of energy and its unconscious repression. There is no reason why one person's repression could not be another man or woman's burden, just as the aggression of the one can be the anxiety of another.

The Foundational Fantasy and the Affects

The idea that containment is constructed, rather than given, is at odds with Freud's own starting point: belief that the individual psyche is the origin of the drives and affects.[28] However, while my argument is a critique of psychoanalysis in this regard, I also draw on concepts that psychoanalysis has made popular, especially the concepts of projection and of fantasy (as well as unconscious processes, although these will be redefined). Fantasy, in psychoanalytic thinking, is a mental activity that allows us to alter an unpleasant reality by making it into something more pleasurable. If the reality is that we have to wait on the mother's good will, the fantasy is that she has to wait upon ours. In this fantasy one's actual situation is projected onto the other, so that if one feels abandoned, one projects the feeling of abandonment onto her. In what I have termed, in *Exhausting Modernity* (2000), the "foundational fantasy," the mother, especially, is seen as the natural origin of rather than the repository for unwanted affects. It is not that we dump on her (all our screaming rage and pain). It is rather that she dumps on us. (For her occasional irritation or distraction she is held culpable, made the cause of all our rage and pain.) We project onto her our helpless and unbearable passivity, our lack of agency. I call this illusion the foundational fantasy because it is the foundation of the fantasy of self-containment: the belief that "we," the passive infant, are the true fountain of energy and life, and the mother is a hapless, witless receptacle. Situating the mother as the passive repository for the child's unwanted raging affects is, perhaps, the first powerful instance of the transmission of affect (excluding the hormonal interactions in utero, which we will also discuss).

It is at this point that the theory I am outlining becomes an alternative to Freud's metapsychology (meaning his theory of the psyche) while, I hope, providing tools to help explain current psychoanalytic practice. My theory is an alternative to psychoanalytic theory or metapsychology in that it postulates an origin for affects that is independent of the individual experiencing them. These affects come from the other, but we deny them. Or they come from us, but we pretend (habitually) that they come from the other. Envy, anger, aggressive behavior—these are the problems of the other. Overtolerance, overgenerosity—these are our problems.

The occasion of the foundational fantasy constitutes the fulcrum upon which our acceptance of the good affects, and our rejection of the bad ones, resolves itself. But from the psychoanalytic perspective, this is not always clear. The moment of the foundational fantasy is the moment when one says either "I am good and powerful. The other is base and abject" or "I am miserable and abject. The other is good and powerful (so good that sometimes they will punish me for my abjection)." Subsequent stable relationships in later life are formed between people who endorse one another's sentiments in these respects: emotionally and/or sexually. But for the exchange of affects to work between two parties, they have to agree unconsciously, more or less, on what is being exchanged. Relationships break up when they disagree, when one party demands more, or another takes less. But how does one study this from the perspective of psychoanalysis? In Freud's economy, only the subject experiences the affects he or she produces. If the subject came to analysis, the subject of the affects—not an object of affects—had to want to change. And, of course, the subject can change. The effects of psychoanalysis on analysands can enhance their resistance to projection, or encourage them not to project, or both. But while the dynamics of transmission here have been studied by the post-Kleinians, by R. D. Laing,[29] Daniel Stern,[30] and other mavericks, they have been studied as exceptions to the rule, or relegated entirely to the psychic life of the infant before "boundaries." Some of the mysteries involved in the transmission of affect have been documented, but how the transmissions come into being has not really been explored. To understand how transmission takes place, metapsychology has to begin again, and from the standpoint that individuals are not self-contained, although the foundational fantasy fosters this illusion. Nor is it enough to claim, à la Gilles Deleuze, that the (energetically fluid) body without organs preexists and underpins the horrors of the Oedipus complex.[31] The point is that energies and affects, after the Oedipus complex, still cross over between us, but they do this in specific directions, carrying a content that varies according to the nature of the affect or affects concerned. The process of the transmission of affect does not stop because we, like Oedipus, become blind to it.

The foundational fantasy, which can be analyzed in psychoanalytic terms up to a point, explains how it is that we come to think of ourselves as separate from others. But it does not account, of itself, for the energetic level at which we are not separate from others—the level at which my affect enters you and yours, me. For this there needs to be a theory of the transmission of affect. But what the foundational fantasy does, as well as explaining why on earth we think of ourselves as self-contained, is explain why we are likely to judge the other, to project certain affects on the other. It explains why we are willing to see the other as the origin of negative affects, such as envy and aggression, which we would rather disown in ourselves. In terms of the history of ideas, the foundational fantasy, or foundationalism, also explains the strong tendency to think in active/passive terms, as we shall see. As an aside, let me stress that there is a difference between the fantasy as a psychical event and the intellectual work affected by it. For instance, Aristotle, as a father of foundational thought, does not himself accept that activity and subjective agency, or passivity and matter, are necessarily associated, although his thought tends to this end. It is the *tendency* that is fantasy-imbued: the fantasy will limit thinking unless it is actively resisted. It also limits practice.

The first rule of foundational thinking is to blame the mother, and it is honored in most schools of therapy. But what is attributed to bad or not-good-enough mothering can also be the result of the failure to find a mother—or a woman to substitute for her—to carry one's own negative affects. Women, I hazard, regardless of whether they are mothers, have carried the negative affects. But a better term than "women" would be "feminine beings," by which I mean those who carry the negative affects for the other. These are most likely to be women, but the disposition of the negative affects varies, especially when racism is a factor. By disposition, I mean the direction of negative affects such as aggression. The question should be: To whom is the affect directed? Because whoever that object is will be prone to anxiety and then depression (both the effects of aggression turned inward).

In the 1990s, depression was the most rapidly growing disorder in Europe and the United States,[32] while concern with boundaries was also proliferating.[33] Could these things be related? Have boundaries come to matter because self-definition by projection is less available than it was during the last few sexist and colonial centuries—there are now too few willing receptacles—or because of an accumulation of environmental-inflected affects?[34] Either way, boundaries may matter now because there is too much affective stuff to dispose of, too much that is directed away from the self with no place to go. As Julia Kristeva has shown us, there is an increase in what she calls "new maladies of the soul"—psychosomatic and narcissistic disorders that are not matched with a language that reorders the copious and nameless affects underpinning them.[35] But this increase of affects is also a real thing, historically produced. The reality of the increase makes the Western individual especially more concerned with securing a private fortress, personal boundaries, against the unsolicited emotional intrusions of the other. The fear of being "taken over" is certainly in the air, although the transmission of negative affect generally is not recognized for what it is. Boundaries, paradoxically, are an issue in a period where the transmission of affect is denied.

A Brief Historical Orientation

Boundaries, like identities, were not an issue when the transmission of affect had more currency historically. The historical dimension of this inquiry is only preliminary, but I shall use the remainder of this introductory chapter to sketch out how the concept of transmission appears to fade as we go forward in Western time. Some of this I have already discussed elsewhere; some of it will be documented in more detail below.

Ideas of the transmission of affect were scattered across premodern European history and were still current in sixteenth-century France: thus Montaigne's well-known observation that an old rich man would find his energy enhanced while the younger man (Montaigne himself) in his company would find his energy depleted.[36] Similarly, the seventeenth-century discussion of the passions is explicitly concerned, in part, with transmission. In Susan James's interpretation, Nicolas de Malebranche thought that emotions such as sadness could circulate among people.[37] Malebranche was also concerned with a form of transmission in which the mother is supposed to affect the fetus. The "theater," as I will term the *deliberate* creation of an atmosphere, is one thing. Of more direct interest here is the idea that the mother's imagination and affects influence the child. It is interesting for two reasons. First, this form of hypothetical transmission and the transmission of affect were discussed in the same context, and not only by Malebranche. Similar instances also fascinated Montaigne, who called this transmission "the power of the imagination." For him, this power worked in utero as well as between people. Just as the mother's imagination could affect the shape of her child, so too was it likely that the rich old man could deplete the energy of the younger one by feasting on his company. "Everyone feels its [imagination's] impact," he wrote, "but some are knocked over by it. On me it makes an intense impression."[38] The imagination is clearly linked to images, and it is equally clearly a physical force. The old man is invited "to feast his senses on my [Montaigne's] flourishing state of health,"[39] while the mother may produce a "monster" if her imagination has too much effect. The nature of this imaginative force will concern us again, when we return to maternal transmission and draw out, on logical grounds, how the denial of maternal transmission is tied to the denial of the social transmission of affect between people. For there is contemporary evidence suggesting that maternal transmission is also a fact. As with the facts of hormonal entrainment and other forms of the social transmission of affect, various uterine findings challenge the idea of a division between individual and environment. But the common sense view of persons as discrete beings gets in the way of the logical conclusion.

After the seventeenth century the concept of transmission lost ground. In science, transmission between beings was neglected, while political philosophers denied that the fledgling individual was indebted to those that came before. It was born, this new individual, free and equal in the market place. The original meaning of affect and affection was minimized, and the notion that the mother actively *affected* her child was lost, together with the idea that persons were also *affected* by the emotions of others. At least, the idea loses ground in the official record, the philosophical canon. What ideas were entertained in popular culture (then as now) is another story.

Notions of animal magnetism in the eighteenth century contributed to the subsequent decline of interest in the transmission of affect. Variants of the idea became feminized, a sure symptom of slipping status. Only women suffered from the vapors (although the idea that one suffers from odors affectively is correct). Any concept of transmission would have fared badly, however, with the emphasis now on sight as the key sense in human relations. Sight, as noted earlier, is the sense that renders us discrete, while transmission breaches individual boundaries.[40] The eighteenth century was so preoccupied with vision that it was known as the *siècle des lumières*. Nonetheless, there was no easy or clear-cut victory for sight over the other senses. Or rather, sight itself was not yet viewed as somehow immune from transmission. In discussing entrainment, I suggested that sight also has physical effects. To an extent, this idea is prefigured in the ocular theory of extramission. Extramission, the notion that the eye gave off light and, by this light's merging with the air, "touched" its immediate environs, was not officially disproved until 1704.[41] But by the nineteenth century sight was the first of the senses, and to this day the only sense, to attain objective status.[42] Nonetheless, the transmission of affect, especially in its energetic dimension, lingered on in its conceptual effects.

The nineteenth- and early twentieth-century work in France on the "group mind" (*âme collective*) takes the transmission of affect for granted, although it does not specify its mechanisms. Part of the reason why this literature is so problematic is that it takes a group mind as a given, but its procedure is essentially romantic. The group mind is invoked, much as pantheism might be invoked, with no argument but powerful "intuitive" appeal. Indeed, it is worth adding that nineteenth-century romanticism is the place where transmission re-treated to, and like most retreatants, lost touch with social reality, for ill as well as good. The idea that the emotional connections between beings have an energetic force of their own, by dint of magnetism and romantic association, became less scientifically respectable.

In one respect the nineteenth-century studies of the group mind do make a bid for scientific status: they designate the group as patholog-ical precisely because it is affectively imbued, and because the distinc-tiveness of individuals is swamped by the affects of the group. It fol-lowed that those who are most susceptible to transmitted affects are those who are least socially desirable.[43] This prejudice survives in the psychiatric and psychoanalytic clinics, as we will see shortly. By con-trast, recent studies on the group mind or crowd mentality attempt to rescue those who participate in gatherings from the accusation of pathology. At the same time, these studies are steeped in the cognitive bias of twentieth-century psychology. In contemporary discussions of the group mind, now called the "crowd" or "gathering," transmission is discounted at the outset. By definition, it seems that the stress on the cognitive is a turn away from affect, and so, necessarily, away from questions of the affect's transmission. So invisible became the idea of transmission that it had to be rediscovered in the psychoana-lytic clinic, dredged up from the unconscious.

The striking thing about the historical turns adumbrated so far is this: It seems that the experience of transmission was once conscious to some degree in Europe (we do not know how far) but is now (gen-erally) unconscious there and throughout the West. Transmission is the only consistent explanation for a variety of phenomena, but it is no longer transparent to common sense. Now it is the case that those who think they have experienced the transmission of affect will be more sympathetic to a logical argument for its existence, but that should not prevent an undecided reader from following the logic of the argument independently of personal experience. The challenge, in the end, will be bringing sensation together with reason in the under-standing of transmission, extending consciousness into what is now unconscious. In a sense Michel Foucault was right to claim that the re-pressed unconscious had been invented, but the effects of repression are real. Repression, after all, is the energetic repudiation of an idea.

The name or the concept of the transmission of affect does not sit well with an emphasis on individualism, on sight, and cognition.

These things are all associated with the subject/object distinction, with thinking in terms of subject and object. This thinking, while it long precedes mechanism, gives rise to a particular understanding of objectivity that is coincident with it, based on the notion that the objective is in some way free of affect. Once this notion is accepted, then the affect, as a vehicle connecting individuals to one another and the environment, and for that matter connecting the mind or cognition to bodily processes, ceases to be a proper object of study. In other words, to be a worthy object of study, the individual has to be severed from affective connections with the surrounding environment and others in it. But how did this notion of objectivity come to the fore? If we understand this, we will be able to grasp why a rigorous distinction between biological and social explanation, as well as between individual and environment, is maintained even when it makes no sense. (This is not an argument against attempting impartiality.)

The peculiar elisions characteristic of subject/object thinking entail objectivity as a condition a subject should ensure when studying either an object or another subject. Subjectivity means studying what one has experienced oneself and valuing it, or valuing the subjective side of one's interactions with the object studied. But whether one insists on the subjective or the objective, whether one believes that the object can be known in itself or for itself, one tacitly assumes the foundational associations between mind, form, activity, will, and the subject, on the one hand, and, on the other, body, matter, passivity, lack of agency, and the object. When affects and feelings force themselves into consideration, they will be allocated a status that either makes them subjective or makes them part of the object, as in the physiology of the affects when bodily changes are measured—something to be studied, but not by means of feeling and sensing. Just as unconscious bodily processes are not meant to be intelligent or intentional processes, so are feeling and sensing ruled out as methodological tools for studying the object, because they cannot be seen, of course, and because they constitute a connection with the object. By feeling and sensing, I do not mean vague emoting. By "sensing," I mean the deployment of smell and hearing as well as open vision, while by "feeling," as implied above, I mean the accurate and rapid interpretation of this information via language. Feelings are sensations that have found a match in words.

I will try to show that the subject/object distinction is shaped by the same foundational fantasy that leads us to project affects on and into the mother (or another who stands in for the mother), the same fantasy that denies that the transmission of affect exists. The reason for thinking that a fantasy shapes those most basic of categories, subject and object, is that on analysis, the distinction between the categories is incoherent. But bypassing the fantasy's effects requires a new paradigm, and that requires a theory of the psyche and the maternal environment that is not premised on self-containment.

The Argument

The first part of the book fills out some of the parameters outlined in this chapter, in that it reviews evidence for the transmission of affect from psychoanalysis, psychology, and social science. Chapter 2 analyzes work on the transmission of affect in the clinic and shows how the closest we come to a modern theory of transmission lies in Wilfred Bion's and Daniel Stern's accounts of the mother/infant relationship and Jean Laplanche's particular understanding of the child as the symptom of its parents. Chapter 3 turns to how the transmission of affect operates in groups, gatherings, and crowds. The idea of an "atmosphere" in a room tells us at once that the transmission of affect does not only work between two persons, let alone only between parent and child. As noted, the concept is potentially relevant to understanding the behavior of groups and gatherings, despite the way in which ideas of emotionality in groups have been associated with largely discredited ideas of the "crowd." This chapter links a discussion of the communication of the affects in groups with recent and contemporary research on entrainment and chemical communication, suggesting that these be considered as mechanisms for the transmission of affect.

On this basis, chapter 4 then turns to the matter of a new paradigm. The way the psyche conceptualizes its self-containment means, as we have seen, denying the mother's agency.[44] But as this chapter shows, the foundational fantasy does not only make the mother a passive repository for unwanted affects after birth. The same fantasy distorts the inquiry into maternal agency in utero. By pursuing an inquiry into the in utero research, chapter 4 draws out the homologous way in which conceptualizations of the relation between the individual and the environment and that between mother and fetus have been limited by the foundational fantasy and the fantasy's effects on theory and science. In both areas, the results of recent experiments confirm that the maternal environment and olfactory factors in the social environment shape human affect.[45] This returns the discussion to questions of free will, agency, and intentionality. After analyzing how the distinction between individual and environment is allied with the distinctions between mind and body, subject and object, activity and passivity, and consciousness and unconsciousness it should be plain that the idea of the transmission of affect turns any reductionist preconception about the priority of biological causality in social explanation on its head. The problem, as was established in the discussion of entrainment, is how to conceptualize the information biology uncovers. Honest neo-Darwinians are unable to account for the evidence of hormonal interactions in utero and subsequently, insofar as they seek explanations for maladaptive hormonal responses in our genetic evolution. A paradigm based on the transmission of affect encounters no such difficulties, or so it seems to me as an outsider surveying relevant scientific research. Such a paradigm also offers an alternative to the supernaturalist explanations that hold demons responsible for sudden changes in disposition.

As far as I can tell, the negative affects (understood as mobile rather than endogenous forces) are identical with demons and/or deadly sins—the earliest incarnations of the idea of negative affects in the West. The seven deadly sins are not acts. They are affects: pride, sloth, envy, lust, anger, gluttony, avarice. Early Christian writings, like rabbinical writings, speak of the demon of despair and the demon of shame. Toward the end of chapter 5 I will discuss the origins of these affects in relation to the foundational fantasy, thereby extending the explanatory use of this theory as a logical account that is both consistent with the known facts and that offers a reasoned account of supposedly supernatural entities. *Exhausting Modernity* established that the foundational fantasy is prompted by envy (the affective constituent of the need for control and power over others), objectification, narcissism, and anger or aggression. Additionally, it demonstrated that the psychoanalytic account of early life offered a microcosmic version of theological accounts of the Fall and an economic, environmental notion of judgment.

Here we shall see that envy, pride, anger, and other negative affects are identical with the seven deadly sins, which were originally cast as demons. But there are vast scholarly gaps between the appearance of those affective constellations as sins and demons and their reappearance in the clinic, and it needs to be quite clear that this book is not a history of the affects. While I wish it could be more comprehensive in this respect, the project I am outlining will have to be a collective endeavor because of the research needed to take it farther, as well as simply drawing together all that has been done.[46] In particular, there is scope here for more convergence in theology and the history of philosophy and science. However, I do explore the relation between the old lacks and sins and how those that have gone underground most deeply reemerge as pathology. For instance, sloth, which once featured as a major sin, seems to disappear when we turn to psychoanalytic formulations of equivalent affective states . . . unless we remember that depression is marked by inertia. It is also apparently marked by anxiety and inward-turned anger, and in this it constitutes a different complex of affects. Depression is more likely (although this is not its only cause) to mark the reception of, say, an envious or paranoid projection, which works as the markers of depression usually work, namely, through negative judgments.

While agreeing that what defines the significant affects varies, especially across time or through history as well as cultures, I also argue that there are constant potentials at work, and they are universal—for now—in that they are potentially present in all human psyches as we know them. I do not think they are universal forever, for reasons we will come to in the end. They are universal as potentials in that they devolve from the quasi-geometric positioning of human perception that occurs as humans come to see the world from their own standpoint. But while this imaginary positioning is a product of fantasy (a fantasy whose origins are wrongly ascribed to the infant rather than the world into which it is born), such positioning becomes material and physical when it is constructed in external reality. It can be constructed in the external realities of social and economic orders.[47] In such cases, the force of the negative affects clustered around postures and positions, in any given domain, will increase. These negative affects increase especially in relation to the present global economy, and their obvious proliferation in violence has to be related to the physical toxicity and stress of daily life in the West.[48] Yet whether the negative affects are increased by a social order that abets their production or diminished in a civilization that counters them, their potential is present. Nonetheless, that potential can be unfulfilled, resisted economically, just as it can be personally.

At the personal level, the transmission of these affects can be resisted, provided they are discerned, as we will discuss in chapter 6. One discerns with the feelings that are sometimes confused with the affects but that are, in fact, basic to discerning or perceiving by sensation. As stressed at the outset, the things that one feels are affects. The things that one feels with are feelings, which can also feel and even discern the energy of the life drive and/or love.

The seventh chapter argues that the suppression of consciousness based on discerning, or finer, feelings (not the same thing, as will be clear, as in "feeling angry") is the suppression of information from the body's divers systems. It is the suppression of knowledge gleaned precisely by feeling or sensing. Such knowledge is a chain of communication and association in the flesh (with its own anchors in the brain) that is also structured like language and functions in a parallel way. But such knowledge, whether it is gleaned by smell or touch or sound, does not always, or even habitually, penetrate the modern consciousness. The subject/object categories that order the world of visual perception override it. When these categories thicken together with the negative affects that fuel them, the ability to feel information from the other senses diminishes.

In consequence, the split between thought and real feeling, which will be seen as another product of the same forces that bring you the subject/object distinction, deepens historically at the same time as the subject/object method captures the investigative high ground. The split is a lived thing, insofar as humans are swamped by negative affects in a way that leads them to calculate more and feel less. At the same time, this swamping by the affects has consequences for theology, philosophy, social theory, and political philosophy. Explanations favoring biological determinism and neo-Darwinism are in vogue, and social facts are often reduced to biological factors. What is overlooked, in the rearguard actions of those who defend the social construction of persons, is the way that certain biological and physical phenomena themselves require a social explanation. While its wellsprings are social, the transmission of affect is deeply physical in its effects. It is moreover the key to the social and scientific understanding of what have hitherto been theological mysteries.

CHAPTER TWO

The Transmission of Affect
in the Clinic

In theories of psychiatry and psychoanalysis, the healthy person is a self-contained person. This healthy being has established "boundaries" in early childhood, having successfully negotiated the relationship to the mother. From a state of narcissism, if not omnipotence, he or she played with "transitional objects," such as teddy bears, which helped him or her to realize that the mother was a separate person, and eventually passed the transitional point. This being now realizes where he or she ends and the other begins. He or she has boundaries. Yet most non-Western and nonmodern theories of mental illness posit the transmission of affect, meaning that the emotions and energies of the one can cross over into another.[1] It is primarily modern and Western approaches to mental illness that assume that the individual is an energetically self-contained or bound entity, whose affects are his or hers alone. This is explicit even in, especially in, theories about how boundaries are constructed, with no sense of contradiction. If boundaries are constructed, they cannot be the same as the energetic containment these object-relations theories have assumed. For the boundaries theorized in object-relations theory, while cast dynamically and interactively, have been theorized in nonphysical terms. My hypothesis is that the psyche's sense of its self-containment is indeed structured, but that therefore the state of experiencing both the "living attention" and the affects of others is both the originary and in some way the natural state: the transmission of energy and affects is the norm rather than an aberration at the beginning of psychical life.[2] The

Western psyche is structured in such a way as to give a person the sense that their affects and feeling are their own, and that they are energetically and emotionally contained in the most literal sense. In other words, people experience themselves as containing their own emotions.

Of course, it is not only comparative forms of psychiatric treatment that are at issue. At issue is the formation of the individual. This and the next chapter cull individual observations of the transmission of affect from the work of various thinkers. These come from two major disciplines: psychoanalysis, with its emphasis on the clinic and other relations between two people; and group psychology, with its study of the interactions of groups and crowds. It is important to note that this psychoanalytic evidence serves as the basis for a *critique* of psychoanalysis. This will be plain in the next chapter, where crowds and groups and hormones are discussed. But it should also be apparent in this chapter, where I argue that the idea of "boundaries," fundamental to psychoanalysis after the rise of the object-relations school, is a culturally specific idea. The Western mode, modern psychiatry, presupposes a self-contained individual. This individual is more likely to be treated successfully by methods premised on self-containment. On the other hand, the person forged in a culture in which the transmission of affect and energy is taken for granted is more likely to be treated by methods that accept that such transmissions take place. This means methods that accept that the traffic between the biological and the social is two-way; the social or psychosocial actually gets into the flesh and is apparent in our affective and hormonal dispositions. The bounded individuals of the modern West, regardless of their race, are by virtue of their *social* construction physically different from the persons who live elsewhere. Below, I will outline a theory that would make those cultures—with various systems of healing that assume the transmission of feeling, energy, and emotion—explicable in psychoanalytic terms. I have tried to do this by treating them as the rule, rather than as exceptions to the Western model of self-containment. By contrast, the Western self-contained subject is seen as one whose self-containment is constructed rather than naturally given. In his hubris, this subject, and the psychological theories about him, have assumed that he is the norm, rather than the historical aberration he is in fact. The real origins of this subject are evident in the disparate and contradictory approaches taken in the psychiatric clinic and psychoanalytic consulting room. There, it is taken for granted that the affects of a patient can quite literally enter into the analyst or therapist involved. But the usual emphasis in informal accounts by clinicians is on the idea that it is the "borderline" patient who transmits his or her affect more freely. If the borderline client lacks boundaries, such a person should be more susceptible to the impact of the other, susceptible as well as liable to "leakage." While the borderline patient, the patient without clear "boundaries," is most often held responsible for projecting "into" the analyst, there is a contradiction here. Analysts are meant to have their boundaries in place, and yet they feel the other's affects. This contradiction may have preempted a thoroughgoing inquiry into how one feels the other's affects. But there is no doubt that there is ample material, and widespread conviction, warranting that inquiry.

Emil Kraepelin, psychiatry's first taxonomist, wrote: "At the beginning, work on the ward upset me very much. . . . The intensity of unusual, disturbing impressions and the first feeling of personal responsibility pursued me into my sleep and caused irritating dreams."[3] By the mid-twentieth century, the understanding of the transmission of affect as a pathological event was formally complicated by the recognition that clinicians too could experience it. One clinician who discarded the clinic in favor of a study of neurology did so precisely because he was too susceptible to transmitted affects. "During my psychiatric residency, I noted that certain patients aroused extremely uncomfortable sensations within me. These sensations often persisted for hours and sometimes even several days after my last contact with the patient."[4] Similarly, and at more theoretical length, the Kleinian school of psychoanalysis claims that a new understanding of countertransference is required, precisely because analysts directly experience or pick up on the affects of their patients. Countertransference, in the original meaning of the term, meant the affects and ideas an analyst had regarding a particular patient. It was comparable to the analysand's transference. Like the analysand's transference, countertransference "transferred" an emotional pattern developed in earlier life. Countertransference was dealt with, or meant to be dealt with, by the expedient of self-analysis. In short, neither transference nor countertransference was allowed to be anything beyond the experience of repetition engendered by the process of analysis.

Among the Kleinians, Paula Heimann argued for a new understanding of countertransference in which the "feelings" an analyst had about the patient were not only (if at all) a repetition of past loves and hates. These feelings could also be transferred directly to the analyst from the patient;[5] they could be a product purely of what the analysand was feeling then and there, which meant that the analyst's prior psychohistory had nothing to do with them. Heimann meant that the patient's affects got inside her, and she evidently regarded this lodgment from without as a communication. It was information about the patient's state, a way of communicating what an analysand was feeling. The analyst felt this feeling in relation to the patient. In this sense, the feeling was "countertransference," but the feeling did not originate through the analyst's failure to self-analyze. Let us note at once here that this notion of countertransference is open to ready abuse. In the worst-case scenario, an envious analyst feeling full of hatred might absolve himself of envy and hatred alike, concluding that these feelings were his analysand's. Indeed the ready abuse to which the new idea of countertransference lent itself made Melanie Klein herself dislike it. One story goes that when a young doctor whose training Klein was supervising told her that he had "interpreted to his patient that she was putting her feelings of confusion into him," Klein replied, "No, my dear, you are confused."[6]

Klein's own substantial doubts aside, it is more and more taken for granted by various schools of therapy that the feelings an analyst or therapist has in the presence of a patient are information about that patient's state of mind. The question becomes, how does the analyst come to feel the other's feelings? In one of the early (pre-Heimann) papers on the new countertransference, analyst Mabel Cohen wrote: "It is a well-known fact that certain types of persons are literally barometers for the tension level of other persons with whom they are in contact. Apparently cues are picked up from small shifts in muscular tension as well as changes in voice tone."[7] Here, the extent of the prejudice in favor of sight or hearing is evident in the way that when Cohen recognizes transmission, she assimilates it, however unlikely the assimilation, through sight or sound.

Examples from other analysts are less susceptible to a visual or aural interpretation. In 1992 Darlene Ehrenberg wrote: "We have all had experiences such as one I had with one patient, in which I found myself having a fantasy of her arriving for a particular session with a gun, only to have her reveal in the very same session, without my having said anything, that she was having murderous fantasies about me which she had been terrified to share. In those instances where patients do not tell us such fantasies, sensitivity to this level of our own experience can be essential."[8]

Christopher Bollas is even more explicit about the visceral nature of transmission:

> I am sure, however, that many interpretations with certain patients originate from our soma. I may ache from psychic pain affecting soma, and my interpretation will come from there—the ache. Or a patient may be so overwhelming, my anxiety so high, that I am more a creature of my respiratory system, so that some interpretations will evolve out of this somatic distress . . . I seem to be saying that analysts are mediums for the psycho-somatic processing of the patient's psyche-soma. . . . I may be working with someone in my soma—in the stomach, the back, or in my respiratory system.[9]

But Bollas is clear that there is precision in the feelings that are transferred from the patient. "If I am with an obsessional analysand, I may feel a sense of seemingly unresolvable frustration and irritation as a result of being the object of such a person's aseptic relating. With a manic patient, I may feel frightened by the murderous quality of the patient's grandiosity. The borderline analysand's chaotic internal world may well preserve in me a prolonged sense of confusion and disorientation, while the narcissistic patient lulls me into the grip of the sleepmaker as I fight his obtuseness to remain alert."[10] Of another patient, who presented himself as cold and unlikable, while cheerfully insulting Bollas for being too politically correct, Bollas responds that he was never really insulted. "In fact I liked him. I knew, therefore, that my affection for him was a countertransference state that provided some evidence of dissociated loving feelings in him."[11]

So far, it is clear that the analyst or therapist is the *recipient* of affects from the patient. As I have suggested, this is contra the idea that it is the patient who has weak boundaries and therefore projects out affects. But psychoanalyst Harold Searles, who also experienced the transmission of affect, is interesting because he turns the pathology around. Searles regards the schizophrenic patient, the patient without boundaries, as especially susceptible to the unconscious processes of the analyst. In line with Freud's theory, Searles had considered hallu-cinations to be projective phenomena:

> But in the course of my work with a certain schizophrenic man I discov-ered that, in at least some instances, to understand why a patient is hal-lucinating we must see this as having to do with not only *projection* but also *intro*jection. To be specific, in this particular instance, I found that the patient's evident hallucinating of murderously threatening figures connoted not only his projecting, in the form of hallucinatory figures, his own unconscious murderous impulses, but connoted also his struggle against the introjection of *my* own unconscious murderous impulses toward him. . . .
>
> one of the sessions . . . I noticed that as he came in and sat down he said to himself in a hushed, quavering, very frightened voice, "Careful!" as if he sensed an ominous presence in the room. It was only a few ses-sions after this that an incident occurred that showed me how much dis-sociated rage there had been in me, presumably for a long time.[12]

We will return to Searles in the discussion of entrainment. His idea that hallucinating may mean *receiving* information from another's un-conscious will be borne out by the discussion of vision. But what are we to make of a situation where borderline and psychotic patients are held responsible both for transmitting affects and for receiving them? While there are concepts bearing on the projection of affects, the con-ceptual armory concerning their introjection is undeveloped. More-over, the concepts bearing on projection are also limited, although of course they need to be discussed.

Projection and Projective Identification

By common consent, but no clear definition, the affects received by countertransference are termed projective identifications, as distinct from projections. A projection is what I disown in myself and see in you; a projective identification is what I succeed in having you experi-ence in yourself, although it comes from me in the first place. For ex-ample, with my projection, I may see you as unimaginative, to avoid feeling that way myself, although somewhere I probably do. With my projective identification, you actually feel unimaginative, while I do not.[13] This is a version of dumping, in that I have evacuated my unpleasant feeling and deposited it in you, except that dumping as a concept has a wider compass. You dump when your voice tones are violently angry and another's sense of well being is shaken by those invisible violent vibrations. They have taken on your disturbance and have to adjust to the disequilibrium (by retaining it for you or perhaps by finding ways to "give it back").[14] But the envious glance and the ill wishes that accompany it may take place in silence, unheard and even unseen by the object of that envy.[15] Envy is more likely to find its way into a projective identification, but it need not. It can be refused, just as anger can be refused, and this refusal marks the difference between dumping and projective identification. Projective identification requires unconscious complicity. Dumping may be retained, or it may not. When a person is, in fact, not the problem, not the origin of the negative affect in question, the realization of this can be occluded by feelings of worthlessness (guilt and depression). Those who consistently blame the other are more likely to be projecting on the other, while those who do not, obviously, blame themselves. Tendencies to allocate affective responsibilities themselves encapsulate the direction in which the negative affect is pointing, and both parties more or less agree as to who carries it.[16]

Projective identification is an essentially primitive form of communication. Klein believed it was characteristic of infancy before boundaries (although "boundaries" was not one of Klein's words) were established. If you did not like a feeling or an attitude, you "put" it into the other. You then believed that the other had that feeling or attitude toward you. Subsequently, Kleinians took projective identification further. Primitive communication (olfaction?) meant that you let someone else know how you were feeling by getting them to feel the same way. Projective identification (projector hormones?) was how you did it. The fact that psychical complicity was not presupposed, and that an equivalent concept of introjective identification was not mooted, reflects the biased starting point in which "affects" and drives are held to originate from a subject, although this view of things was modified by the greatest of the post-Kleinians, Wilfred Bion.

Bion does not style his theory an account of the transmission of affect (although I will argue that he should).[17] Rather, he presents us with a theory of groups (to which I shall return) and a theory of container and contained. This theory is based on the mother-infant relationship and how the mother is, or should be, a "container" for the confused thoughts and feelings of the infant. More than this, the mother accepts (or should accept) these confused notions as projected communications from the infant and returns them, as it were, sifted through, without the anxiety that makes it so hard to connect one thought logically with another. Bion goes further, arguing that the mother also gives the infant a supply of attention that enables it to develop. Bion saw it as the mother's gift to the child. But if we regard the attention the mother gives the child as an energetic force in itself, is there any reason for supposing the gift of attention is any less enhancing in other dyadic relationships? I will return to this in a moment. The idea of attention is of more immediate interest, because this capacity is associated with the cognitive rather than the emotional dimension of human affairs.

For Bion, the mother-child relationship is not the only instance of the relation between the container and the contained. An effective analyst-analysand relationship—in the treatment of psychosis especially—is another:

> The patient had been lying on the couch, silent, for some twenty minutes. . . . As the silence continued, I became aware of a fear that the patient was meditating a physical attack on me, though I could see no outward change in his posture. Then, and only then, I said to him: "you have been pushing into my inside your fear that you will murder me." There was no change in the patient's position, but I noticed that he clenched his fists till the skin over the knuckles became white. The silence was unbroken. At the same time I felt that the tension in the room, presumably in the relationship between him and me, had decreased. I said to him: "When I spoke to you, you took your fear that you would murder me back into yourself; you are now feeling afraid you will make a murderous attack on me." . . . It will be noted that my interpretations depend on the use of Melanie Klein's theory of projective identification, first to illuminate my countertransference, and then to frame the interpretation which I gave the patient.[18]

Hypothetically, the analyst, or more probably and usually the mother, absorbs thoughts in the confused form (Bion termed them "alpha" elements), confused in the rage and aggression that accompanies them, and returns them. In the process she somehow transforms these aggressive alpha elements into "beta" elements of thought. Beta elements are capable of being connected with one another in the same way that impressions and sensations, once adequately connected with one another, yield more comprehensive interpretations than those that cannot. The thing about these elements is that while their relation to thinking has salience for Bion, what interferes with the ability to think are the affects of rage and anxiety. This is not to say that Bion ignores affects, not at all. It is only to say that we should be aware of a bias toward thought and cognition at the expense of affects in accounts of transmission. Such a bias prevents Bion from seeing that love should not be listed as an affect *simpliciter* along with envy, greed, anxiety, fear, and rage. Love is different in that it directs positive feelings toward the other by attending to the specificity of the other (rather than seeing her or him through idealizing or demonizing projections). As we will see, it has now been established that love, as living attention, literally and physically affects biological and intellectual growth in children.[19]

If Bion's premise in relation to why thinking can be difficult was to be simply stated, it would have to be that the transmission of affect is a fact. An idea of transmission is also demanded by the more recent work of Laplanche, who sees the child as the repository of the unconscious of the parents. Laplanche believes the unconscious in the child is only created by the parents' fantasies, which the child then carries.[20] His difference from Bion is that while Bion focuses on what the mother carries for the child, Laplanche is concerned with what the child carries for the parents. Laplanche's idea is radical not only in relation to what it implies for notions of the self-contained individual but also with regard to psychoanalysis overall: from the time of Freud's discovery of "psychical reality" onward, the child was shaped by the way its drives sought out its objects and its parents. Laplanche reverses the child-to-parent logic of psychoanalysis. But it is at least as radical in that this theory, like Bion's, demands a mechanism of transmission.[21] After all, how exactly does the unconscious of the parent get into the child?

One might answer, through language and caress. And that answer might be partly right, provided we note that there are physical dimensions to both touch and words. We will return below to whether the sweat traces and modulations in a caress, or the quavering notes of language, are sufficient to carry the unconscious from one being to another. The thing to note now is that this problem is like the one Searles observed. The unconscious of the analyst is likely to get "into" that of the psychotic patient because the psychotic patient lacks boundaries. Similarly, on the face of it, a child is also unable to resist the forceful projections of the parents.

The question of boundaries returns us to the school that has said most about how boundaries are formed, the mainstream object-relations school of psychoanalysis. This is a hugely diverse school, ranging from the insights of a Daniel Stern or Maud Mannoni to the strictures of a John Bowlby. But mainstream object-relations theory has entered popular culture through all those works that blame the mother if the "inner child" is unhappy in later life. I am calling this school "mainstream" to distinguish it from Klein's, which is also based in object-relations, but which holds the child's fantasies concerning the mother to be of more note than the mother's actual conduct. One of the fathers of the mainstream school, Donald Winnicott, credits Melanie Klein with being the founder of object-relations thinking in psychoanalysis. But he distances himself from the priority Klein gives to fantasy over reality in psychical life and from her attachment to Freud's idea of the drives (Klein, like Freud, believed in a death drive). After Winnicott, non-Kleinian object-relations theorists more or less dispensed with any notion of the drives.[22] But a brief discussion of the drive in Freud's account shows it is inseparable from the affect, especially in the energetic context of transmission.

Drives and Objects: Affects and Attention

The tremendous work done this century in object-relations theory generally, and specifically on the mother-infant relationship, is premised more and more on the assumption that an infant psyche develops not on the drive-ridden "egg" model Freud presupposed, but through the interaction with, and internalization of, significant others. But while object-relations theory developed in opposition to psychoanalytic drive or instinct theory, it stresses the affect before all else.[23] An object-relations clinician probably regards the life and death drives as myths, but her and his work cannot proceed without a concept of love. Love is critical in mothering, in analyzing, and in development overall. This stress on the affect should pose an object-relations dilemma: for while there is a difference between the notion of affect and the idea of the drives, the two are intimately connected. The drive propels the affect; it is in large part the stuff out of which the affect is made. This is the case not only for love and libido but also for those other object-relations foci: hate, aggression, greed, and envy. (These are derivatives of the death drive, of which more shortly.)

In the received Freud, priority in psychical life is given to the drives or instincts. The libido is constructed out of tributaries whose character is forged by their interaction with their oral, scopophiliac (that is, relating to the perverse pleasure of spectating), anal, and other objects. These drives seek out an object, but just about any object will do. Indeed, this is why the term "object" is used in psychoanalysis. Formally it has no instrumental or objectifying connotations. It is used in preference to "person" precisely because the drive could seek out a shoe or a corset more than, or as much as, the person to whom either accessory is traditionally attached. Whatever the case, the drive comes before any object.

The indebtedness of the affects to the drives is plain if we reflect on the way that affects, like the drives they are derived from, are carriers of energy. If I am depressed, it may be because I have turned the affect of anger back against myself rather than directing it toward another. And in turning it back against myself, I automatically become more inert: my energy is less. In other words, it is the energetic dimension of the affects that reveals their partial origin in the drives most directly. This energetic dimension is not only evident in the negative affects. Just as the negative affects may deplete energy, so can the positive affects enhance it. If I receive another's love, I receive their living attention; and this attention, logically, is a biological force in itself, as palpable an energy as adenosine triphosphate (ATP), the bioenergetic basis of life and consciousness.[24]

It is difficult to draw any other conclusion from studies on the failure to thrive in neglected children. Such studies show how children with adequate food, but no love or personal attention, do not grow at an average physical rate. The most dramatic instance of this was a comparison of two German orphanages in the years following World War II. The children in both received comparable material care—nutrition, doctor's visits—but very different personal care. In the orphanage run by the "warm, attentive" caretaker the children grew significantly faster than in the orphanage run by the caretaker who had time for only a few.[25] Sociologist Mary Carlson has made similar observations concerning her more recent work on Romanian orphanages.[26] Accepting that love and positive attention are inseparable, I suggest that attention, as an energetic and profoundly material additive is missing when children fail to thrive, in the same way that nutrition can be missing.[27] Exactly this has been argued in relation to recent research on maternal rodents. Nurturing by these mothers "stimulates neural connections in their babies brains and enhances learning. . . . [Their] offspring subsequently scored higher in intelligence and memory tests."[28] A summary of this series of experiments ("broadly applicable," say its authors, "to humans") is worth quoting at length. The experiment divided thirty-two female rats into two groups:

> One group provided a high level of care to their offspring, including stroking, grooming, licking and attentive nursing. The other group included mothers that were more indifferent. When the baby rats matured, they were tested in a swimming maze in which they had to find a small platform submerged in a shallow tank. The rats were tested fifteen times over three days. . . . The rats scored about the same on the first day of testing. However, the offspring of the attentive mothers scored higher on days two and three. The smarter rats also scored high on other tests throughout their lives. . . . Researchers then examined cells extracted from the hippocampus, a brain region vital to memory and learning. . . . They found extra synapses, or connections between nerve cells, in samples from the nurtured offspring. They also found more receptors for growth hormones and the NMDA neurotransmitter that is crucial to learning. The cells of the neglected offspring did not show similar enhancements. . . . In a second round of experiments, the researchers switched the offspring between the good and neglectful mothers. Rats born to neglectful mothers but raised by good mothers also scored well on the maze test and showed more neural connections. But rats born to attentive mothers but raised by indifferent mothers scored well, too.[29]

In other words, one can either find attentive love or energy in utero, or find it after birth. Either way, the brain responds. Cast in Freudian terms, in responding to the living attention of the other, one is responding to the life drive. That is to say, for Freud, one's basic driving energy is sexual, but it is also and simultaneously a life drive. The life drive is not something whose relation to the libido was elaborated by Freud. He assumes they are the same, although one is constructed and the other is in some way originary, like the death drive. As a principle and a force, the life drive is something that furthers vital unity (as opposed to the death drive, which destroys the unity necessary for life to exist). The aim of the life drive "is to establish ever greater unities and to preserve them thus—in short, to bind together." The death drive, on the contrary, aims "to undo connections and so to destroy things."[30] Freud allied the force of the death drive with the force of anxiety as the factor that undoes connections. It works against connective growth rather than for it. Demonstrably, anxiety, envy, and aggression work against bodily well being through stress-related illness. Hence my earlier indication of a distinction between love and the other affects. Love is tied to the life drive; the other affects are full of disconnecting or deathly impulses. They work in different directions, one for unification, the other against it.

For Freud, the life drive operates at all levels from the cellular to the sexual as a principle of union and organization. The affinity and assumed identity between the life drive and the libido is evident not only in the sexual drives, but linked as well to the "attention" used in intellectual concentration. Attention has also been shown to be the condition of thriving and connected by Bion and others with love. Freud is insistent that the libido is, from the very beginning, shaped in its interactions with its objects, whether these objects exist in reality or in fantasy. Given that the libido is anchored in the life drive, the same should be true of it.

The drives continue to be shaped by their interactions with fantasies and objects, but also reveal their origins in the life drive insofar as they drive the subject toward others and organize its psyche toward that end. At one point, I sought the distinction between the affects and the drives in the difference between the internal and external direction of energy. I have also sought it, more correctly, in the idea that the phantasmic has less energy than the real. Each composite of imagery, of fantasy, memory, and energy, modulates the energy of the life drive. It does not invariably reduce it. It can release it. But I hazard, following Freud, that the energy available to the subject is reduced whenever it constructs a viewpoint, or an experiential pathway from its own standpoint. Alternatively, when it attracts the attention of another, that energy is enhanced because an actual living force is added to its literal well being. Moreover, the subject is more free to direct the life drive in its various modulations toward aims other than its own ego when another attends to it or loves it.

The life drive is diverted inward in the repression of the hallucinations that are supposed by Freud to occur in infancy.[31] The foundational fantasy as such is cemented in place when the first hallucination is repressed. The essence of the fantasy is the reversal of positions: the projection onto the mother of one's infantile passivity and dependence; the arrogation to oneself of the imaginary maternal ability to meet one's needs instantly. In turn, the belief that the mother can gratify those needs at once has, I argue, a basis in reality. It is a carryover, a fleshly memory, of the in utero experience in which there was no delay between the perception of a need and its fulfillment. The first hallucination is the conjuring up of an immediate satisfaction (in the form of the breast) of one's needs. But because the promise of relief is false, because this falsity registers in the flesh in terms of excitement that has no energetic release, the hallucination has to be repressed. At the same time, the confusion between maternal and infantile capacities carries over for the infant to its understanding of who or what causes the unpleasant repression it experiences after it hallucinates. It confuses the experience of the mother's living attention with its self-caused repression.

It may also be the case that an image (or imprint) received from the mother, or the father, works similarly to the bondage effected by the repression of a fantasy. But the infant has no means of distinguishing between the sense of bondage occasioned by the repression and the imprint it experiences at the hands of the other. Nor is it aware of the other as a source of facilitating energy, as one who transmits attention. So the infant blames the other for the bad feelings occasioned by repression, feelings that are felt as aggressive (for any bondage is aggressive). The infant then projects this aggression back onto, or literally into, the other. The repression of fantasies gives birth to more fantasies about bad mothers, supposedly responsible for experiences that are felt as punitive. That is to say, because it does not yet have a sense of its own boundaries, the infant is necessarily unclear as to what comes from where. The fixity it produces through its own repressions can be attributed to the other. The attentive energy it receives from the other can be felt as its own production. Nonetheless, it can be the case that the imprint from the other is also draining. Most of us are familiar with those prematurely aged children whose faces bear the marks of the experience and stress of a much older person, an older person who may not be shouldering the burden of his or her own life.

The imprint from the other is never, or very rarely, pure facilitating energy, the pure attention of disinterested love. It is energy laced with the other's own affective agenda, but it is not always uniform in its effects. The times when we are especially open to the imprint of others correlate roughly with the "plastic" periods described in psychiatry. Preeminent among these periods is infancy. We are never more vulnerable to the imprint of the other than then. And yet, as I noted, there is a degree of resistance to the other's imprint. As we shall see, it is in the interaction between the imprint and the forces propelling a resistance to it that the unconscious is born.

What this means for now is that the unconscious is not only a matter of the imprint of the other. It is also formed through the projections of the subject-to-be. First among these projections is the wish to expel fixity, which is felt as deadening or confining. Fixity is attributed to the other's imprint; the imprint "makes" you feel confined. But fixity is also produced by oneself. It is produced when we repress fantasies or hallucinations. Any repression involves fixing something in place, holding it still, preventing it from coming forward. The good news is that this newly bound energy provides fixed points of reference in the world of transmissions and moving energy into which the infant is born. From these fixed points the nascent psyche begins to get a sense of its own distinctness. The bad news is that this bound energy is felt in the flesh for what it is: a repressive experience. Instead of being available for use, that energy is now permanently tied up in keeping a repression in place. As the infant cannot distinguish between inside and outside, it blames the other for its repression.

Because fantasy is present from the beginning, we should conclude that the affects are always passive and always negative, insofar as they obstruct, deregulate, and divert the life drive and force of love (which arguably, and originally, are one and the same thing).[32] This conclusion (which echoes a long tradition in which the affects as passions are passive) follows from the way hallucination and primary repression, and fantasy and secondary repression, divert the drives.

Freud saw repression as a twofold phenomenon linked to the acquisition of language. The first phase, primary repression, attracted subsequent secondary repressions toward it. Primary repression is the repression analyzed in the defense against hallucination: it occurs when we repress a visual image that would otherwise lead to a perceptual disorder (confusing hallucinations conjured on command with the spatiotemporal reality inhabited after birth). Secondary repression occurs afterward as the organism acquires language, in that it involves repressing an idea that has had words attached to it at some point ("I wish Daddy was dead"). This is essentially different from repressing an idea that presents itself visually (the floating signifier of the breast). The theory then is that the primary repression (as in the breast) would then attract similar secondary repressions toward it ("I wish Daddy was dead, so that I could sleep with Mommy"). In a famous metaphor, Freud compared the process of repression to the construction of the pyramids—repression has to be pulled, as well as pushed. There is a relation between the puller (the primary repression of the visual image) and the pusher (the named categories of secondary repression), but, here, the thread of reasoning breaks off. It does so, I think, because Freud, who was deeply synthetic regarding the logic of his findings, was unable to pursue the relation between primary and secondary repression in terms that work within a self-contained energetic system. He was working from evidence provided by a system with that appearance, insofar as he hypothesized the nature of repression from the interpretation of dreams in the first instance. He hypothesized on the basis of evidence that had already been organized in visual and linguistic categories. Everyone hallucinates in dreams. But Freud did not only infer the existence of infantile hallucination from comparing dreams, as he did, to the most primitive stages of psychical life. As we have seen, infantile hallucination is prompted (in part) by hunger in the first instance. The relation between the primary repression of the hallucination and subsequent oral fantasy is prompted by drives modulated by that initial hallucinatory experience. If such oral fantasies come too close to the mother's breast, then, on the one hand, they are repressed, while, on the other, they structure subsequent desire. This simultaneous operation is performed by the Oedipal splitting of the sensual and affectionate currents, so that sensuality is shaped in a way that minimizes associations between the breast and the need for nurturance and affection (the mother or woman on whom one depends), while exaggerating those that affirm the breast's obedience to masculine desire (the whore or woman one may use at will). Again, this Oedipal moment will concern us subsequently. The immediate point of its use here is to serve as an illustration of how energetic drives are shaped from the outset through social interaction. That is to say, given that the oral drive is formed in relation to the breast (or any subsequent drive is formed in relation to its objects), then it is also formed in relation to fantasy. Because, as I have shown, fantasies either divert living attention inward, or, like hallucinations, require the expenditure of energy in their repression, they slow us down. They passify us relative to the state of energy before repression. Insofar as they drive fantasies, affects always block energies, but for most working purposes affects and fantasies are only known via their combinations with the life drive and/or death drive. Passionate love, for instance, can embody aggression as well as loving attention and living energy, and depending on the proportions of the mixture, we find it good or destructive. In short, the affects as such are always negative, but as we know them only in admixtures with energy, we are forced to speak of positive affects from time to time.

Moreover, the distinction between the drive and the affect as such is not a pure one. It may seem that the one has an active aggressive drive, while the other suffers from passifying anxiety. But if the other is carrying the anxiety the aggression attempts to dispose of, or if anxiety is the registration by the other of projected aggression, then this distinction is in question for reasons additional to those already adduced. That is to say, there is no such thing as an affect-free drive, for all the drives are shaped by their interaction with fantasies and objects. But the shaping of the drive by its interaction with the object also affects the object once the transmission of affect is taken into account, just as the object influences the subject. The object, as the mother, returns living attention for anxious aggression, enabling thoughts to make connections. Making connections, organizing ideas and experience into unities, is the essence of the life drive as Freud defined it. Living attention hereby emerges as the thing that directs the affects to certain objects; this or that affect conjures up this or that object (owing to entrenched patterns of fantasy and experience). But the thing that gives that affect energy is the living attention it absorbs, while the thing that depletes it is the lack around which affective pathways congregate in directing that attention to specific ends (such as itself, its appearance, its reputation).

Inasmuch as intersubjective relations are affect-ridden and therefore drive-ridden, not only in the obvious sense that every instinct must have an aim but also in the sense that the affect of the one carries over into the other, then the opposition between classical drive theories and object-relations theories breaks down. To replace it we need a distinction resonating with that between the life and death drives. For reasons that are becoming plain, we find that resonance in the distinction between attention and affect. Attention to something other than oneself, or the living energy that enlivens another without affective penalty, is not the same as an affect directed toward another, because the affect carries a message of self-interest along with the attention it rides on. Nonetheless, unless it has captured a supply of attention, an affect fades into insignificance. A passionate and obsessional hatred, for instance, can capture a great deal of living attention in the service of the thought it is directed toward.[33] Kant saw passion (by which he meant something like obsessional fixation) as the result of error on the part of reason. St. Augustine saw all passions as species of love. But reason and love are both names for aspects of living attention; living attention is the condition of reasoning and the embodiment of its connective ability as well as the gift from the mother to the child or the lover to the beloved. It is only the attachment to the idea that the subject is self-contained, and the related prejudice against the energetic physicality of ideas, that stops this from being obvious. As the psychoanalytic thinker Jessica Benjamin has pointed out to me, there is a wealth of empirical material in intersubjective analytic theory that could be drawn on in developing the theory of the transmission of affect, insofar as affective transmission is effectively presupposed in various intersubjective accounts of the infant's development; this is notable in the work of Daniel Stern, who also discusses the energetic dimension of the affects.[34] However, there is an evident reluctance to think "physically" in object-relations theory, precisely because of the theoretical heritage to which I have just referred. Bion at times does put the question of affects more in physical, biological terms, possibly because his theory of the container and the contained is an explicit theory of the acceptance, transformation, and return of the infant's affect, a transformation modulated by living attention. Moreover, Bion's sympathy for physical, biological thinking is evident in his construction of a table of the elements of thoughts, paralleling the periodic table that is basic to chemistry. Whether a union with the life sciences can be fostered by imitating their taxonomies (if indeed fostering such a union was Bion's intention) is open to doubt.[35] Nonetheless, it may be through biochemical and neurological research that we will locate mechanisms for the transmission of affect and understand more of the energetic force of attention.

Colonized and Colonizer

As mothers and analysts contain the thoughts and affects of infants and patients, the same process, or a version of it, probably occurs outside the container/contained relationships. In *Interpretation of the Flesh* I argued that the missing dimension in the analysis of femininity and masculinity is an understanding of how the masculine party (a being of any sex) projects his or her unwanted aggression into the feminine other, who experiences this projected aggression as anxiety and depression. But, at the same time as one carries these negative affects for the other, one can, much as Bion's mother did, give a form of living attention to the other.[36] The feminine party, while carrying the masculine other's disordered affects, also gives that other living attention. Following Freud, I cast the question of femininity in terms of an economy of this form of basic energy. For Freud, energetics was the key to health. Put at its simplest: the more neurotic you are, the more repressed you are; the more repressed you are, the less energy you have. He observed that his feminine patients were more repressed and more rigid than his male patients. But he also observed the mysterious masochistic workings of femininity in men, as well as the fact that women have weaker superegos than men, although the superego is the agency of repression, and women or feminine beings are meant to be more repressed than men or masculine ones. But by my argument, such contradictions, together with the rigidity that marks femininity and the repression that accompanies it, are constituted in relation to the other through an energetic exchange. The transmission of affect, although it has all but been named as such in psychoanalytic studies of the parent-child relationship, is not restricted to that relationship. The transmission of affect also works between individuals who are coupled as partners or peers, between not-exactly-consenting adults in private and in public.

But transmission does not account for all affects; parties bring their affective histories into relationships with them, and these histories are perceived as their endogenous affects or emotional dispositions. We can consider the difference here in terms of case material on depression. Depression, in men or women, is a feminine affect, aggression a masculine one. These are also things that can be brought into a relationship by one or both parties. The idea that depression is anger turned inward is common to both endogenous and relational (for want of another term) depression. To take an apparent example of the former: In a study of recovery from major depression, which appeared to be endogenous, it was found that when the recovery group was compared with the group who had never been depressed, the recovery group reported holding anger in and being afraid to express it far more than the control group.[37] In another sample of 270 depressed patients reporting on their responses to stress, four-fifths of the patients acknowledged "acting in" (internalizing) behaviors—most commonly withdrawal.[38] Similarly, an examination of adolescent psychiatric patients showed that adolescents who "internalized their anger were more likely to be depressed and to experience feelings of hopelessness."[39] Turning to relational depression: The literature discusses a phenomenon known as "interpersonal depression," where the person's depression depends on his or her relationship with a particular person, and disappears when the relationship disappears. Other studies demonstrate a significant, positive correlation between depression and various types of hostility, including "intropunitiveness" and "extrapunitiveness." Interestingly, analysis of the statistical data showed that women tended to have higher scores on most hostility measures, despite the fact that women do not tend to act out in violence.[40]

The explicitly interpersonal process view of depression has been formulated by researchers evaluating subjects' reactions to a supposed depressed or nondepressed person. "Requests from depressed persons elicited significantly more anger and social rejection than from nondepressed persons." The authors believe that these findings support a view advanced by James Coyne that "rejection of depressed persons results from the negative mood they induce in others."[41] The notion that such negative moods can be induced again suggests that the dynamic between aggression, anger, and depression (or masculinity and femininity) is one in which an external or secondary structure replicates a primary one. That suggestion entails endorsing the idea that seemingly endogenous depression—where one's own anger is turned inward in anxiety and guilt—can be overlaid by secondary depression, which results from carrying another's anger, aggression, and anxiety. But about the mechanisms here we have to speculate. Perhaps the depressed person emits a chemical constellation that invites aggression and rejection. Perhaps antidepressants work by reordering that constellation so there is a smell of guilt-free confidence, within and without. Is this why convulsive electric shock therapy works, because it shifts off or breaks the connection with the negative affects, from wherever they arise?

There is some indication that the prolonged use of antidepressants is tied to sociopathology (the absence of guilt or remorse), but antidepressants also relieve sufferers of "free-floating" guilt, anxiety, and inertia, which they would not deserve in any just allocation of the negative affects, "just" insofar as the affects are distributed in relation to the acts that generate them, or lend them energy they lacked hitherto. If we follow this line of speculation further, the appropriateness of an antidepressant would depend on whether affects fixed in place needed to be released, or whether relational affects needed to be redirected. But the question of analysis is complicated by the manner in which preexisting depression attracts more aggression toward it. If one party's depression originates in unconscious anger, the other may well pick up something that makes his or her own hormonal networks quiver in response. Accordingly, the other may become anxious, even aggressive, in response to a preexisting state that is thereby reinforced. There is something in human depression that calls out the worst in others; perhaps it is only the wounding smell of sadness, whose kinship with anger draws out angry fellow feeling. There is also a certain *jouissance*, a wheezing pleasure, in the acceptance of the other's negative affect via depression. In such depression one lives out the projected anger or anxiety or general aggression of the other. In either preexisting or relational depression, evidently one is better off refusing the affect than enjoying the trespass. That very refusal is an act of self-constitution, but it is self-constitution directed toward refusing what should be refused. This refusal also affords a pleasure that is easily abused—the ability to cut off emotional contact by breaking off empathy with the other. In some cases, cutting "empathy" does indeed cut off affective cycles in which we should not participate; however, we can also cut off cycles in which we should participate—that is to say, cycles in which we are in debt, as the recipients of others' energetic attention.

The New Maladies of the Soul

Socially, the transmission of energy and affect is at the partial root of—and perhaps the whole explanation for—the new diagnostic disorders: attention-deficit/hyperactivity disorder (ADHD), chronic fatigue syndrome (CFS), and the disease of painful muscles, fibromyalgia (FMS). I would point out that these are all disorders of attentive energy: either the absence of energy, as in chronic fatigue, or an excess of it, imbued thoroughly with the affects of aggression as in the impulsive-hyperactive form of ADHD.

Attention-Deficit/Hyperactivity Disorder

Three to five percent of school-age children suffer from attention-deficit/hyperactivity disorder (ADHD). ADHD is associated with altered brain functioning and is characterized by the inability to focus on tasks and/or by impulsive hyperactive behavior.[42] The etiology of these behaviors is not understood. Nonetheless, "increased levels of environmental adversity [have been] found among ADHD children compared with controls." Adversity was defined as "exposure to parental psychopathology and exposure to parental conflict."[43] These findings about adversity may be real or imaginary. Adolescents with ADHD "endorsed more extreme and unreasonable beliefs about their parent-teen relations [than another group], and demonstrated greater negative interactions during a neutral discussion compared to the control group."[44] A study comparing the prevalence of psychiatric and developmental disorders in the family members of children with ADHD compared with a control group of children with Down's syndrome (DS) concluded that "by parental report, children with ADHD were significantly more likely than the DS group to have a parent affected by alcoholism, other drug abuse, depression, delinquency, and learning disabilities." Similar patterns were also evident in first- and second-degree kin relationships. A nearby abuser meant a child was less able to concentrate, yet had abundant energy.[45] Current research is tending to uncouple the ability to concentrate from hyperactivity (meaning undirected or constantly distracted expressions of energy).

This literature supports the contention that parents, or parental negative affects, are implicated strongly in ADHD. But it is also written from a standpoint that blames parental psychopathology for problems in their offspring as a matter of course, ignoring the extent to which the parent (and the parent, demographically, is more and more the mother alone) is also dumped on. Specifically, the mother can have aggressive affects projected toward her in adolescent interaction, especially with boys. More generally, if the transmission of affect is a fact, a person in one (say, violent) environment or familial, communal context will encounter a different barrage of affects than a person in another (kinder) one. But explanations culled from an individual context blame individuals rather than contexts. Despite this, there are significant social patterns. The vast majority of ADHD patients are boys. Something clearly is off here, something marked strongly by sexual difference. That something, I will argue later, is not so much the presence of attention as such; it is more that the predominance of negative affects increases, and the affect of love and the force of energetic attention no longer provide sufficient boundaries or shields against it. In other words, the problem may not be that mothers love less. Incidence of depression among mothers of ADHD children suggests otherwise. It is rather that the force of the negative affects—the hate, envy, and aggression that inform violence—is growing throughout society.[46]

Chronic Fatigue Syndrome

Chronic fatigue syndrome (CFS) and fibromyalgia (FMS) are also linked to depressive and anxiety disorders. Fifty percent of CFS subjects have them. Moreover, approximately 80 percent of CFS subjects fulfilled criteria for sleep disorders (which is significant insofar as sleep is the leading candidate for the rejuvenation of attention).[47] Significant risk factors for CFS included three or more sources of stress in the patient's life, loss of interest in daily activities, and panic attacks, all things brought on by and through social interaction.[48] The correlation between psychogenic and social factors and the onset of physical symptoms is clearly indicated. Researchers have also attempted to clarify the associations between several socio-demographic and psychosocial variables in the onset of unexplained chronic fatigue. One British survey showed that subjects with psychiatric complications had *higher* rates of fatigue, a fact that is consistent both with the idea that they receive less love or living attention from others and with the idea that they are unshielded, or less well-shielded, from the negative affects.[49] Another study confirms this, showing that the lifetime prevalence of depressive and anxiety disorders among patients with chronic fatigue was 54 percent; current depressive and anxiety disorders were identified in twenty-eight out of one hundred patients, who exhibited more psychopathology and "functional impairment" (energetic work and relational capacities) than other patients.[50]

Fibromyalgia

The story of fibromyalgia (FMS) takes on similar contours, with many patients reporting psychological or emotional precursors to what is another disease in which the musculature and nervous system are trapped in debilitation. An overview reports that "emotional trauma was associated with the onset of FMS independently of demographics, physical trauma and sexual/physical abuse." Among patients, emotional trauma was correlated to a high number of physician visits, functional disability, and fatigue.[51] One study found that "compared with patients with rheumatoid arthritis, those with fibromyalgia had significantly higher lifetime prevalence rates of all forms of victimization, both in adult and childhood, as well as combination of adult and childhood trauma." Similarly, "Sexual, physical, and emotional traumas may be important factors in the development and maintenance of this disorder (FMS) and its associated disability in many patients."[52]

Trauma, very directly, is linked to the transmission of affect. Some of its victims testify with extraordinary acuity concerning the experience of something infiltrating their psyches as well as their bodies. Jane Caputi has gathered together several accounts resonant with knowledge of the transmission of negative affect among those subjected to the trauma of rape and incest. In such cases, trauma (originally, a piercing of the brain) becomes a piercing of the psychical shield as well as a dumping. But it does not fade in the way that physical and mental abuse (that is to say, the transmission of negative affect) fades with time or distance, provided the intersubjective context alters. As a growing and interesting literature documents, it is as if the psyche has incorporated the very structure of abuse in some malformation, which keeps the trauma current by repeating it in the imagination and thereby seems to keep the perpetrator linked to the victim. Psychoanalytically, the musculature is identified with the ego. It would be too much to say on the basis of limited evidence that somatic expressions of trauma carry the physical or psychical memory of inflicted pain in the musculature, or ego. But it does seem as if the affects of the perpetrator are in some way negatively affixed to the victim in such cases. As long as trauma is unhealed it keeps the victim open to the same affects (and attracts them from a variety of sources); there is something in trauma that permits such affects a permanent entry. Of more direct interest in closing this chapter is that the contemporary psycho-disease epidemics indicate that on the one hand, there is an increase in enervation and depression and, on the other, there is an increase in aggression and lack of attention combined. The way that the incidence of violence and aggression is paired with an increase in enervation is striking because it echoes the dynamics of transmission between masculine and feminine, colonizer and colonized. But as we suggested, this aggression may no longer be contained or containable by those who once carried it. An increase in aggression is evident in the waves of violence that sweep over whole populations in active persecutions, as well as the increasing incidence of individual rage. Both suggest additionally that violence can be contagious, that it is an affect that is readily transmitted either directly or through anxiety and depression, which in turn affects a person's ability to think clearly about connections and causality. Drives, it seems, as the embodiment of life energy, are increasingly disconnected from attention, so that energy carries on without focus, much like Schopenhauer's blinded will.

Energy is known to us through the drives, but it is rarely known simply as energy. The drives are the energies modulated by the affects. This modulation inevitably decreases the energetic force of the drive and to this extent makes it passive—relative to the active force of the drive—when it is not tied to memories, fantasies, and associations. These slow it down, as do all cognitive and affective formulations of the aim of the drive when these are made from one's own standpoint. But some slow us down less than others, while others seem to give us energy. This is where the energetic depletion that is contingent on depression, and evident in psychogenic diseases such as chronic fatigue, lends support to this general formulation. It is consistent with the notion that aggression directed toward the one by the other increases the psychical stress of the recipient, who thereby carries an additional repressive burden because of that projection. It is also consistent with the idea that the projector benefits in that he or she is then free, or relatively free, of the disorder that hitherto disrupted his or her capacities for thought and action (witness Bion's formulation of alpha and beta elements). Yet in a situation where aggression is no longer contained in dyadic transfers, it will spread by contagion, by episodic violence that is and is not connected, that occurs at the same time in individuals and groups.

The notion of contagion, and critiques of that notion, will be considered next. This consideration encompasses a literature on the phenomenon known as entrainment—the olfactory and rhythmic means whereby one person's affects can be linked to another. These biochemical and neurological literatures have not, to my knowledge, been linked to the study of the transmission of affect, an omission that reflects prejudices concerning the biological and the social, on the one hand and, on the other, the belief in self-containment. But in approaching these literatures and the study of contagion in groups and crowds, it will be useful to make a distinction between what we may term "simple affective transfers," in which your aggression communicates itself and I become aggressive in consequence, and "dyadic transfers," marked by projection and introjection. Contagion is a form of simple affective transfer. That is to say, simple affective transfers are not only discerned in rooms. They can be discerned in crowds as well as in that most mimetic state of identification in which one begins to act like the other, to do as they do, to wake up at the same time, for instance or go to the fridge or the bathroom at the same moment. This state of rhythmic identification (for that is what it is, identification or the simple transfers effected through chemical and nervous entrainment) is generally short-lived, but it seems to be brought about by proximity ("now I am feeling your nervousness," "we are both yawning," and so forth).

In dyadic affective transfers, whether they hold between two people or two groups (genders, races), one party benefits from the other's energetic attention, the other who is also carrying the depression. In other words, as this chapter has established, the key to these chronic fatigue syndrome-structured transfers is the relation between energy and affect, drive and object. When a certain affect captures a thought, or the thought attracts the affect, the thought then holds the attention, and with it, under normal circumstances, energy. Whether the thought then redirects that affect toward the other is another question. But we cannot conclude without noting that withdrawing attention from another (shifting focus from a child or beloved to a book) often draws forth attempts to regain that attention.

CHAPTER THREE

Transmission in Groups

A group, in sociology and social psychology, is two or more people. The theory of the transmission of affect is always and already, given this definition, a theory of the group. But it is also a theory of the group based on what is produced by the "group," as well as the individuals within it: the emotions of two are not the same as the emotions of one plus one. If I emit one emotion and you emit another, we may both of us take onboard the effects of this new composite. This should yield the basis for a contribution to group psychology, because we are beginning with an idea of how a gathering is constituted, in part, through the transmission of energetic affects (which may add up to something more than the individual affects of the group's members). The specific waves of affects generated by different cultural constellations could lead to a different and altogether more interesting characterization of stable, as well as temporary, group phenomena. It follows from the idea that affects can be compounded by interactive dynamics that some groups will carry more affective loads than others will. Similarly, codes of restraint where the affects are concerned also vary, with emotional displays being looked upon favorably in some contexts while they are discouraged in others.

I would like to develop that theory now, but it will have to wait until we have surveyed the existing literature. Also, the following survey of the debates on groups will show that there once nearly was a theory of the transmission of affect; ideas of the "group mind" and the emphasis on emotion in later nineteenth- and early twentieth-century writing on group or "crowd" psychology come close to it. We will see this in the next section, which focuses on the three theorists of the group and the crowd whom Freud, and later Bion, relied on: Gustave Le Bon, Wilfred Trotter, and William McDougall.

In the end, none of the principal contributors to the first discussion of group psychology explained the mechanism of transmission. And when we turn to the more recent work on groups, gatherings, and crowds, as we do in the second and third parts of this survey, we find that any such mechanism has become ever more elusive. Le Bon's first critics credit the individual rather than the crowd with the madness that crowds are meant to show. Subsequent contributors argue that the "group mind" theorists tend to pathologize and neglect the rational motivations of groups. But these sensible criticisms do not apply to all the phenomena of crowds and to even the most intelligent groups, within which a difficult idea can spread as if it were indeed contagious, as Le Bon contended. Our focus, then, is on the phenomena this literature records but does not explain. In this regard, Bion's theory of pathology offers more ways forward. Bion's group work was premised on the notion that psychotic defenses were more evident in, in fact critical to, group behavior. As Bion is known as a theorist of the group, let me introduce his relevance to the present discussion by stressing that while he believed that group phenomena do not by definition require that a group has gathered, these phenomena are easier to observe when the group is meeting. In other words, what ties the group together, what makes an individual a member of a group, holds regardless of whether the group is gathered together in one place. I turn to Bion in the third section, after Le Bon and other theorists of the crowd and group mind. What all of these thinkers demand in different ways is a mechanism or mechanisms for the transmission of affect. The fourth section draws out a literature that answers that need, a biochemical literature on a phenomenon known as entrainment. Entrainment is a name for the process whereby human affective responses are linked and repeated. Research on entrainment has not (to my knowledge) been linked to the study of groups and gatherings. But we will see that research on entrainment by olfactory and other sensory means accounts for situations where people act as of one mind. It also points to a reevaluation of evidence for the postnatal social shaping of factors we think of as biologically given: human hormones. I suggest these are the leading candidates for how affects are transmitted, as they involve the deployment of all the senses. Smell is significant here, but hormones, especially testosterone, can also be visually stimulated. I conclude this chapter with an analysis of the relation between image and olfaction in the production of group violence. This phenomenon prompted Le Bon's initial work on the crowd, to which we now turn.

The Theorists of Crowds

Le Bon's 1895 *La Psychologie des foules* (*The Crowd: A Study of the Popular Mind*) claimed that groups have heightened affectivity and a lower level of intellectual functioning and regress to the mental life of "primitive people." Groups have an unconscious irrational component, the pathological substratum to which I have already referred. But, above all, people in crowds lose their individuality in favor of a common mind:

> The most striking peculiarity presented by a psychological crowd is the following: Whoever be the individuals that compose it, however like or unlike be their mode of life, their occupations, their character, or their intelligence, the fact that they have been transformed into a crowd puts them in possession of a sort of collective mind [*âme collective*] which makes them feel, think, and act in a manner quite different from that in which each individual of them would feel, think, and act were he in a state of isolation. There are certain ideas and feelings which do not come into being, or do not transform themselves into acts except in the case of individuals forming a crowd.[1]

How does this come about? Le Bon's explanation relies on the phenomena of hypnosis, suggestion, and a kind of social contagion. Hypnosis, in Charcot's (and Freud's) France, was a popular explanation for just about any inexplicable action. According to the theorist Gregory McGuire, hypnosis, like suggestion, testifies to an enduring French interest in "animal magnetism."[2] Similarly, contagion, as an idea, is medically derived: "Ideas, sentiments, immersions and beliefs possess in crowds a contagious power as intense as that of microbes."[3] But contagion, for Le Bon, was only an effect of hypnosis. He wrote that:

to understand this phenomenon it is necessary to bear in mind certain recent physiological discoveries. We know today that by various processes an individual may be brought into such a condition that, having entirely lost his conscious personality, he obeys all suggestions of the operator who has deprived him of it, and commits acts in utter contradiction with his character and habits.[4]

The individual "is no longer himself, but has become an automaton who has ceased to be guided by his will."[5] Freud notes that one of the problems with Le Bon's explanation is that he does not mention *who* the hypnotist is in the case of the group, while, at the same time, he clearly distinguishes between the influence of hypnosis, or "fascination," on the one hand, and its contagious effect on the other.[6] This is fair, but not fair enough. Le Bon does accord great power to the image as an organizer of crowd responses; and I suggest that the "image," as Le Bon understood it, stands in often for the "leader." Consider the following:

> The power of words is bound up with the images they evoke, and is quite independent of their real significance. Words whose sense is the most ill defined are sometimes those that possess the most influence. Such, for example, are the terms democracy, socialism, equality, etc. . . . They synthesize the most diverse unconscious aspirations and the hope of their realization.[7]

The emphasis on the pathological and irrational was used by Le Bon to condemn all entirely "popular movements, democratic institutions, and collective aspirations."[8] But Le Bon also said that a crowd was capable, ethically, of far more than an individual. An individual would put his own interests first. A crowd need not.[9] On the other hand, the just accusations of elitism leveled against Le Bon often fail to take account of how, for him, all groups, even groups composed of the "most learned," became fundamentally less intelligent than the worst of their individual members. This may become significant for us later, as will Le Bon's emphasis on how it is that in a group an unconscious substratum takes over, a common unconscious substratum, as distinct from the individual distinctness of the group's members.[10]

Trotter, the next major contributor to the question of groups, saw group phenomena in more positive terms. Unlike Le Bon, whose focus was on transient group formations, Trotter concentrated on that "most generalized form of assemblage in which man, that [political animal], passes his life."[11] The fact that Freud included Trotter, as does Bion (and that many writing in between also do so), testifies to a difficulty in separating the study of groups from that of crowds. What unites both groups and crowds for Trotter is the idea of "suggestibility." Suggestibility, for Trotter, is one of four primary instincts: self-preservation, nutrition, and sex being the other three. For him, the association of suggestibility and the pathological is "unfortunate."[12] Suggestibility is critical to gregariousness, and gregariousness underpins his herd instinct.[13]

The last of the three thinkers who most decisively influenced Freud and later Bion was McDougall, whose book *The Group Mind* appeared in 1920. Suggestion also figured for McDougall, who substituted it for hypnosis and criticized Le Bon accordingly. But like Le Bon, he stressed the emotionality of the crowd and adopted the idea that the group lowers the intellectual level of its members. McDougall did, however, do two new things: First, he concentrated on more stable group phenomena. Second, he tried to explain exactly how suggestibility takes hold. To this end, he proposed three candidate mechanisms that may account for the phenomenon: a collective consciousness, "telepathic influence," and (related) the "principle of direct induction of emotion by way of the primitive sympathetic response."[14] He pointed out that one need not stop at telepathy as an explanation because of the significant role (he supposed) the senses must play. "The consideration of the conditions of the spread of emotion through crowds affords evidence that this mode of interaction of the individuals is all-important and that telepathic communication, if it occurs, is of secondary importance. For the spreading and the great intensification of emotion seem to depend upon its being given expressions that are perceptible by the senses."[15] In turn, that idea returns us to the "principle of sympathetic induction." With this principle, McDougall came very close to my argument, although it is unclear what his "primitive sympathetic response" consisted of, partly because he did not free himself from the rhetoric of "suggestibility." Yet, in trying to explain the response, he made a connection between contagion and energy:

It is well recognized that almost any emotional excitement increases the suggestibility of the individual, though the explanation of the fact remains obscure. I have suggested that the explanation is to be found in the principle of the vicarious usage of nervous energy, the principle that nervous energy, liberated in any one part of the nervous system, may overflow the channels of the system in which it is liberated and re-enforce processes initiated in other systems. If this be true, we can see how any condition of excitement will favor suggestibility; for it will re-enforce whatever idea or impulse may have been awakened and made dominate by "suggestion." The principle requires perhaps the following limitation. Emotion which is finding an outlet in well-directed action is probably unfavorable to all such "suggestions" as are not congruent with its tendencies. It is vague emotion, or such as finds no appropriate expression in action, that favors suggestibility.[16]

Also, and this is very significant (for we will find a variant of it as late as Clark McPhail in 1991), the received McDougall is one who sees the "primitive sympathetic response" in visual terms. The mechanism, in other words, is one of mimesis. Thus, the potential for an understanding of the direct transmission of affect is undercut by a stress on the sense of sight as the principle sense involved. More accurately, it is undercut by a particular understanding of sight (which is not quite the self-contained sense it is usually assumed to be). Consider Freud's reflection on the "primitive sympathetic response" in McDougall's work:

> The manner in which individuals are . . . carried away by a common impulse is explained by McDougall by means of what he calls the "principle of direct induction of emotion by way of the primitive sympathetic response," . . . that is, by means of the emotional contagion with which we are already familiar [as postulated in Le Bon]. The fact is that the perception *of the signs* of an affective state is calculated automatically to arouse the same affect in the person who perceives them. The greater the number of people in whom the same affect can be simultaneously *observed*, the stronger does this automatic compulsion grow (emphasis added).[17]

The emphasis on sight as the principal mechanism in the communication of affect goes unchallenged in the literature on groups thereafter. There is also stress on hearing, but, as with the emphasis on sight, the idea is that the communication of affect takes place between individuals whose affects are self-contained: one individual has the affect, other individuals see it, or sometimes hear it, they then drum it up within themselves, and so the affect, apparently, spreads. The emphasis on sight as the preeminent sense rendering individuals discreet to one another has been extensively criticized in writings on modernity. But the emphasis is not really challenged, or not consistently challenged, unless one takes account of the role of the less valorized senses, as we shall see below.

Freud himself approached the communication of affect through concentrating on the drives. He did this after stressing that Le Bon's, Trotter's, and McDougall's explanations were circular. The circularity was evident in "the magic word 'suggestion,' which explains nothing" (*Group Psychology*, 88). Nor was circularity the only basis for Freud's objection. "There is no doubt that something exists in us which, when we become aware of signs of emotion in someone else, tends to make us fall into the same emotion; but how often do we not successfully oppose it, resist the emotion, and react in quite an opposite way? Why, therefore, do we invariably give way to this contagion when we are in a group?" (89)

We will return to whether and how individuals "invariably give way" shortly, and subsequently (chapter 6) to that thing in us that resists. In Freud's own theory, the individuals in the group put the group's leader in place of their own ego-ideals and then identified with one another. Their libidinal drives were then, in sublimated form, directed toward both the leader and one another. This is how Freud tried to overcome the circularity of "suggestion." He attributed his forebears' circularity to the failure to recognize exactly how it was that the "leader" held the group together (the leader for Freud could be an idea as well as a person). The mechanism of identification itself, Freud was happy to add, is still in many respects obscure to us, but it is clear that a "path leads from identification by way of imitation to empathy" (110, n. 2). More critically in Freud's model, suggestion, like hypnosis, works in the same way that being in love works. "There is the same sapping of the subject's own initiative" (114), although under certain circumstances, "the moral conscience of the person hypnotized may show resistance" (116). Be that as it may, Freud thought he had explained suggestion and contagion in the same way as he explained hypnosis: the subject falls under the spell of the other who is the object of the libidinal drive. He loves himself in the other and is as bound to the other as he is to himself.

Freud's explanation works well enough for stable group phenomena (such as the church or the army), but it does not really explain the character of the short-lived group. As Freud also pointed out, most of the assertions of Le Bon and others on the irrational character of the group relate to the short-term group, not the stable group. But as far as Freud's own explanation for the short-term group goes, it is limited to the case of panic. He argues that it is the absence of libidinal ties that is evident in panic (96), when it is "each individual for himself and the devil take the hindermost." The deflected self-love or narcissism involved in the tie to a projected ego-ideal in another, and a bond with others who share the same ego-ideal, enables a stable group to exist. But without this love there is a reversion to hatred and aggressiveness, springing from the death drive as opposed to the life drive. When this occurs, organization—which for Freud also characterizes the life drive—disappears (102, n. 1). Freud's association of Eros with organization recalls our earlier link between love and living attention. The life drive, for Freud, is basic to the libido, and he regarded love as a derivative of the libido. But he also regarded the erotic as linked to living attention and to coherence. The extent of the life drive, with its derivatives, makes for organization or harmony in the group to the extent that it dominates over the death drive. The more love there is in a group, the less formal leadership it needs. The life drive also appears to bind groups without significant leadership, or none at all. As anyone who has participated in social movements is aware, the effect of moratoriums for instance, is to intensify emotions of collectivity, not of panic. And this intensification happens in situations where leaders are marginal. Moreover, it withstands incursions from the state apparatus designed to disperse groups, even to make them panic. In situations of panic, the absence of libido or life drive is also the presence of aggression and anxiety, where the anxiety is a response to aggression that may be imaginary or real.

The consideration of affects and notions of group minds did not end with Freud. While its popularity is contested more and more, the idea that there is a pathological component and a form of common response in groups and crowds has also persisted. It is found in the works of Robert Park (1904); Park's student, Herbert Blumer (1939);

Leon Festinger, Anthony Pepitone, and Theodore Newcomb (1952); Neil Smelser (1962); Philip Zimbardo (1969); Edward Diener (1977); and Serge Moscovici (1981). Blumer is interesting for the reason that his notion of a "circular reaction" in crowds perpetuates, while making explicit, the problem of circularity we have already mentioned. Following Park, he stressed the individual component in crowd behavior to the extent that he believed that the thwarting of the satisfaction of routine individual impulses contributed to the communicative restlessness of crowd behavior. This restlessness led to a circular reaction, "a type of interstimulation wherein the response of one individual reproduces the stimulation that has come from another individual and in being reflected back to this individual reinforces the stimulation."[18] The question is precisely how this "interstimulation" works. Blumer's suggestion was the process of "milling," which makes individuals "increasingly preoccupied with one another" and less responsive to anything or anyone beyond the milling group.[19] Milling suggests that touch is important, as indeed it may be, but "interstimulation" is, nonetheless, vague. It is also thoroughly circular as an explanation as well as a description, unless one gives a communicative power (a power of communicating affects) to the sense of touch, which Blumer holds back from according it.

Crowds Are Composed of Mad Individuals

As the century progressed, a shift away from notions of a group mind and toward an emphasis on the individual gathered steam. The irrational individual, or even the rational individual with his or her own reasons for acting irrationally in crowds, came to prominence in crowd psychology (he had of course been prominent everywhere else, ever since Marx added his analysis of why the rational individual was the right man for the market to the chorus of seventeenth-century political theory). Floyd Allport was the first to reject Le Bon's and McDougall's "group fallacy" or "the error of substituting the group as a whole as a principle of explanation."[20] Only individuals, Allport believed (as did others) have minds. Nonetheless, these individuals are predisposed in similar ways to satisfy their basic drives. Crowds sometimes offer them an opportunity to find this satisfaction: "The menacing and the drives of a large number of individuals simultaneously both draws them together and incites them to common action."[21] "The individual sees with his own eyes that others are delivering the blow he longs to deliver, and are thereby expressing, not disapproval of acts of violence, but the strongest kind of approval."[22] Critically, the crowd adds nothing new to what the individual would do if he were by himself. The individual "behaves just as he would behave alone, only more so."[23] He behaves "more so" because "the sights and sounds facilitate an increased fervor in the responses of each."[24] In other words, as with Freud, any intensification of individual drives in a crowd is the result of observation and hearing. It is based on sensory forms of communication that present individuals to one another as separate self-contained entities: the response is imitated; it is precisely *not* transmitted.[25] While Allport noted that individuals in a crowd received stimuli from all sides and that this increased "social facilitation" (the way individuals come to be "more so"), his crowd did not make individuals mad. Rather, the people in it had some madness in common; that was why they were there. "The thought process in crowds is used only to serve the prepotent interests, and not to direct them."[26] Crowd behavior consisted of the intensification of responses that had been individually learned. Allport was followed by two thorough behaviorists: Neal Miller and John Dollard. Borrowing from Blumer's idea of a circular reaction, Miller and Dollard posited that a crowd, by virtue of the proximity and increased exposure to the mutual stimuli of its members, would increase the individual predisposition to act in various ways.[27] The individual predisposition depended on the circumstances of personal biography. Miller and Dollard explained the behavior of participants in lynch mobs, for instance, on the basis that these participants had been individually deprived in their upbringing, and hence were more frustrated. They explained mutual stimuli and intensification in the usual terms: that is to say, Miller and Dollard couched their account in terms of visual and auditory cues, with some concessions to touch.[28] Even leaving aside its problematic logic, the individual deprivation-frustration explanation has not been borne out empirically. An initial finding to the effect that the incidence of lynchings decreased when the cash value of the cotton crop rose was subsequently overturned.[29] In addition, the hypothesis did not hold for the individual participants in race riots.[30]

The Crowd Is Composed of Rational Individuals

In the time of Le Bon and his predecessors, the idea that there could be a group mind affecting a crowd was taken for granted. Their work faltered when it came to identifying the mechanism, which was assumed to be pathological. In the early studies, pathology is coupled with emotionality. It is generally assumed or explicitly stated that, in McDougall's words, the most significant consequence of the formation of a group is the "exultation or intensification of emotion" in each member of it.[31] But from the 1960s onward, there has been a marked shift away from the affect, associated most of all with the names of Carl Couch (1968), Richard Berk (1974), Charles Tilly (1978), and Clark McPhail (1991). The direct genesis of this work lies in an attempt to rebut Le Bon and like-minded critics of the "gathering," whose class-biased and race-imbued assumptions led to a politically reactionary view of crowds. In the more recent studies, crowd behavior in demonstrations, rallies, and so forth is seen as rational attempts to achieve goals. Given the proximity of my argument on affect with nineteenth- and early twentieth-century theories of emotional intensity and a common mind, I state that my intention is not to claim for the transmission of affect a monocausal explanation for group psychology, or to discount the complexity of empirical, real crowds and the intelligence and conscious motivations of persons within them. Rather I intend to introduce the transmission of affect as one factor, a crucial factor, but still one factor among others. To respect the complexity of the work that has already been done here, I add here that following Erving Goffman, I am using the more neutral term "gathering" rather than "crowd" for any organized group event.[32]

I will try to make it clear that the negative side of the recent research is that it has gone too far away from concerns with group affect. Like the first generation of critics, they focus on the individual, a rational individual rather than a mad one, but an individual nonetheless. This means they are unable to account for the contemporary incidence of soccer violence, among other things. This social-movement scholarship rejects the spontaneous emotional images of crowds, and it is has done so in part through substantial empirical research on what crowds actually do, and partly through defining what a crowd is meant to be. It has shown that violence is unusual in political demonstrations, in a variety of common crowds or gatherings, and even in sports gatherings. But it has led to the view that the meaningful division is between the mad crowd and the rational crowd.

I submit that, on the contrary, it is between the collective and the individual explanations of group and crowd phenomena. Although they emphasize the political effectiveness and rationality of gatherings, the more recent scholars of group psychology perpetuate an emphasis on the individual as the unit of analysis. In doing so, they lose sight of possibilities inherent in the notion of collective understandings and a collective drive. For there are other possibilities. Collectivities may have more—rather than less—intelligence, deductive speed, and inventiveness than the individuals within them. While this is obliquely recognized in Freud's, and even Le Bon's, references to the courage and self-sacrifice of which groups and crowds are capable, the recognition is somewhat back-handed in that it focuses on emotional changes alone, as if there was no corresponding lift in intellectual capacity. There have been gains in the work emphasizing the rationality of gatherings. There are also losses. The shift to cognitive science[33] in the analysis of the crowd is part of a shift away from the affect that is characteristic of the twentieth century, a shift with its own historical explanation. That shift is complicated by the separation by disciplines between social and biological explanation and the related notion of affective self-containment. In short, the turn away from affect in the more recent work on group psychology is related to the turn toward the self-contained individual. It is related insofar as the individual's cognitive capacities are held not to desert him in a group. The group individual is not, in Le Bon's terms, "an automaton who has ceased to be guided by his will," or Freud's "individual who has lost his distinctiveness."

The bias toward the cognitive individual is entirely in line with the prominence of ideas of unilateral self-containment. If the belief in the self-contained state as the natural state has hardened, then the social movement literature, however good its intentions, can be read as another instance of the same escalating prejudice. As I said at the outset, it is caught up in the very process it should be analyzing. It is caught up in it because the self-contained individual could only rise to power through severing affective ties, in theory as well as practice. In other words, the idea of self-containment is tied to the belief that cognition, more than emotion, determines agency, and it is not surprising that as the one (self-containment) comes to dominate in the history of ideas, so does the other (cognition). That said, the cognitive scholars' criticisms of the assumptions about the use of emotionality and its tie to pathology are not only often right, they are also useful. One of the problems with the "group mind" theories is that they reverse the logic of the transmission of affect in the clinic. The early crowd theorists effectively made the one who feels the other's affect pathological, whereas the clinicians tend to see the patient who projects affect freely as the problem. Such patients are often "borderline," meaning that they lack self-containment, or boundaries, and are thus on the border between neurosis and psychosis. And if the implication here is that self-containment is not only a delusion but also an achievement, it is an implication I am willing to entertain. However, it would be a mistake to see either the tendency to project or the inability to resist projection as the mark of pathology. All depends on how containment comes into being, as we shall see.

Bion on Groups

Bion's major work, *Experiences in Groups*, was published in 1961. His starting point in groups, as in his individual analyses, was the work of Melanie Klein and the mechanisms she ascribed to the earliest phases of mental life, mechanisms that involve psychotic defenses. These psychotic defenses persist in the life of all normal individuals to a greater or lesser extent, but they are especially characteristic of groups,[34] and revealed in the context of the "basic assumption" that binds the group together. Generally, basic assumptions are about the affects Bion groups together: "anxiety, fear, hate, love."[35] Specifically, by "basic assumption," Bion means an assumption such as "the group exists for fight or flight," or the group depends on a leader, or the group has hope based on its belief that through it a new messiah or solution will emerge.[36] How thoroughly such an assumption holds varies, but an assumption always exists. All the basic assumptions can be running through a given group at any one moment, but one will usually dominate. And all the basic assumptions are in some way oedipally derived (where Oedipal is understood with the full Kleinian resonance of an Oedipus complex that begins in early infancy and transitions by stages, if successful, from psychotic to neurotic anxieties).[37]

The fight/flight assumption is fuelled by hate. Hate, for Klein, is a derivative of the death drive, as is its close relative, envy. They are also related to anxiety and aggression, for Klein, "products of the death drive working within." The affects of envy, hate, and aggression are directed toward the breast and the mother, whose creativity is envied in earliest psychical life. To deal with aggressive hatred and envy toward something that is also loved and essential to survival, one splits the good breast from the bad. One then fears, or has anxiety, that the breast that is subject to aggression will retaliate in turn. One is also overwhelmed with hate and envy by the sight in fact or fantasy of others merging without one.[38] This also leads to anxiety about being left out. Anxiety, in turn, exacerbates the paranoid-schizoid defense of splitting. The results of splitting range from the psychical disavowal or denial of reality to the inability to make links between ideas. In the ideal case, the split is healed through the recognition that there never was a bad breast; there was only the aggression within oneself, and it is this that made the breast "bad." With this recognition comes the initial passage from the psychotic mechanisms of splitting—and affects of hate and aggression—to the neurotic mechanisms of inhibition.

As in psychosis, and for that matter the unconscious, time plays no part in basic-assumption activity. "The basic-assumption group does not disperse or meet."[39] In fact, if the awareness of time is forced on a group in basic-assumption mode, it "tend(s) to arouse feelings of persecution."[40] At some level, the group is always in its basic assumption, which means, in effect, that no member of the group can cease to be in it, even when the group is ungathered. While Bion did not say so, a further implication of this is that it is the strong emotions, the psychotic, persecutory anxieties or affects rather than the normal ones that are "in the air." From this standpoint, the group remains a group when it is ungathered because it is linked always by these basic assumptions, by the resonances they trigger, and the positions they assign. We noted that whereas for Freud the group resolved neurotic anxieties, for Bion it resolves psychotic ones. Potentially, the seeds of a very positive view of groups and gatherings lie here, but Bion's own concern is with how the group is far more likely to evoke the earliest, psychotic anxieties. This is because forming a relation to the group in which one lives is "as formidable to the adult as the relationship with the breast appears to be to the infant."[41] The implication is that that relation is only satisfactorily resolved when the work (organizational, and hence restraining) functions of groups dominate, just as inhibitions come to dominate over psychotic mechanisms.

But perhaps the real question is why it is that the psychotic bits of us should emerge in groups but not in individual behavior. Given that Bion believes we are all of us, whether we like it or not, in a group, and all of us, whether we will it or not, gripped by basic assumptions from time to time, and that basic assumptions are about affects, one could infer that we are born into affects that exist independently of us—affects that are organized around patterns of splitting and paranoia. Even though Bion draws no such conclusion, I hazard that his theory is compatible with this notion, and thus with the notion that affects are preeminently social. And they are there first, before we are. They preexist us; they are outside as well as within us. Now if this is true, and later our argument for the transmission of affect will support this likelihood, what happens when a group gathers is that psychotic affects are either intensified or offset (bound and restrained).[42] They can be intensified, as with Nazism or a lynch mob. They can be restrained as in the collective resistance to imperialism and globalization. Globalization, after all, is quite mad in the technical sense ("a danger to oneself and others"), insofar as it is destroying the long-term conditions of human survival. But I am moving too far ahead of the argument. Backing up a little: Bion's excursus into group psychology was conducted in relation to Freud's interlocutors in the same field: Le Bon, Trotter, and McDougall. He does not mention subsequent writers on groups. Le Bon, McDougall, Freud, and Trotter all concentrate on the affective ties that bind the group together.[43] But Bion himself (like many of his contemporaries in the sociology of the crowd) did not believe that the "basic assumptions" are all there are to group behavior. We have seen that he makes a distinction between the work aspect of groups, which does the job for which the group was formed, and the basic-assumption aspect, which acts on the basis of the affects. The same group is simultaneously a work group and a basic-assumption group; one or other of these aspects—work or basic assumption—will dominate from time to time. This dual definition allows us to define a group in a way that recognizes that the group can be quite mad and yet apparently stable, organized, and purposeful in its outward forms, as in the case of the suicidal Heaven's Gate cult. Al-

ternatively, the group can be apparently sane (a university department for instance) and yet occasionally irrational or persecutory in its
dynamics. For the group can be, and usually is, organized around its
work function. But, as it is also bound together through its basic assumption, it should be stressed that organization and basic-
assumption bondage are radically different.[44] This counterposition,
the organization of energy versus the imposed directions of the affects, will return in a discussion of a similar counterposition in the
psyche.

> In contrast with work-group function basic-assumption activity makes
> no demands on the individual for a capacity to co-operate but depends
> on the individual's possession of what I call valency—a term I borrow
> from the physicists for instantaneous involuntary combination of one in-
> dividual with another for sharing and acting on a basic assumption.[45]

Later, Bion is more specific. "Valency [is] used in physics to denote
the power of combination of atoms. . . . By it I mean the capacity of
the individual for instantaneous combination with other individuals
in an established pattern of behavior—the basic assumptions."[46] The
idea of valency should take us directly to the transmission of affect,
but Bion explicitly avoids the question of mechanism, stressing that
we can only explain quiescent basic assumptions on the basis of a
"proto-mental system" that is physical as well as mental. But this is
all, except for a remark later in the same paper that valency is "a spontaneous, unconscious function of the gregarious quality in the personality of man."[47] (As we have seen, "gregariousness" is fundamental in
Trotter's definition of the herd instinct, a concept that Bion rejected).
The problem with "valency" as a term is that it captures a truth but
does not differentiate between what one is valent toward or what one
is valent with (although the term connotes the activity of the senses).

Bion's idea that there is a duality of approaches within a group
(work and the basic assumption) makes it possible both to recognize
that a group can be cognitively responsive in relation to symbols and
to see that something else is going on affectively. "The work group
understands that particular use of symbols which is involved in communication; the basic-assumption group does not."[48] Verbal communication is a function of the work group, although it is also the case
that the more the basic assumption takes over in the group, the more

words become mere sound. To say that a group is cognitively aware at the individual level of its task is to say that its work-group aspect predominates, even though its affects are undoubtedly heightened as well (as in a successful demonstration). On the other hand, in Bion's terms, the crazed British soccer crowds of the 1980s were very basic in their "fight" assumption (and were incidentally a group in which the basic-assumption affect clearly overrode any work function). The study of these groups has been truncated (I can find little on them) perhaps because their existence flew in the face of the newly dominant paradigm on crowd behavior: the paradigm emphasizing the cognitive, reflexive capabilities of the crowd. But soccer spectator violence does exist, or perhaps one should say it happens, and it is not antidemocratic to say so.[49] Whatever generates this violence, it seems that here the image of aggression does act as an immediate trigger for some, and then spreads more slowly to others.

Rather than ignoring these crowds, it might do more service to class politics to note that from the perspective of the theory of energetic transmission many of the working-class participants are carrying the affective refuse of a social order that positions them on the receiving end of an endless stream of minor and major humiliations, from economic and physical degradations in the workplace to the weight of the negative affects discarded by those in power.[50] Having said this, let me immediately differentiate my position from that of Konrad Lorenz, who argued that aggression results from the catharsis of pent-up hostility, and that this catharsis is abetted by vicarious or direct participation in competitive sports. Rather, I am making two different points here. The first is that while aggression may be fuelled by the attempt to relieve oneself of the weight of the other's exploitation, the experience of that exploitation involves more than a nebulous "hostility"—the weight of the other is more likely to be experienced as depression, which can also be released through aggression. The second point is that in a group or crowd, the aggressive response spreads through the transmission of affect, and this can influence anyone in the group. This idea is compatible with the empirical findings against Miller and Dollard, also with findings that Lorenz's claim is not borne out empirically, in that the personal profiles of those involved did not match up with Lorenz's predictions as to their backgrounds,[51] just as they did not match up with Miller and Dollard's deprivation-frustration explanation for race riots. With our explanation, the history of a particular individual's aggression profile in the first case, or deprivation profile in the second, matters less. It is relevant insofar as it establishes the "attractors" to which similar affects are drawn. But to be caught up in an affect is to be caught up in it, sometimes to the extent that the unconstrained ego, the ego riddled with basic assumptions, once more appears to be "in the air" in the violent crowd. Without containment, whether it is containment by another or genuine self-detachment, what we are left with is an affective force in common that says "me" precisely when it is most lacking in individual distinctiveness. The affect can override an individual's personal affective response, and in the case of a group aggressive response it does so, for some more than others. A non-occultish explanation of this focuses on entrainment via hormonal factors in aggression and other mechanisms of the transmission of affect.

Entrainment as Mechanism of Transmission

Our brief in this section is the exploration of concrete mechanisms of transmission, also known as entrainment. If contagion exists (and the study of crowds says it does), how is it effected? Images and mimesis explain some of it (as we have seen), but olfactory and auditory entrainment offer more comprehensive explanations.

If I walk back into the atmospheric room in which I started (and so return to the example with which this inquiry began) and it is rank with the smell of anxiety, I breathe this in. Something is taken in that was not present, at the very least not consciously present, before. But no matter how thoroughly my system responds to the presence of this new affect, it is the case that something is added. Whether this in itself makes me afraid, or whether I respond to fear by producing it within myself after I have smelt it around me (and probably both things occur) the phenomenon cannot be explained by the simple postulate that I am acting out something I already felt or was driven toward feeling by my "individual drives." The affect *in the room* is a profoundly social thing. How exactly does it get there? We are not entirely in the dark when it comes to answering this question. Research on chemical communication and entrainment suggests answers centered on the analysis of pheromones, substances that are not released into the blood but are emitted externally. Pheromones have been proven to exist in animals, and researchers think they have confirmed their human presence.

> Unlike hormones, which are secreted into the blood stream, ectohormones or pheromones are substances secreted by an animal externally with specific effects on the behavior or physiology of another individual of the same species. These substances may be secreted rather generally by the skin or by specialized glands and, similarly, their detection by the recipient individual may be simply by ingestion or by specialized chemoreceptors.[52]

A more recent definition claims that pheromones are "pollenlike chemicals that when emitted by one creature have some effect on other members of the same species."[53] One detects pheromones by touch or smell, but smell is more common. To smell pheromones is also in a sense to consume them. But the point here is that no direct physical contact is necessary for a transmission to take place. Pheromones are literally in the air.

The concept of pheromones and all it implies has been popularized in relation to sexual behavior. Even in this field, the research subjects for pheromones have generally been drawn from the animal kingdom, although there is a growing body of research on human beings, and some of the work is comparative.[54] But pheromones have a wider compass, extending beyond sexuality and reproduction. They "also have a communicative function . . . a distinction is made between pheromones that affect the endocrine system (which produces sex hormones), pheromones that facilitate physiological changes of various kinds (*primer pheromones*) and pheromones that directly provoke a certain behavior in the observer (*releaser pheromones*)."[55] For our present purposes of understanding transmission, all these are significant insofar as they are tied to affects. The connection between pheromones and hormones is established: a pheromone in one member of a species may "cause" a hormone to be secreted in the blood of another.[56] But hormones are not only produced by smell, nor is olfaction the only means for the transmission of affect.

As chemical entrainment also involves touch, we should note that contagion by this means has been mentioned by group theorists from Le Bon to Blumer (compare Blumer's understanding of "milling"). What remains surprising is that communication by touch in groups has not been linked by social scientists to research on chemical entrainment (as far as I know). But there are indications of social interest in work on "electrical" or nervous entrainment, "the driving effect one nervous system has on another" effected by touch, sight, and sound.[57]

Nervous entrainment may also depend on body movements and gestures, particularly through the imitation of rhythms (effected by sight, touch, and hearing).[58] In understanding the aural rhythmic component evident in the vocal interactions of a parent and child, Richard Restak suggests we attend to the study of prosody—"the melody, pitch, and stress of human speech"[59]—where auditory cues clearly have priority over visual ones.[60] Rhythm is a tool in the expression of agency, just as words are. It can literally convey the tone of an utterance, and, in this sense, it does unite word and affect. Rhythm also has a unifying, regulating role in affective exchanges between two or more people. The rhythmic aspects of behavior at a gathering are critical in both establishing and enhancing a sense of collective purpose and a common understanding. This can be done consciously, whereas chemical entrainment works unconsciously. That is to say, rhythm unites within a more conscious frame of reference, which is why it may transmit more complex states.

In addition, the sense of well being that comes with a rhythmic entrainment with one's fellows (in dancing for instance) is entirely compatible with mutually directed activity of a most intelligent order. By contrast, nonrhythmic or dissonant sound also separates. It leads people to stand apart from one another and generates unease. Fear can also have this effect, although fear and anxiety are also communicated by smell. We can hypothesize that the effects of nervous entrainment are furthered by chemical means as well. But the point to stress is the neutrality and socially determinant factors in nervous and chemical communication. Of itself, they can lead either way—to coordinated well being or to anxiety.[61]

While the auditory has priority over the visual, the visual has a place in the process of entrainment. First, let us note that the process of registering an image is also an anatomical process, rooted firmly in brain physiology. Second, the *registration* of the image in the mind's eye is only one side of things. The image is also, necessarily, *transmitted*. It is transmitted as surely as the words whose sound waves or valence register physical effects in the air around the ears of those who hear. In the last analysis, words and images are matters of vibration, vibrations at different frequencies, but vibrations. The significance of this is easily underestimated in that we have failed to consider how the transmission through physical vibration of the image is simultaneously the transmission of a social thing; the social and physical transmission of the image are one and the same process, but (once more), if we have to make a distinction pro forma, the social, not the physical, is causative. In addition, the social, physical vibrations of images, as much as words, are critical in the process of electrical entrainment, although they lack the rhythmic dimension of auditory entrainment.[62] If the image is violent, this means one is not indifferent to its effects, however indifferent one feels. But the immediate point is simply that sights and sounds are physical matters in themselves, carriers of social matters, social in origin but physical in their effects. Every word, every sound, has its valence; so, at a more subtle level, may every image.

More concretely (as speculations about imaging are only that), the manner in which the image has a physical, chemical effect on individuals and groups is evident in the work showing that testosterone is elevated in relation to an aggressive image in the form of a photograph. In one experiment, when subjects of both sexes were shown pictures of angry and tense faces, they responded by raising their levels of testosterone.[63] In other words, they responded to an image, felt "anger and tension," and elevated the hormone they call upon for aggression in consequence. Earlier experiments on men revealed similar effects in terms of erotic movies raising male/masculine hormones, while films of dental surgery decrease them as anxiety or stress is registered.[64] The hormone elevation or decrease is accompanied by affective shifts: both the hormone testosterone and the affects of aggression (and affects of arousal in the movies) rise or decline in response to visual images.[65] But it is not only the case that individual men and women respond physiologically to a socially contrived image. It is also the case that testosterone levels can be elevated in a group. One study measured various hormonal levels in men who were threatened by unemployment. Significant increases in testosterone were recorded for the entire group, including a few women, suggesting that interactive factors do play a part.[66] This particular experiment did not attempt to isolate variables tied to group interaction, and hence did not attempt to see whether testosterone is "contagious," so to speak. The focus was on individuals responding to the threat of unemployment and the rise or decrease in various hormones produced in response. But there are experiments that show that another member of the androgen family, androstenedione, identified as a human hormone hitherto, does double duty as a human pheromone, producing shifts in affects or moods.[67] A pheromone, it will be recalled, differs from a hormone in that a hormone is an internal molecule, while the pheromone serves to communicate among members of a species externally; its existence is shown or inferred because of behavioral and affective changes in other members of the species. The affective shifts generated by androstenedione are pleasant and caution us accordingly against making rash assumptions about the action of androgens or masculinizing hormones. The point here is not to claim a property for this or that hormone, or to claim that it inevitably affects us all the same way. I do not have the expertise to make such a claim. The point rather is to use particular instances (even if some of them have been misinterpreted, as a layperson is likely to misinterpret any technical field) to frame hypotheses. If olfactory communication turns a hormone into a pheromone and changes another's affects, does it also change their hormones in a way that (temporarily) changes their habitual affective disposition? Are such changes, in turn, communicated by additional pheromones? If such cycles can be shown to hold in groups, then the contagion of affects has been explained.

Crowd violence is attributed to the action of images in the first instance, and it is clear that an image itself will trigger an increase or decrease in certain hormone levels. But it is also clear that the transmission of violence does not take place by visual observation alone, although the shift effected by the (socially constructed) image is very significant and helps us reconcile many of the claims that are currently on the table. The role of visual identification and the identification with the perpetrator of the aggressive act brings in Freud and like-minded analysts. The idea that, affectively, the crowd becomes more than the sum of its parts brings in most of the affectively oriented psychologists (Le Bon, McDougall, Trotter). In addition, it brings in the more recent theorists of affect, those who have argued that drives determine what crowds do. But it does not do so necessarily, which brings me to the final points about the claims surveyed here.

I have argued that the empirical difficulties with the arguments of, say, Miller and Dollard are the result of the way in which the transmission of affect can mean that individuals are affected by a feeling in a group, even though their own histories might not lead them to the same feeling, left to themselves. At the same time, the image of aggression does not always result in an identification, or an identification in a partaking of the relevant affect. This has been established in the recent research used to suggest that groups, meaning the individuals who compose or sometimes deviate from the group, are capable of resistance.

But, as the following chapters show, the nature of this internal resistance can only be grasped in a context where the transmission of affect is acknowledged. Research on hormones supports the realization that the environment, especially the environment in the form of other people, changes human endocrinology, not the other way around. It also changes the affects accompanying those hormones. That otherwise good science holds back from this conclusion testifies to the power of the illusion of self-containment. In relation to its paradigmatic conclusions (although these are contradicted by disparate bodies of research) science is constrained by the foundational fantasy that threw philosophy and early modern science off course, and whose effects linger on as conceptual difficulties. Chief among these difficulties is the denial of the affective impact of the (social and maternal) environment.

CHAPTER FOUR

The New Paradigm

What is at stake with the notion of the transmission of affect is precisely the opposite of the sociobiological claim that the biological *determines* the social. What is at stake is rather the means by which social interaction shapes biology. My affect, if it comes across to you, alters your anatomical makeup for good or ill. This idea, perhaps more than any other, stands neo-Darwinism on its head. It is directly at odds with the premise on which neo-Darwinian biology is based. In neo-Darwinian biology especially, the individual organism is born with the urges and affects that will determine its fate. Its predisposition to certain behaviors is part of its individual genetic package, and, of course, these behaviors are intrinsically affective. Such behaviors and affects may be modified by the environment, or they may not survive because they are not adaptive. But the point is that no other source or origin for the affects is acknowledged outside of the individual one. The dominant model for transmission in neo-Darwinism is genetic transmission. It is the main model for transmission in the life sciences as they stand at present, and the critical thing about it here is that its proponents ignore the claims of social and historical context when it comes to accounting for causation.[1] Even when factors such as Richard Dawkins's hypothetical "meme" (the ostensible ideational equivalent of a "gene," or the unit of an idea) are introduced into neo-Darwinism, suppositions about an individual and socially impervious mode of genetic transmission are preserved.[2] The meme can be transmitted, but only through the birth of new human subjects, only as part of the genetic package that officially marshals the action in the development of an embryo.

Rather than the generational line of inheritance (the vertical line of history), the transmission of affect, conceptually, presupposes a horizontal line of transmission: the line of the heart. The affects are not inherited, or not only inherited. They also flow from this one to that one, here and now, via olfaction and the circulation of the blood.[3] The relatively new discipline of psychoneuroendocrinology shows us this much. As noted in chapter 1, recent research in this field has demonstrated an immediate effect of airborne chemicals on human mood, although its significance goes unsung and attempts at disproving it (if any) remain unpublished.[4] These facts may be neglected for a time as they signal the end of the hegemony of neo-Darwinism, which is anchored in assumptions of self-containment. They also provide a way of rethinking some assumptions about human motivation from the experimental standpoint that have eluded complex studies of the mind (depth psychology, continental and analytic philosophy) to date. These experiments do these things (once their implications are thought through) because they point to the power of an unconscious process in determining actions that are rationalized subsequently as one's "own intentions." In addition to their implicit challenge to neo-Darwinian thinking, these experiments render obsolete philosophical arguments against the idea of unconscious processes based on the notion that intentionality has to be conscious.[5]

The evidence gathered in research on hormones and pheromones points to the heart of the problem by supposing that intentionality is restricted by the skin. As Walter Freeman, a scholar of the neuroscience of emotion, points out, "Serious students of the evolution of brains have long believed that the nature of brain function in consciousness and intentionality will not be solved until olfaction is clearly understood."[6] And by this account, the problems in the study of olfaction and intentionality will not be solved until it is realized that the intentionality of a given subject can be influenced or shaped by factors originating outside that subject. Pheromones act as direction-givers which, as molecules, traverse the physical space between one subject and another, and factor in or determine the direction taken by the subject who inhales or absorbs them.

Changes in direction constitute intentionality in the most basic sense. This is the level at which intentionality connotes *conatus*, or the striving to fulfill one's nature and persevere as a distinct being, and the passions or "vitality affects" that lend themselves to this end. At this level, intentionality is unconscious as well as conscious. At the more familiar level, intentionality is the mark of the subject's particular will or agency. For our purposes, the most relevant of the many debates on intentionality are those that suppose the subject is motivated by intentions that are not his or her own, on which that subject imposes a meaning after the fact.[7] One illustration, from Hippolyte Bernheim's 1887 study of the effects of hypnosis, will suffice. After performing an action as the result of a previously implanted hypnotic suggestion, the hypnotized subject gave reasons for why the action made sense from his own standpoint, and why he intended to do it ("It was so boring; I felt like taking off my clothes").[8] Human beings feel obliged to claim responsibility for their actions, even when those actions are the result of drug-induced or hypnotized behavior.[9]

In the same way, I suggest, hormonal intentions other than our own may be rationalized by us after the fact, or may govern our agency unconsciously in other ways. But the example of hypnosis should signal that I am not reducing affects as such to hormones, and certainly not saying that pheromones, by influencing hormones, are the only means for their transmission (although it may turn out that their projector/receptor structure is at the heart of how transmission takes place). Rather, the point is that the behavior of hormones has a profile that fits with what we have learned so far about the transmission of affect; and what we have learned is that such transmissions affect the subject's intentionality, insofar as the subject's agency is composed of its affects or passions.[10] Influencing the subject's intentionality means influencing the subject's will or agency in ways that make it unfree (following a psychoanalytic definition of freedom).[11] Nor am I saying that the directions that move us intentionally, against our will if we knew of them, and which we rationalize after the fact, are all there is to agency. Later chapters are devoted to establishing that visiting intentions are eluded by memory, ethics, and honesty (themes that take us well beyond the subject matter of this chapter). However I am saying that faith in a fantasy undermines the ability, both scientifically and practically, to detect directions that work against or for the agency we are meant to express: that which is distinctive in each of us.[12]

Because of this fantasy, our self-contained individual believes he acts of his own accord, and that his impulses and desires come from nowhere other than the history embodied in his genes. He is wrong. The self-contained individual driven by a genetic motor has antecedents of his own. His origins appear to lie in a complex of Platonic and Aristotelian views on form and matter, activity and passivity, subject and object, views that merge with seventeenth-century Cartesianism to give birth to the self-contained individual whose mind and body are separate. These views distort science to the present day, so their investigation demands a little attention.

While sociobiology has no difficulty with the idea that hormones influence human agency and the direction of human will, the idea that this influence is anything other than a genetically determined and endogenous one, nonetheless, challenges the neo-Darwinian paradigm. Richard Dawkins, for instance, insists that we are lived by forces beyond our conscious control.[13] But at least they are *our* unconscious forces, perceived as such because perception has also been structured in such a way as to mean we do not see or conceive of an alternative way of understanding, let alone one that means we are not (necessarily) masters of the house.

Having said that, there is a peculiar affinity between Freud's original speculations on the workings of the unconscious and recent findings in neuroendocrinology and in work on how the environment shapes the brain. This affinity is only apparent once assumptions of self-containment are abandoned. Only then does olfaction emerge as a material force adequate to Freud's hypothesis that actions are willed through unconscious intentions.

This much should be more apparent if I sum up what has been deduced so far. The affect might, indeed, be the passive perception of a bodily motion (as William James surmised), but this need not mean the motion caused the affect, or the affect the motion. In some cases both affect and motion (hormones in these cases) are responding to a third factor altogether: the social environment, whose air can be thick with anxiety-provoking pheromones (or "human chemosignals," to use the preferred term). In one of the experiments surveyed in the last chapter, it appeared that anger and tension (whether they originate in a reasoned response, such as the response to unemployment, or from other causes) lead to the elevation of testosterone. Testosterone leads to aggressive as well as sexual feelings (and, as we shall see in a moment, feelings of well-being, confidence, and mania). But here the inquiry breaks off, as the influence of hormones on the emotions has been calculated in systemic, functional terms rather than in terms of factors that interfere with systems as well as facilitate them.[14] This means that all hormones are meant to work for the overall good of a self-contained system, and to be explicable as the fruit of human evolution. The idea that hormones might be thrown off-kilter by their pheromonal counterparts does not sit with the neo-Darwinian worldview. As the next section will show in more detail, assumptions of successful evolution are manifestly at odds with the behavior of hormones in stress and related situations—their behavior shows that the organism does not always, or even habitually, act in its own best interests. Explaining these and other anomalies (and the transmission of affect) requires a new paradigm, one capable of handling intentional and affective connections between and among subjects and their environment.

Now a new paradigm has been snapping at the heels of neo-Darwinism for some time. But it has done so in relation to mounting evidence for some form of inheritance of acquired characteristics, at the very least in relation to the immune system. Evidence of maternal activity in the formation of the embryo and the fetus, especially in relation to the transmission of affect and energy, has also supported the need for a new paradigm. When I referred to a new paradigm at the outset, I had in mind not only the facts on transmission in couples and groups but also these pregnant facts. As with material on the transmission of affect, these facts cannot be assimilated easily into a self-contained, genetically determined account. Indeed, maintaining the fantasy of self-containment requires that neither the womb nor the world penetrate the flesh of the individual as intentional forces in themselves. But just as self-containment is in question because of the transmission of affect, so it is in utero, and for a similar reason. There is evidence supporting the assumption that the maternal organism, like the environment, affects and may even shape the subject.

A discussion of recent literature on pregnancy and uterine life canvasses evidence pointing to the maternal environment as a potential solution to what Colin Blakemore describes as one of biology's longstanding problems: the problem of differentiation. From D'Arcy Thomson onward, others have referred to this as the problem of how the organism acquires its form.[15] Blakemore describes it more concretely: How, he asks, does a cell know that it is destined to be part of a pancreas or a heart, given that all cells carry the same genetic information, and other mechanisms for encoding messages for cell differentiation remain obscure?[16] I shall suggest mechanisms for the transmission of this information, based on superficial commonalities. In technical terms, for this lay reader, the implantation of the days-old fertilized egg—or blastocyst—provides an opportunity for the maternal organism to transmit instructions concerning cell differentiation. The implantation of the blastocyst is one occasion when the embryo-to-be comes in direct contact with the mother's blood, in the form of the endometrial lining. Subsequently, such contact is mediated by the placenta. But this suggestion is more tentative than those brought up in the discussion of hormones and the evidence for their transmission. More exactly, as we saw at the outset, chemical signals from humans have now been shown to affect the behavior of other humans. These may be the human version of pheromones and may be direct expressions of hormonal states. My argument in the next section is that research in this field, as shown in the preceding chapter and at more length in this one, provides confirmation that there is a horizontal line of affective transmission, and initial confirmation that neo-Darwinism cannot accommodate it. This much is clear from Blakemore's analysis of recent work on how the environment shapes the brain, when it is read together with Robert Sapolsky's study of endocrinology. Partly because his major work was written for a general (market) audience, Sapolsky comes as close as anyone in modern biology to a synthesis of current knowledge of hormones. That this neo-Darwinian book honestly records many of the anomalies revealed in psychoneuroendocrinology provides an ideal foil for my present purposes. But here, too, if my interpretations of these anomalies in terms of the transmission of affect may have misidentified the actions of classes of proteins, neurons, and hormones on the basis of insufficient understanding, I submit that the error lies not in the general logic that deduces entrainment and chemical communication between beings but in a premature identification of the action of particular players. But philosophy led scientists to this place, where they are unable to see what is not before their eyes, and necessarily will stumble in freeing science from the errors for which it is responsible.

Hormonal Entrainment

Psychoneuroendocrinology arose through the study of hormones and their effects on emotions as well as the nervous system and, conversely, the effects of affects on hormones and neurotransmitters. Hormone production and secretion in the stressful experience of age, pain, and significant other situations bears no necessary relation to the well-being or survival of the organism, and is often detrimental to it. Stress has proved an ongoing challenge for neo-Darwinism as it strives to explain exactly why stress mechanisms are so dysfunctional. Sapolsky's study draws on this research. It also continues work in the tradition of W. B. Cannon, Hans Selye, and Seymour Levine on stress, focusing on the recent discoveries in this field concerning glucocorticoids (GCs), the adrenal steroids secreted in stress responses. These hormones are involved in the regulation (or lack thereof) in stress and depression. Glucocorticoids can help in survival during brief, intense periods of physical stress, but having too many of them leads to suppression of the immune system and to negative effects on the nervous system.

Half of the autonomic nervous system is activated and half is suppressed. The activated half of the autonomic nervous system is termed the sympathetic nervous system. It connects with almost every organ, blood vessel, and sweat gland. It is the system that is connected with vigilance, arousal, activation, and mobilization, and which releases epinephrine, commonly called adrenalin. It shuts off certain restorative functions (digestion in particular) in order to divert energy to immediate needs. The parasympathetic nervous system, by contrast, diverts energy to those functions. Activation of the autonomic nervous system is involuntary in that it is unconscious.[17]

By contrast with the sympathetic system, the parasympathetic system mediates calm vegetative activities. It works during sleep to regenerate—for growth, energy storage, and rest. The sympathetic system speeds up the heart; the parasympathetic slows it down. The sympathetic system diverts blood flow to the muscles; the parasympathetic does the opposite.[18] Whereas adrenalin pertains to the sympathetic nervous system, it seems that glucocorticoids pertain more to the parasympathetic, although they also back up the action of the sympathetic. Glucocorticoids, members of the steroid class of hormones that also includes estrogen and testosterone, appear to be produced in traces in certain organs at the pituitary's command. They are the class of hormones most liable to overproduction, or underproduction, under stress. The association between glucocoticoids and the parasympathetic system is more a matter of this system inhibiting action and slowing us down, leading to sleep, digestion, and so forth, as glucocorticoids also do.

To complicate matters, nervous communication works by means of neurotransmitters—chemical molecules—and follows synaptic pathways that activate the autonomic nervous system. Hormones do not work in the same way as neurotransmitters. Neurotransmitters are connected directly to the brain or spinal cord and ganglion organs by specific pathways and responses, but hormones percolate throughout the blood stream. The difference between adrenalin (under the control of the adrenal glands) and noradrenalin (which originates in the peripheral glands) is illustrative. Their chemical signatures are almost identical, but they first appear in different places and are registered by different means.[19]

In some cases hormones appear to cooperate with the responses of the nervous system. In other cases they work against it. The origin of hormones has been contested in the brief history of endocrinology. The current position is that they, like the nervous system, are regulated by the brain, with the hypothalamus containing vast numbers of what are termed "releasing and inhibiting hormones."[20] It is assumed that these releasers and inhibitors regulate other hormones—in the glands, for instance. The brain may trigger a releasing hormone to activate another hormone or it may send another hormone to the reverse effect. But when it comes to the origin of the glucocorticoids (and steroids in general) it seems that these are—and yet are not—produced by the sympathetic nervous system. Glucocorticoids work in ways similar to adrenalin, but whereas adrenalin acts within seconds, glucocorticoids "back this activity up over the course of minutes or hours."[21] But in backing it up, they can also, it seems, backfire, leading to a situation where high levels of glucocorticoids and depression coexist. For example: "A socially subordinate rodent that is vigilant and trying to cope with a challenge . . . activates its sympathetic nervous system. . . . In contrast, it is the glucocorticoid system that is relatively more activated in a subordinate rodent that has basically given up on coping."[22] So it seems that glucocorticoids can either work with the sympathetic nervous system constructively, in which case they contribute to the activation of the central nervous system, or they can take on a life of their own. In this case there may be too many of them pumping, leading in extreme cases to the apparent atrophy of the hippocampus, an organ with vast responsibilities in receiving glucocorticoids and interpreting their meaning for the organism overall. This is the reason, or one of the reasons, stress responses pose a problem for the neo-Darwinian, evolutionary paradigm. Zebras, as the title of Sapolsky's popular book tells us, do not get ulcers . . . as a rule; but rats, like humans, get ulcers, and these do the organism no evolutionary good. They will impair the chances of survival of the otherwise fit. So why do we get ulcers and have stress responses that inexorably lead to illness and exacerbate aging? The neo-Darwinian answer is that nonadaptive responses are leftovers in our evolutionary heritage. It was right and proper for a besieged zebra to pump out adrenalin, but foolish for a department head to respond the same way, meeting after sedentary meeting. In such cases, stress can affect the rate of production of hormones, with deleterious, if not dangerous, effects.

An alternative explanation for the maladaptive response of the besieged lies in the transmission of affect. Studies of stressed or depressed humans have shown what may be a human analogue of the rodent dichotomy between sympathetic arousal and hormonal depression or inhibition. "Sympathetic arousal by means of neurotransmitters' sending a release message to the adrenal glands is a relative marker of vigilance, while heavy secretion of gluco-cortoroids is more a marker of depression."[23] Suggestively, certain subjects have noradrenalin levels in brain locations (although this is produced by the peripheral glands), as well as higher levels of glucocorticoids.[24] The production of glucocorticoids necessary for the organism to regenerate is also regulated by the autonomic nervous system. Yet that production is overlaid in its effects by hormones circulating freely throughout the blood. It is the levels of these hormones that are taken to be markers of illness and depression.

Let us now pick up a thread laid out in the last chapter. I supposed that "interpersonal depression" could be explained in terms of the one taking on a "pheromonal overload" from the other. This would explain why distance or travel served to relieve the depressee, or introjector, of the depression they carried for the aggressor, or "projector." A "subordinate rodent" at the bottom of a "stable dominance hierarchy" is more likely to have the symptoms of chronic stress responses (or, in our terms, more likely to be on the receiving end of chemosignals) with no opportunity to redirect them. My question then becomes whether the depressant levels of glucocorticoids are linked to whatever hormones are projected and activated in the one who is vigilant or aggressive—and received or inducted into the other. This presupposes that hypothetical glucocorticoids are responses to human chemosignals. The question becomes: Are some measurements of glucocorticoid levels actually measurements of the other's projection of dominance? Is the socially subordinate rodent exhausted from coping, or carrying—anchoring—dominant (pheromonal) projections or chemosignals?

In addition to the studies and experiments discussed in the preceding chapters, the resurgence of work on human pheromones has already established that gendered factors are at work. Steroids—and therefore glucocorticoids—are closely related to the masculinizing hormone, testosterone, and the androgen family in general, but I do not know if they are direct players in the projection and reception of chemosignals. What is clear is that one of the family of masculine hormones, androstadienone, stimulates human female olfaction. Androstadienone is the most prominent androstine found on male skin and hair. The researchers do not state if it is also found in some women, but they tell us that the administration of the steroid "results in a significant reduction in nervousness, tension and other negative feeling states [in women]. Concordant changes were observed in autonomic physiology."[25]

As already noted, the autonomic, particularly the parasympathetic, nervous system is the area where most glucocorticoid hormones are active in their dampening affects. While their administration is reported to reduce "nervousness, tension, and other negative feeling states," it is unclear how it affects the female/feminine organism in other ways, such as whether it reduces alertness, capacity for concentration, and so forth. This is not to say that there are no circumstances where it would be desirable to have those things relaxed, just that the steroids affecting the autonomic nervous system have already been shown to be those that readily become dysfunctional. In other words, androstadienone is part of the complex of steroids, ranging from testosterone to estrogen and including the glucocorticoids, that are the most vulnerable to stress affects. In such circumstances, production either ceases or accelerates inappropriately.[26] To take another of the very interesting recent studies of hormonal correlates between subjects, it seems that heterosexual couples "exposed to auditory, visual and olfactory cues from newborn infants had similar stage-specific differences in hormone levels." But having shown that the correlations hold *within* the couples the researchers turn away from the significance of that correlation and conclude "that hormones may play a role in priming males to provide care for young."[27] But what they are really concluding is that, apparently, female hormones prime males to care for young. What of a follow-up that compares the partners in gay couples? Or expectant fathers who are coupled with their partners with expectant fathers who are not? Are their hormones also primed in relation to each other, and if so, how? For that matter, what of a comparison of hormonal levels among those who live together as a matter of course, with or without a child?

It is necessary to emphasize again the interpretive difficulties that stand in the way of exploring the effects of hormonal and chemical entrainment (and, potentially, nervous entrainment). I have given one brief, hypothetical explanation relying on a synthesis of some existing findings in one class of hormones only; taking this idea further would mean testing if an overload of glucocorticoids (and depression) in one party is linked to elevated levels of testosterone (and mania) in the environment. I say "environment" at this point deliberately. While testing on partners and close-by relatives is evidently vital, my point (as noted above) is that testing for reciprocal dyads here is only preliminary, as the environment may be equally, if not wholly, at fault.[28] I look forward to olfactory experiments in which hypotheses inferred from the above arguments might be tested. Specifically, does the overproduction of glucocorticoids signify an entrainment to exogenous androgens or chemosignals mimicking their action? If so, it needs to be noted that such chemosignals may also be produced environmentally. The number of hormone-mimicking molecules in the environment has already been demonstrated to have adverse affects on intelligence and fertility in men. At this point I have been unable to demonstrate if these affects are linked to those involved in the overproduction of glucocorticoids or to determine the degree of commensurability between the relevant experiments. Once more, the idea is not to reduce all hormonal shifts and anomalies to a lateral line of affective transmission, any more than it is to ignore the history of affects embedded in the composition of the person and the organism. Taking account of the intersection of the vertical line of personal history and the horizontal line of the heart is the only way that we can make sense of why the administration of steroids affects some subjects more than others. One experiment on the effects of externally applied testosterone on mood and aggression in "normal men" showed that it increased the rate of manic symptoms (overestimating their abilities). "This effect, however, was not uniform across individuals; most showed little psychological change, whereas a few developed prominent effects. The mechanism of these variable reactions remaining unclear."[29] It will remain unclear, I suggest, as long as the variables do not distinguish between what we take in from our environment and what we carry with us in our cumulative emotional baggage. The intersection of the environmental and the historical does not result in a simple addition (x endogenous testosterone plus y environmental testosterone does not equal xy testosterone). As we shall see, it cannot do this if the ability to distinguish an affect is more developed in some than it is in others in terms of the knowledge of it gleaned through resisting it. That psychosocial living organism, the human being, carries within it the pathways it establishes to deal with its affects. The more it resists an impulse, the more it learns about the nature of that impulse. So that if the impulse is violent, "holding it in" tells a person a great deal about how a violent impulse takes hold, provided he or she is able to compare one instance with the last. But one cannot trace the path of an impulse if one does not note its arrival. In other words, if one habitually follows intentions generated by an impulse, one does not distinguish between those intentions and one's normal state. Therefore, there is no awareness of it as something distinct from one's normal nature.

Support for resistance as the means to reducing the presence of a particular hormone and its associated affects is found in a study comparing people in the occupations of ministers and performers. The latter were found to have higher levels of testosterone, which led to the primitive conclusion that choice of occupation was determined by hormone levels, a sociobiological conclusion flying in the face of social variables affecting this and other steroids.[30] What would make more sense of the findings of this study is the notion that the occupational choice of the minister led to more transformation or repression of testosterone-associated affects (aggression, overconfidence, sexual arousal) as a matter of occupational course, whereas the same affects in the entertainer are indistinguishable from those evoked in the course of performance. Being—or identifying—with those in receipt of adulation raises levels of testosterone; monitoring the affects associated with testosterone means those affects have less hold.[31] Testosterone makes some men manic, but not all.

Suggestively, this research lines up with the hypothetical distinction I am making between a vertical or historical line of personal affective history and a horizontal or heartfelt axis of communication that imbibes molecular information directly from the other. The vertical line explains the disposition of the individual and whether he or she is capricious or calm, and so forth. The axis of the heart is the means whereby we imbibe whatever is around in transitory circumstances and may explain why a normally calm person becomes agitated, or vice versa. But if I am right in supposing such axes exist, the question becomes: How do these axes intersect? In considering this question, we can note that hormones appear to have different "signatures." Sapolsky explains that a signature is the language in which the hormone's composition is written. Thus some hormonal signatures involve epinephrine released by the adrenal gland and some involve norepinephrine released by the "sympathetic nerve endings." In addition, "all stressors do not cause secretion of both epinephrine and norepinephrine, nor of norepinephrine from all branches of the sympathetic system."[32] The difficulty for a lay reader confronted with facts such as these is avoiding a premature identification of hypothetical axes of historical and transitory affects with certain hormones. More exactly, I want to argue now that the difference in similar hormonal signatures involving epinephrine and norepinephrine reflects their different points or origin, in historical or transitory affects. As such, the signatures of different hormones are records of the path of their origination. Or, to say the same thing, the signature itself is a record of the origin of the particular hormone, a record of the path by which the hormone was acquired. Adrenalin A (out of noradrenalin registering the hormonal input of the environment) meets with Adrenalin B (out of the adrenal gland of the subject), resulting in signature A/B. A/B has the same effect on the body as B/A, or seems to have the same effect, but the signature is nonetheless significant as information relevant to a corrective (where such is needed). In one experiment, described as "particularly odd," laboratory rats had "different patterns of stress responses depending on which human handled them."[33] This fascinating experiment suggests that confirmation of the relation between stress signatures and their variable activation by others is readily available. The rats brought their own affective, behavioral histories to their encounter with different handlers. But if I am right, those handlers would have contributed their own chemosignals to the encounter, and these would have sent different stress signatures to the hippocampus (through the blood stream). In other words, the differential responses of the rats, and the stress signatures they recorded, are combinations, responses to transitory chemical information from the handler, as well as information programmed by the rat's emotional history.

In a recent paper, Sapolosky notes circumstances in which atrophy of the hippocampus coincides with the prolonged excessive production of glucocorticoids. If I am correct, the hippocampus, as the agency interpreting hormonal information carried by the blood, has to be interpreting chemosignals that did not originate endogenously. But if the hippocampus is struggling to make sense of signatures other than its own, and taking its best guess when it comes to informing the pituitary about radiation, pollution, and so forth, then it might easily be overwhelmed. Its "exquisite sensitivity" to glucocorticoids, the numerous glucocorticoid receptors with which it is lined, are there, from this perspective, for interpretation. The hypothalamus would then be attempting to sniff out what the new molecular information it has imbibed means for the organism's integrity and how it should respond. Too much information from too many unidentified sources and it ceases to function.

Pregnant Facts

The essence of the paradigmatic shift proposed here is that we regard the human being as a receiver and interpreter of feelings, affects, attentive energy. The psychoanalytic study of the mind provides a template for this, insofar as it focuses on the construction of a receiver adequate to receiving language. It is not that all the words ever written are within; all that is within is the means for understanding them. The notion of the brain's response system (cortical as well as hypothalamic) as an interpreter rather an originator of news and information is consistent with Blakemore's account of the development of the peripheral nervous system and the formation of the cortex alike. These are built up by the reception, through the construction of neuronal pathways from the sense organs to the cortex, of environmental inputs.[34] By means of this argument, Blakemore is able to deal with the limited range of input provided by the genes. "Although more than 25,000 of our genes are involved in making the nervous system, this number of instructions seems pitifully small. . . . The blueprint of the brain, contained in the genes, does not seem to match up to the complexity of the object to be built—like constructing the Taj Mahal from a sketch on the back of an envelope."[35]

If one takes the view that the genetic instructions for building the brain are instructions on how to build a receiver rather than a library, their limited numbers are of less concern. Limited numbers may be more than adequate for constructing a system whose primary function is the categorization, recognition, and interpretation of myriad intelligent, intentional messages that flow through the surrounding environs.

However, the instructions are most scanty if one believes that the genes are the fount of every minor variation in mood, intelligence, and inclination. A similar issue arose when it was recognized recently that the human genome had only a few more variations than that of the fly: that is to say, the complexity of human cellular organization compared with that of the fly is not reflected in the genes. Except for the germ cells, all forty-six chromosomes are contained in each cell, which means that there is nothing in their initial genetic endowment that seems to explain why some cells are destined for toenails, some for bits of liver, and so forth. As Ingold and others have noted, there is no warrant for assuming that the capacity to marshal form is genetic; for modern biology, how the organism's form is organized or acquired remains a mystery.[36] Blakemore tackles this issue in terms of how the environment structures the brain through the sense organs, which seem to form the cortex from the outside in, shaping neuronal pathways—axons—according to the nature of the sensory information they communicate. This process begins in utero and continues after birth.

I noted earlier that the cortex is formed from the bottom up, so to speak. In utero, it develops when mysterious cells seem to give the cortex its initial form. These establish a "subplate," or template, whereby the dendrites that grow out of the thalamus take on specific cortical properties, forming a highly specialized division of labor within neuronal communication. However, there are instances where the surface of the cortex does not look as it should: the neuronal pathways or dendrites are a tangled mess on the surface of the brain. This is the case, for instance, in fetal alcohol syndrome. Now, if the dendrites look as they should where alcohol does not affect the fetus, we may suppose that the orderly development of dendrites depends on some chemical constant in the maternal environment. This constant can be conceived negatively—as the absence of toxicity—and positively. The interpretative prejudice in science as it stands is to conceive of the maternal constant negatively. This prejudice has a long philosophical history.

Beginning with Aristotle's perspective on generation, the mother's body has been seen as the passive soil in which the fully formed homunculus is planted. Aristotle's account is particularly interesting when read in conjunction with his views on activity and form (or mind), and passivity and matter. For when it comes to the origins of forms, Aristotle assigns them to a matrix of matter and potential forms, where all potential forms exist in the matrix. His account of pregnancy, however, gives the maternal body no potential or potency. The mother is not the origin of all forms but a passive garden for a form that is implanted from without.[37] Despite the discovery of ovulation, this perspective persists. What justifies the notion of fetal autonomy is not only the idea that the fetus carries its own genetic blueprint but also that this blueprint somehow is sufficient in explaining the growth of its form. Here we have the essence of the problem. This form is meant to call forth the essence of its content, to marshal that content to itself. In fact, what the notion of fetal autonomy assumes is that because the concept of a hand is part of the genetic blueprint, the message "Hey you, grow hand!" automatically issues forth from the fetal package, as do the instructions for marshaling the necessary substance out of which it is to construct itself. Such substances, simply described, are the proteins, sugars, and oxygen that are the chemical building blocks in cells as they divide and multiply—all of them are substances that are supplied by the mother's bloodstream. But while the mother's body is assumed to be passive in the event that a pregnancy progresses predictably, her influence in shaping embryonic life *is* acknowledged if something goes wrong. This point is illustrated by a glance at the expanding literature on the influence of the mother on the fetus. Most of the research examines neurotoxic syndromes and other pathological processes.[38] Chronic maternal anxiety "causes an increased stillbirth rate, fetal growth retardation, and altered placental morphology. Experimental studies have demonstrated a relationship between specific episodes of maternal psychological stress and exacerbation of fetal asphyxia in utero . . . 'psychoactive' interchanges between the mother and fetus are decisive in the ultimate outcome of the fetus' growth and brain development."[39] Similarly, there is evidence that anxiety and poverty and other lacks do affect the fetus as well as the neonate.

At the same time, it should also be clear that the negative affects of anxiety and the stress of poverty are mitigated by something, a positive maternal constant. Another study explored the development of fetal sensory faculties that are the basis for many interchanges between mother and fetus. "The good quality of psychoaffective communication between the mother and her child during pregnancy appears to be decisive for the fetal, perinatal, and later development of the child, especially for harmonious brain growth."[40] As with the living attention responsible for that extra growth variable in postnatal life, so it seems does living attention, or love, foster prenatal vitality.

For instance, there is an ongoing debate over the extent to which the preimplantation embryo or zygote possesses the information necessary for its development or articulation as a human being. Those who claim that the preimplantation zygote does possess all or most of the necessary information necessary to develop as a human being have to reckon with two outstanding sets of facts. The first concerns the manner in which embryos that are not implanted take on a formless or molelike shape if left to develop, so to speak, in the petri dish. The second set of facts focuses on the totipotency of the zygote's cells. Totipotency in this context is another way of referring to the problem of form. It means that each of the cells contains all the information necessary for the elaboration of livers and toes, even if a particular cell is destined to be part of a knee.

But as with the understanding of the transmission of affect, the notion that human intention and intelligence are self-contained stands in the way of recognizing facts that make a self-contained intelligence or agency improbable. That said, just as the existence of human chemosignals breaks down prejudices privileging the inner hormone, the indications that the maternal organism is implicated in the construction of form or organization are growing.

Both sets of facts are amenable to an explanation in which the form-giving capacity inheres in the mother. I want to suggest two related ways in which the maternal environment is active in forming the embryo and the fetus. The maternal regulation of form is effected by the interaction between the zygote's genetic coding and the RNA memory proteins in the endometrial lining at the moment of the blastocyst's implantation in the womb. This is the only point at which the "mother's blood" is not filtered by the placenta, so to speak. Speculatively, I am suggesting that the interaction between these memory proteins and the zygote establishes a link between genetic instructions and the means to fulfill them through cell differentiation and that this link is in some way expressed in patterns or rhythms of blood flow. The immediate prompt to this idea is the fact of thalidomide, the condition in which the limbs do not develop. This condition is explained by the compression of a maternal blood vessel at a crucial point. More concretely, a phenomenon known as "positioning," which works by messenger-RNA proteins ("morphogens") may soon provide evidence of precisely how this occurs. Currently, there is a debate as to whether some morphogens are triggered by the maternal environment. Stressing that a petri-fied zygote can develop into a hydatidiform mole rather than a human being, Carlos Bedate and Robert Cefalo argue that the embryo develops through its own genetically and nongenetically coded molecules, "together with the influence of the maternal environment." Against this, it is asserted that "the domain governed by embryonic information remains well separated from the domain governed by maternal information."[41]

The tradition from Aristotle onward is to conceive of this constant negatively, as an absence rather than a presence. Yet there is evidence for an additive or positive factor. The presence of living maternal attention enhances the cortical development of rats, as we have seen, and there is evidence that such attention has related impacts on human embryos. What stands in the way of taking such ideas further is not the accumulating scientific evidence supporting them. It is the philosophical prejudice against the notion of the maternal environment, or any environment, as constructing persons in this way. The extent to which the maternal environment interacts with the genetic variables in inheritance has been consistently underestimated.

Perhaps it is the case that the embryo does not only carry its own blueprint but that it also unfolds in a way that enables it to direct its own growth. Currently, however, no one knows. Genetic theory has its major explanatory value with respect to the notion of a blueprint, but it provides us with no evidence as to how the zygote implements its own construction. This is simply assumed to be so. The notion of fetal autonomy *simpliciter* leaves several facts unexplained and is in flat contradiction with others. It is clear that alterations in the mother's biochemistry may have the effect of stunting or altering the direction of fetal growth. In other words, the mother may be actively involved in the production of abnormality and, thus, in this instance, is plainly not passive. It is alterations in the mother's chemistry that deform (as in the case of thalidomide), as well as genetic coding. Yet it is also plain that the maternal environment enhances the life chances of the embryo, and the fetus, through energetic attention in the case of both rats and humans.

But the presenting problem of this section remains. Given the various placental screens that stand between upsets to the mother and the fetus, and given that the embryo and the fetus are shielded from the physiological components of anxiety as a rule, how can it communicate itself in exceptional cases? As indicated earlier, a factor in the disruptions of pregnancy is that of a change in circulation or motion. The accident or jolt does this directly; the chemical malformations of thalidomide are produced by a chemical constriction in the maternal blood vessel, which interferes with the flow of blood. If the affects the mother experiences interfere with the rate of pulsation or blood flow appropriate at a given stage of development, it will affect the formation of the child.[42]

But once it is acknowledged that the chemosignals that affect us encompass more than our endogenous productions, once it is realized that these chemosignals also come from others and the environment, Harvey's understanding of the circulation of the blood may resemble Ptolemy's assumptions about the earth's centrality. The Harverian model is one in which everything gets pumped around in a self-contained system with the heart doing the work and the brain in command.[43]

In this psychological equivalent of this model, the senses that locate us in space and time (vision, hearing, and touch) present themselves as the means for drawing the boundaries. The notion that the sense of self is different from that which is outside it (because that which is outside is unconscious, passive, and material) is clearly untenable. It is untenable as a substantial distinction, because, insofar as the self has substance and is embodied, it too is matter. It is untenable as a distinction relying on the active/passive dichotomy, unless we interpret "active" in a very specific sense. That is to say, natural matter is active in certain natural cycles; it is only passive to the extent that it does not have free will, meaning that it does not implement any design or intention other than the one maintaining its place in the scheme of things. Active matter is passive in that it is not individual; its intentional activity does not place it at odds with its surroundings. Only humans have intentions at odds with the scheme of things, but those intentions do not originate within them, as we will see.

It follows that the passivity of matter does not lie in lack of action but in lack of free will or agency. Only the subject of free will differentiates itself from its environment by activity that is at odds with that environment. Intentional activity in harmony with one's surroundings does not stand out from it, in that it is not motivated by a will of one's own. It is only through activity reflecting its will that the environment can reflect the subject's activity and thereby confirm that the subject's activity is something more (or less) than the passive activity of nature. This is why intentional activity, in the sense of an intervention in or an imposition on the subject's surroundings, is also understood as subjective activity. This subjective activity takes the definition of itself as the center of all definition and defines all "activity" as having its own character. It labels "passive" everything that is not active in its own way and which it is able to *bend to its will*, passive if it does not assert itself against the subject. The objects making up the environment are seen as passive because they do not carry out intentions of their own. To be active is to carry out an individual intention, which must, by definition, differ from the intentions of the environment. The active/passive dichotomy, as consciousness understands it, is thus a product of the sense of self that divides itself off from the rest of the world on the grounds of its difference. Its understanding of activity is synonymous with the idea of individual intentionality.

So the distinction between subjectivity and objectivity cannot rest on a distinction between psyche and soma, meaning that it cannot rest on a distinction between ideas and matter. What prohibits the assimilation of the psyche/soma, ideas/matter distinctions to the subject/object distinction is, above all, the fact of feeling and the existence of affects. The first discerns the second. Both feeling, as a process of sensing affects, and the transmission of affects, are material processes. We cannot distinguish between them, any more than we can distinguish between subject and object, by any criteria to do with materiality as opposed to ideality. The distinction can only be drawn on the basis of the nature of the feelings and affects involved. Feelings connect logically (consistently with the information provided by the flesh). The negative affects divide one person from another and then remake connections inaccurately from the subjective standpoint.

The narrative loops in neo-Darwinism occur when biology encounters anything that disrupts the illusions of a self-contained subject negotiating a world of objects. The distinction between the subject and the object is essential to all received views of knowledge and perception, to Western philosophy and to the history and practice of science. The distinction between subjectivity and objectivity is meant to be the essence of the scientific method. The notion that there are objective material processes separate from their subjective observer is the traditional, although not unchallenged, scientific standpoint. I do not disagree with the principle here, insofar as it represents an attempt at impartiality or at seeking knowledge by some principle other than personal convenience. Accordingly, the question becomes: Is there another basis for distinguishing between what can be known or supposed scientifically and what is mere fancy? A basis that, as materiality was supposed to do, exists independently of human subjective awareness and that is not the product of that awareness? In answer to this question, chapter 7 suggests that science that studies the living logic in terms of systems is more likely to evade the restrictions imposed by the subjective standpoint. But first chapter 6 turns to the difference between feelings and affects in terms of a practice of discernment that is based on what is and is not consistent with one's historically formulated intentions. Discernment begins with considered sensing (by smell, or listening, as well as observation)—the process of feeling that also operates, or seems to operate, as the gateway to emotional response. When we do not feel, we open the gates to all kinds of affective flotsam, being unaware of its passage or its significance. We cease to discern the transmission of affect.

Uneducated, unconscious senses are not aware of any psychical, intelligent connection with the internal and invisible body, and this unconsciousness extends to the rest of the environment. They are structured in such a way as to deny or foreclose on sensing information as a conscious process. But the foreclosure is not absolute; it does not govern perception permanently or fully. It is interspersed with feelings that lead to different conclusions and other directions. The foreclosure itself and repression appear to coincide with the projection outward of the negative affects. This projection results from a sense of peril and pain in which the nascent subject is attempting to defend itself by expelling bad feelings outside itself. In this projective defense lies the basis of all its errors of judgment.[44] But one must not, and cannot, forget that these links do make sense from the subject's standpoint, lots of sense. The links between activity, subject, mind, and their opposing chain of associations seem real because at one level they are real, made of matter and twisted energy. When my eye sees what it expects to see, even though it is not there, I have made the image real, given it a tangible and physical existence by the force of my imagination. As we have seen, this imaginative force is not metaphorical.[45] It helps construct apparent chains of reason from the subject's standpoint, especially the foundational links between mind, activity, and so forth (and by a strange derivation, the belief that the social is unphysical).

Understanding the influences to which we are subject in terms of passions and emotions, as well as living attention, means lifting off the burden of the ego's belief that it is self-contained in terms of the affects it experiences. Lifting off this burden liberates it scientifically, allowing it to explore communication by smell and sound in ways that can heal it. It also liberates it physically, in that it permits it to think in terms of extending consciousness through its feelings. But perhaps the most immediate relief it offers is an understanding of our lacks and faults and sins, to which we turn in the next chapter. These are the moments when we are callous or blinded to the facts, when tempers are lost and feelings trampled, when spite dictates the words and envy the vision—all these moments can be revisited in the light of the transmission of affect. These moments are not only self-caused. They are also times when waves of negative affect possess us as surely as anxiety is communicated or love truncated. Both anxiety and living attention can be measured in their effects and understood in terms that are the opposite of the superstition that habitually distorts the interpretation of the invisible. As the remaining chapters show, these affects can now come down to earth, exposed as no more than collections of bad odors or misguided molecules.

The most hardened materialist would agree that ultimately all differences registered through chemical as well as electrical means are differences in the rate of pulsation or vibration, registered in the heart and affecting variations throughout the circulatory system.

CHAPTER FIVE

The Sealing of the Heart

The notion that free-flowing guilt or free-floating anxiety are in the air, and more prone to descend on the anxious, has been expressed in the vocabulary of demons of doubt and guilt and despair. The earliest Western records of the transmission of affect (excluding the Homeric record, which makes them monitions or energies from the gods) make them demons or deadly sins.[1] Insofar as we understand these demons and sins as affective states operating according to their own lazy laws, rather than as maliciously independent entities, their burden on the psyche is less onerous. But that light burden cannot be perceived for what it is when the world is viewed in terms of subjects and objects, perceived in ways that sever and objectify the means for perceiving affects (the feelings) and assigns the affects themselves to a purely en-dogenous place. Yet, prior to the eighteenth century, affects generally were not perceived this way. When they were not styled as demons they were regarded as passing passions that gripped the soul but were not equivalent to the soul. Demons, passions, and affects were entities that visited the psyche, rather than entities that originated within it. Sins were also affects, but affects that had found a secure lodgment. The parallels between demons and affects do not end here. When the history of the deadly sins and the demons is investigated, one finds a tie between the notion of the demon and that of a bad smell. If complex human affects are communicated by chemical and electrical entrainment, and we have every reason for supposing that they are, this was also sensed by the authors of the Talmud, and known to the early Church fathers. "Demons flee from the smell of a good soul," wrote Evagrius (536–594 C.E.), while the Talmud enjoins us to smell that which is pleasant and to avoid those odors that communicate demonic intentions.[2]

First we shall trace the view (as far as I can tell, the oldest view) of the affects as demons or sins. We shall then trace out how the affects, while they ceased to be labeled sins, were nonetheless conceived as entities opposed to the integrity of the organism's expression of its true nature until the seventeenth century. The third area of discussion turns to how the affects more or less won after that, becoming the ego, or "I." The relation of the affects to the ego—how the ego is composed of affects and how the ego grows stronger as the negative affects proliferate—is important here. In the light of this, we see how the transmission of affect works in the present to strengthen the negative affects and the passionate judgments they carry in their train, hence reinforcing the ego with its aggressive barriers of self-containment. I will also extend the parallel—sketched out in *Exhausting Modernity*—between psychoanalytic accounts of the formation of the ego and theological understandings of the fall into sin, where sin is derived from the Latin for "lack." The basis for extending the parallel in this case will not be the similarity between Augustine's account of the Fall and Melanie Klein's ontology of the infant psyche, as it was in *Exhausting Modernity*. It will be the way in which inertia takes hold in the psyche and how the fixed points it creates lead in turn to the seven deadly sins or, in the language of psychoanalysis, envy, narcissism, aggression, and other affective judgments cathecting the other. The concluding section discusses the argument for why the negative affects cut us off from the "positive affects" in a recognizable historical progression, similar to what Judaism describes in the laws of the sealing of the heart and the decline of the generations and which Lacan terms the "era of the ego."

The Seven Spirits of Deceit

The most familiar forms of passion and judgment or constellations of negative affects are embodied in pre-Hellenic concepts of seven spirits of deceit, and the seven deadly sins that more or less embody those spirits. Each of the sins—pride, sloth, envy, lust, anger, gluttony, and avarice—is an affect rather than an act. My comparison of the passifying or negative affective states with the seven deadly sins begins by noting that the sins are all emotions, except for sloth, of which more in a moment. In the official Christian list following Gregory the Great's (died 604) formulation of it, they are: pride (*superbia*), sloth (*accidie*), envy (*invidia*), lust (*luxuria*), anger (*ira*), gluttony (*gula*), and avarice (*avaritia*).[3] There is a fair approximation between this list and the psychoanalytic sins of narcissism, inertia, envy, objectification, aggression, greed, and obsessionality. In the psychoanalytic case, these passifying affects are produced by the ego's confrontation with its other and the realization of its dependence on that other. In the case of the deadly sins, the accounts of their origin are unclear. The idea of seven major sins did not begin with Christianity. In the apocryphal Testament of the Twelve Patriarchs, the Testament of Reuben (109 B.C.E.), a Judaic text to which Christian additions were later made),[4] seven "spirits of deceit" are listed.[5] They are close enough to the later Christian official list (and are called fornication, gluttony, strife, vainglory, pride, lying, and injustice).[6] The Testament of Reuben occasionally adds an eighth vice: the spirit of sleep. The Judaic text, in turn, was affected by Gnosticism and Hellenic philosophy, and both of these bore the marks of Eastern beliefs.[7] Possibly, the Gnostic beliefs had an earlier, ultimately Egyptian, origin. The most ancient list of what to avoid, affectively speaking, may lie with the Egyptians, and there we are back once more with demons, who inhabited the Egyptian world as surely as they did the Jewish, Greek, and Christian worlds to come.[8] Where the different theories (Egyptian, Judaic, and Christian) come together is in the idea that, originally, the sins were evil spirits. For the Gnostics, the guardians of the planets were "aerial spirits," while the things to be shunned in the Judaic Testament of Reuben were, as we noted, the spirits of deceit. Like his Judaic and Egyptian forebears, Evagrius also thought of the sins as demons. For the Egyptian desert monks, sloth, in particular, was an evil spirit,[9] known as the noonday demon. Let me add here that this idea of a noonday demon may be more than just a nice metaphor for capturing the fact that sloth was likely to get hold of you when the sun was high and energy was low. It may be a survival of a way of thinking about good and evil that was more physical than the thought of our time.[10]

Of most import for us in this discussion of affects is the persistent association of the sins with demons. The sins are equivalent to primary repression, insofar as they then function to attract demons, or the affects the psyche attracts to itself in secondary repression. Indeed, all that would seem to distinguish the demons and sins on the one hand from the passifying affects on the other is that the latter have a genealogy tying them to the birth of the ego in a game of comparative advantage, while the derivation of the demons is at present lost to us. But, for what it is worth, there is a limited parallel between the role played by inertia in the formation of the ego and the sin of sloth, the sin to which inertia is most closely tied. Sloth for a time was significant in the deadly sins, although it never had the status that Gregory and others, including Augustine, gave to pride. Nonetheless, in the medieval and early Renaissance literature, we are often told that "the slothful provide a comfortable resting place (*hospitium*) for the devil."[11] But is sloth the same thing as inertia in the formation of the ego? Inertia, in this theory, is the *condition* by which all the passifying affects—or sins—come into being. It is like an eighth sin. The idea of an eighth deadly sin is not new. The fourth-century Egyptian desert fathers, who were the first Christians to formulate a list of deadly sins, listed eight, not seven, of them. The eighth sin has been a matter of controversy, basically because no one is quite sure what it was. When asked what the eighth sin was, Serapion, bishop of Thmuis in the Nile Delta in the middle of the fourth century, said that it was "the elementary condition of the soul under the influence of sin, the condition symbolized by the captivity of the Israelites in Egypt."[12] We may regard this eighth sin as equivalent to the repression of the first hallucination: this constructed inertia holds captive human souls in fixed form, leading them to see the world from their own viewpoint (vanity, narcissism), to compare themselves with others (envy), and so on.

The fact that what is repressed is nothing, an empty hole, means that the affects take direction from a dead thing. They take direction from something that does not exist. What does exist is an affect-driven parody of creation that mirrors it in reverse. By studying the mirror we have made, we will learn the difference between the original and the imitation and learn, too, that all that holds the imitation together is the dead mirror that inverts the path of life. That said, while inertia is not the same as sloth, it nonetheless resembles it. Inertia also, especially in the modern understanding of depression, connotes sadness. When we are depressed, we are likely to be inert; when inert, sadness may be the underlying cause. Moreover, inertia is tied to depression, again reflecting an ancient tie, in that sloth is a species of sadness, which is why Gregory felt able to amalgamate the two sins (sadness and sloth) into one.[13] But the further back we go, the more it seems that inertia is prominent and a candidate for the missing eighth sin. As we saw earlier, the occasional references to the eighth sin in the Judaic Testament of Reuben were to the "spirit of sleep." We are never more inert than when we are sleeping, unless we are dead. Horace's list of the vices actually includes inertia (*iners*),[14] and Servius speaks of how the planets bestow evil gifts, listing torpor as the unwanted gift the soul receives from Saturn.[15] Inertia and fixity are the condition of the other sins being magnified,[16] the means whereby souls are made captive.

In the medieval emphasis on literal immobility and sloth or inertia, sloth (*acedia*) is symbolized by slow physical movement. Dante has *acedia* punished by an "incessant running on the fourth cornice of *Purgatorio*,"[17] an image that reminds one irresistibly of joggers on treadmills. In a similar vein, when *acedia* is compared with illness in medieval writings, the illness it is compared to first is actual paralysis.[18] The slothful are inert. They literally cannot move. They are symbolized now by a century that began with hysterical paralysis as a most popular disorder and ended with the syndrome of chronic fatigue.[19] The sins are deadly because of the affective constellations they embody, the objectifying and "abject-ifying" images they impose on others, as well as on oneself. They are the means by which repression is actualized along certain channels, through the diversion of life energy or life drive in the service of repression.

Passion and Action

The notion that the affects are invaders that work against our true natures is expressed in the early modern understanding of passion as a passifying force opposed to action, meaning the activity of the soul. As Susan James draws out, up to and including the seventeenth century, to be the object of affects is to be passive in relation to them. "For early modern writers, desire—and feelings such as love, anger or sadness—are all states of a single kind."[20] Such passive states are contrasted with those in which one is active. Thus, when Spinoza talks of an adequate cause, he means a cause that accounts for actions that take place within us or that follows from our natures. "On the other hand," Spinoza says, "we are passive (*pati*) when something takes place in us or follows from our nature, of which we are only the partial cause."[21] Nonetheless, the passions are also and essentially "a manifestation of a striving to persevere in our being, which is our essence."[22] This striving, or *conatus* for Spinoza, is the most basic of our passions. Building on this base, he dynamically integrated the familiar passions of joy (*laetitia*) and sadness (*tristitia*). When our striving to maintain ourselves leads to an increase in our power, we feel *laetitia*. When it diminishes, we feel *tristitia*. This experience of the passions also embodies individual history. History is embodied as the basis for comparisons concerning whether our power is diminishing or increasing. Faced with a diminution in power compared to where we were, we experience *tristitia*.[23]

As we saw in chapter 4, matter officially is passive. Action, by contrast, is defined in terms of actuality, actually realizing one's potential by realizing one's form and hence fulfilling one's purpose. By extension, one could suppose that the passive affects hinder us from realizing our form and acting in accord thereby with our natures—or one could suppose this until the eighteenth century. While all things are composed of form and matter, actuality and potentiality, the soul is something of an exception. It is form, but it is also the power that makes a body a living thing. As James notes, "A form . . . can be understood as the set of powers to behave in certain characteristic ways that make a thing what it is."[24] (The form-giving role of the soul is similar to that which we hypothesized belongs to the mother or maternal environment; the soul, like that maternal capacity, shapes a blob of formless matter into something morphologically familiar and able to think and act.) Passions, by contrast, may work against actions and actualizations. James goes on, "Rather than conceiving of appetite as containing desires *for* states that are pleasurable and aversions to states that are painful, we do better to think of it as consisting of desires and aversions that are *already* pleasurable or painful, which give rise to actions that in turn produce further kinds of pain and pleasure." The short argument, then, as to why these passions and passionate judgments are passive is that they are the result of being "affected by the world around us."[25] We are not acting to actualize our distinctness, but reacting, and in this sense losing the initiative relative to the things that affect us. Desires and affects, in this view, are both passive. Yet it is in the peculiar nature of their passivity that they also affirm the ego. Aristotle notes that "the emotions [*pathe*] are those things through which, by undergoing change, people come to differ in their judgments and which are accompanied by pain and pleasure."[26] It should follow that the distinctness of our judgments depends, then, on the extent to which we are passified by various affects and how far this passification or the resistance to it marks one person as different from another. It also depends on the soul or anima that resists those passions.

In essence, Aristotle's understanding of action and activity contrasted with passivity remains throughout Aquinas's work, together with what James describes as "the view that the soul is the form of the body."[27] Aquinas was a major influence on seventeenth-century philosophy of the passions, and through him the Aristotelian understanding of the passivity of both affects and desires is perpetuated. Aquinas also proposed that "evil cannot be known simply as evil, for its core is hollow, and can be neither recognized nor defined save by the surrounding good,"[28] which is a notion we pursue when we turn to Lacan's very similar definition of the ego as nothing but lack.

The notion that passifying passions work against the soul or form they affect is also a statement that the essence of the self is something other, something distinct from the passions. It is this distinctness that is later lost. First, the insistence on form as the origin of powers and motion comes to seem absurd.[29] While passion as passivity and action are retained as the key categories, they are recast in a mechanistic worldview that "explains nothing" (Descartes); action, rather, is the transfer of motion from oneself to another, and passion is being acted upon.[30] With the mechanistic turn, it seems that bodies have a "power to resist change," as well as the ability to impart motion.[31] For Descartes, the soul is not the form that is the body's power, it is the capacity to think. While the soul exists, as James notes, "it is always thinking,"[32] but as it thinks it loses more of the physicality it had hitherto, joining the body only at the pineal gland.

The alignments we analyzed in the last chapter between the body, passivity, the object, matter, and the unconscious are cemented with the mechanistic turn. At the same time, Malebranche's notion of passions as communal and as a form of communal bonding fades as the impassioned individual comes to the fore. It is not Malebranche who is the ancestor of the presumptions governing contemporary assumptions about the passions and the affects. It is Thomas Hobbes. The abandonment of the idea of form as the motor of the agent's activity means that the contrast between action and passion is destined to be lost in Hobbes's determinism. For Hobbes, the process of thoughtful deliberation consists not in the thinking-action of the soul but in an alternation of passions. Because it is passions that move us to act, not action seen as arising from the soul as will, Hobbes refused to distinguish between sui generis action and action resulting from being moved or affected by passions. The will itself is moved by passions. Voluntary actions become those that are willed by some appetite or aversion or passion, while involuntary actions are brought about by an external force. In this way, individualism is reconciled with determinism, and the passions are made equivalent to the soul or psyche.

During, and especially after, the seventeenth century, the idea that one struggles to reorient the passions fades, together with the association of passion and error. For Rorty, the eighteenth century marks a shift. "Instead of being reactions to invasions from something external to the self, passions became the very activities of the mind, its own motions. . . . During this period [roughly, from Descartes to Rousseau], emotions also cease to be merely turbulent commotions; among them appear sentiments, ways of feeling pleasures and pains as evaluations and, so, as proper guides to action."[33] Rorty adds that as the emotions change, so too do the prime examples of the passions. This is entirely consistent with the view advanced in the last chapter: there is no such thing as a raw emotion nor an unconstructed passion. These are always modulated, both because they have an aim conceived from one's own standpoint and because they are infused with words and images, and such things can only be socially derived.[34] But the immediate issue is that the predominance of the affects means it is harder to struggle against them, and when that predominance is complete, one no longer knows that there is anything to struggle against.

Awareness of the passions as a site of struggle, as Amélie Rorty and Alisdair MacIntyre point out, fades in the eighteenth century in that the affects, more or less, win. They win insofar as they succeed in presenting themselves sympathetically, as the constituents of our true natures, entitled to an equal say, if not to rule. Since Hume, they have edged toward the position that all ethics, insofar as they embody passionate convictions, are no more than passions or emotions, affects or sentiments (terms that were to become, at various points, synonyms). Even the most destructive of affects can justify itself under the guise of expressing one's feelings. The term "feelings," which used to be allied with sensations, is another victim of the increasing lack of precision in affective language. No distinction parallels Aristotle's between emotions and sensations. Passions or affects now claim to be a class of feeling, rather than something discerned by feeling. They seem to be part of one's drive in the sense of energetic motivation, and, with this illusion, the original understanding of the passions or affects as passifying or passive is lost.

Rather than passifying forces that to be struggled with in an attempt to assert the voluntary course of the soul over them, the passions become gradually equivalent to our true nature. The inevitable accompaniment of this in philosophy is the ethical slide to which I have alluded, and which MacIntyre analyzes so well.[35] The twentieth century conclusion that the difference between good and bad is no more than the difference between "I like it" and "I don't like it" follows logically from a situation in which human action has been explained in terms of a succession of passions and passionate judgments mediated by more or less deliberation. In these deliberations the guiding principle is self-interest. The sensitivity to amour propre and one's bad faith in terms of projecting emotional judgments, or ceasing to struggle against them, is lost. Concerns with the nature of the will, its relation to the intellect, understanding, and so forth depart from the scene together with a concept of the immortal soul, whether as the form or power animating the body or the more tenuous connection between thinking and the pineal gland. Ultimately, the concept of self-interest dominates because there is no felt principle other than the prosecution of pleasure and the avoidance of pain governing human action.

At the same time as the passions become the ego, the category of amour propre takes off. So does the recognition of and distaste for grandeur. "Grandeur, as [French thinker] Nicole insists," writes James, "is opposed to almost all the Christian virtues."[36] What is significant about this seventeenth-century interest is that the notion of grandeur—as a passion increasing the likelihood that other passions will lead us to err—anticipates the role of the narcissistic ego in the modern perspective. As we will see, the disposition to grandeur and the ego are similar in that they make a property of what is, as James describes, "an initial disposition to evaluate comparatively and a susceptibility to scale."[37] Like the ego, grandeur makes us opinionated and prone to "the conviction that our own emotional responses are correct."[38] If we see similar responses in others constantly, we take the battles over esteem and envy to which we are disposed by grandeur more as the norm and the stuff of life. Lacan dates the era of the ego from Pascal's dissection of these battles in the late seventeenth century. Foucault assigns an intensification of knowledge as the will to power to the same period, as does Adorno.[39] Both were aware of how the passion to control the other causes a person to seek knowledge as a means to control and that the exercise of such knowledge is aligned with discipline imposed from without, or objectification. Taken to its objectifying extreme, this process leads to our present madness, which is the destruction of future life, even our own, for the sake of immediate gratification.[40] But, to understand this, we need to see how the negative affects cohere in an egoistic constellation, why judging or projecting affects onto the other and the self is fundamental to this coherence, and why that egoistic constellation solidifies as the Western centuries progress.

Affects and the Unconscious

We can begin showing how affects bear on the ego by noting that the repressions and fixations structuring drives, affects, and the ego, itself, are also forms of judgment. They are judgments based on images, memories, and fantasies about how to avoid pain and increase pleasure. The response to hallucination is to repress it, because its false promise leads to unpleasure, unpleasant excitation, or pain. This repression is simultaneously a judgment about the consequences for pleasure of the hallucination, for judgment is the attempt to expel what is painful while enhancing what is pleasurable: "I should like to eat this. I should like to spit it out."[41] But what is most significant in terms of Freud's energetics is that, whatever the judgment, if it leads to repression it involves a persistent expenditure of energy, which obstructs the life and libidinal energy of the body concerned. This does not mean that all repressions are bad. They are necessary if the individual is to have a sense of its distinct self and if it is to avoid harm to itself. But they nonetheless take place at the expense of the drives and driving energy otherwise available to that individual.

Not enough repression? Psychosis is likely. Too much? Excessive and misplaced repression was believed to be critical in the formation of the neuroses. These neuroses in turn were seen as affective and nervous disorders, which disabled the sufferers by enervating them or in other ways making them unable to act upon reality. Neurotics were made passive by their passions and their repression. The essence of the talking cure was reuniting the repressed with the words that expressed the affect attached to it or which converted the affect from one state to another in which a drive was likely to be expressed (as when depression is converted to anger). With that conversion, the energy locked up in the repression was released. Thus the life drive, or energy in motion, would counter the repression that shapes the desires and passions of the subject concerned.

The role Freud gave to the life drive is similar to that hitherto accorded the soul as the animating power within us by seventeenth-century thinkers and their predecessors. Another similarity is that the life drive is constitutive of acting and thinking and allied with or expressed in living attention (as the soul is meant to be). What is most different in Freud's account is that this power may itself be repressed or made unconscious. The conflicts between it and the unconscious repressions and fixations constituting the ego may result in symptoms, by which the body tries to express itself in visual, linguistic terms, making its wish known to the conscious linguistic subject, and thereby freeing its drive. At the ordinary level of nighttime dreams, there is a similar effort to communicate, but it is repressed by a visual censor that substitutes misleading images for the words needed to understand the communication. For instance, if I dream of a seabed that will disguise the fact that my body was telling me to sleep more. "See! Bed." Such censorship keeps a conflict unconscious. But even if the conflict is now unconscious, it is present as a version of the old struggle between the passifying affects and action.

While the last chapter demonstrated that smell and chemical and electrical entrainment, more broadly, communicate affects, the construction of the thing that attracts and regenerates those affects is another story. The essence of this construction lies in the quasi-geometric positioning of human perception that occurs as humans come to see the world from their own standpoint. In turn, the key to this geometry of positions resides in reformulating the birth of the psychical apparatus and understanding delay and spatial causality as its nucleus. Positioning is observational. It sees the other and the self from its own standpoint. It sees the other in the light of its own shadow. This shadowy light is the essence of the imaginary, not the absence or presence of physical components in the affects clustering around certain imaginary positions. This spatial, observational standpoint, grounded in delay and pain, may be nothing in itself, but it attracts defensive and protective mechanisms away from their proper functions, thereby causing them to be exercised unnecessarily in the positional dynamics of humiliation and grandeur.

What needs to be established is that these potentials only have actual power, meaning energy or drive, to the extent that they serve as the locus for affective constellations or clusters. For instance, pride or megalomania implies control of the environment: one measures one's position, at first literally, in relation to one's agency. The extent of the rejection of a passive position measures the extent of one's need for control. But where does the force come from? As argued above, all energy is a derivative of the life drive or love, in whatever combination these things existed before they were split into the sexual-aggressive and affectionate streams of that drive. In turn, the energy of all the drives is constructed by splits and repressions as the organism seeks to protect itself both in the real world of its logical senses and the imaginary world of the ego's perception. By imaginary, I do not mean unphysical, just that the origin of the threat is misperceived and its force, often, accordingly overestimated. For example, if I were to perceive that someone was deliberately withholding a pleasure—food— from me in order to keep me in a state of pain, then I would react. But if they were doing no such thing; if, say, they were not feeding me because it would make me sick, then the aggressive energy I direct toward them is based on a misperception.

As Maurice Merleau-Ponty and Jean-Paul Sartre understood, the subject is situated as a subject by a spatial operation. As Lacan understood, that spatial operation introduces *méconnaisance*: misrecognition or misperception. Lacan caught its nature in the mirror-phase or moment when the subject has an image of itself in the eye of the other. The identity founded in one's self-image is simultaneously a spatial construction. That image is deflected back to the self from an other, one's ideal image, which also gives one a perspective on oneself. One sees oneself through the eye of the other, so three factors are at work: one's self, one's image, and the other who validates the image. For

Lacan, the interlocking of self and other constitutes an imaginary space, which is imaginary in that fantasies interlock within it. By my argument, these interlocking fantasies are also physical, just as the force of the imagination is material and physical. In this respect they can be either an endogenous or an exogenous matter, something the self does to the self, energetically speaking, or something that is also directed toward the self by the other's goal-seeking aggressive projections.

The foundation stone of inertia, the subject's repression of the first hallucination, consists of energy turned inward. This inward turning hinges on a misperception: the first fixed point is founded by the repression of a hallucination—the primary misperception. Yet perception has to be constructed from the subject's standpoint if the subject is to function in a three-dimensional world. It conceives of this world from its own position, although the logical structure of that biological world cannot be understood from that standpoint. In this respect, the structuring of perception in subject/object terms, or from a subject-centered standpoint, is illusory, although it is also accurate. It is structured around a lack or a gap or a hole, the empty place of longing that led the subject to formulate its needs from its own standpoint. On this basis, inertia comes into being.

The repression results from hallucination, and hallucination results from a feeling of lack. But because this repression brings a fixed, still point into being, it also brings comparison into being. All the negative affects result from a disabling comparison. The notion of comparison requires another, a yardstick separate from the self. We have seen that the repression of the first hallucination constitutes a fixed point of reference and a fixed or still point energetically. By this point of reference the ego gets its bearings as a being distinct from its environment. But the price of this orientation is a loss in the energy hitherto available to it. The price of its nascent sense of self is a relative passivity, relative in relation to the freely mobile energy into which it was born, as well as a newborn sense of comparison. Before that repression, there was no comparison from one's own standpoint. There can be no notion of comparison, of bigger than or smaller than, without a still fixture.[42] Without comparison, there can be no envy or humiliation nor the narcissistic sense of superiority; without this sense, and the imaginary threats to superiority accompanying it (always comparative threats), there can be no real fear, anxiety, or that imaginary fear, paranoia.

Without these there is no need to direct aggression toward the other, for this, too, is a response to threat. Without aggression toward the other or the self, there is no guilt or shame. Without feeling separation from the other, which one must also feel as a consequence of becoming distinct, there is no greed or lust or anger at being separate and, therefore, lacking. One is prone to all the lacks that come with comparison, after lack introduces comparison.

Comparison is effected by and mediated through images of others and fantasies concerning them. The history of an imaginary slight—in envy or wounded narcissism—can be built into a fantasy or psychical memory, and that history can be conjured in an instant together with its affective associations. This is why we can also speak of these affective states or passions as passionate judgments. The passionate judgment is what gives the other or the self a negative image, embodying the objectification of narcissism or the contempt of envy. These judgments are also at odds with the life drive, insofar as they disable the other or the self by depositing aggression, which the other feels as anxiety or guilt and worthlessness—all modulations of the aggression directed toward the other or the self. (I note in passing that aggression can only be the cardinal force here, and hence the thing that is modulated, if it carries the force of the life drive with it. The idea that aggression is connected with the life drive in this way reminds us of Augustine, for whom all the passions were species of love: "The love that shuns what opposes it is fear, while the love that feels that opposition when it happens, is grief.")[43] If Augustine's passions as forms of love were to be understood as modulations or directions (and I think there is a strong argument for seeing them as directions of a specific energy), then Augustine's view would have much in common with this theory of energetics. But whereas love-life connects things to one another, aggression separates them. Nonetheless, aggression carries the energy of life or love in its train, at least for a time. But when that intelligent energy encounters obstructions, experienced in terms of desires related to lack such as envy or frustration, it is diverted from its original aim of unity and changes its connecting logic and nature accordingly. It becomes divisive and destructive.

The life drive is also modulated and associated in patterns that might impede it with memories but, nonetheless, enable it to discern what moves it for good (its own good and that of others) and what impedes that good. The ego, originally the arbiter of conflicts between one's own good and that of the other, is less able to discern this when the ego itself becomes a distorted arbiter, an arbiter that judges in order to arbitrate. Each of the affective constellations known to us as desires related to lack or sins is a state of the ego in which its self-protective function has been distorted by imaginary factors. Thus, envy can result from an imaginary belittlement, anger can result from imaginary insults, and so forth. The ego, in other words, is not only a perceptive preservative function but a constellation of memories and desires associated with imaginary threats to its prestige as well as its existence. Once the fixed point of comparison is provided through re-pression, the negative affects come into play as measurements of one's standing in relation to others.

The ego, it will be objected, is not only a response to imaginary threats based on imaginary comparisons. The ego is also the vehicle for preserving the organism. This is true, of course. Yet self-preservative functions are easily confused with imaginary matters. Consider the (necessary) fight or flight responses, responses that may be the only means for preserving the life of the organism. The fear or anxiety that prompts flight is the most easily distorted of the self-preservative motions. It can be distorted by imaginary threats, as we have already indicated, and these threats grow as the imaginary ego's sense of its comparative importance becomes inflated or slighted. I want to suggest now that there is also some necessary relationship be-tween the fear of the threat and the materialization of that fear or threat. As noted in the discussion of smell and attractor pheromones, members of the same chemical families (such as anxiety and aggres-sion) attract one another. Fears, from this standpoint, can be the means for attracting what they fear—the aggressive drives that ap-pear to justify the anxieties.

The acting out of the foundational fantasy (which founds the sub-ject in its sense of superiority and separation) passifies the self or the other precisely because the fantasy is a passionate judgment directed toward that other in order to maintain a certain relational position. The need to project intensifies as the affects, and the drives promoting it, accumulate. The person projecting the judgment is freed from its depressing effects on him or herself. However, he or she is dependent on the other carrying that projected affect, just as the master depends on the slave. For the one who is projected upon, the drive becomes an affect, a passionate judgment directed inward, a judgment that consti-tutes a kind of hook on which the other's negative affect can fix. As noted earlier, if I take your aggression onboard and turn it back against myself as depression I have less energy and you have more, because you are not inhibited by a drive that limits you when it is turned inward. In this case, the affect appears as the passive manifes-tation of the other's active drive. It may also be the passive recognition of one's own drive turned inward (self-pity, masochism), but this pas-sive recognition differs from the drive when it is directed outward. The sensations registering the former leave one less able to act, whereas the latter is action and the release of energy. This is true for narcissism, envy, inverted aggression or depression and anxiety, and the inertia accompanying all of them.

As I indicated earlier, what I am proposing here is a variation on Freud's theory of primary and secondary repression. In Freud's model, a primary repression attracts subsequent or secondary repres-sions toward it because they are similar in nature to the primary re-pression. In my energetic version of this model, I am proposing that inverted aggression, whether it is felt as anxiety or experienced as anger and depression, attracts more aggression toward it. This attractor-receptor model parallels the psychical process and may be identical to the hormonal-pheromonal model in certain cases. But the exploration of the mechanisms of entrainment and responsiveness is recent. As argued in the last chapter, I do not mean to imply that hor-mones alone are the only positional and directional markers and givers, anymore than are the pheromones with which they are linked chemically. They function at this point to illustrate a philosophical thesis.

Nonetheless, as far as it can be done, the above account completes a theoretical outline of how projective affective transfers might work. While there are no neuronal or chemical maps of entrainment that can guide us readily through the complex physical territory of these inter-locking affects, there is evidence that supports a relation between the incidence of aggression, depression, and further aggression in rela-tional depressive disorders, ADHD, and CFS. If the general thesis of this book is right, that evidence also shows that the prevalence of these disorders is relationally and socially exacerbated. We construct our own attractors, but the force of what we attract varies according to affective circumstance.

The Sealing of the Heart

Thus far, I have tried to tie the negative or passifying affects to the affective judgments that were once known as demons and sins. These affects increasingly dominate life in the West. In doing so, they increase the sense of self-containment. The self-contained subject maintains itself by projecting out the affects that otherwise interfere with its agency (anxiety and any sense of inferiority) in a series of affective judgments that are then carried by the other. As these affective judgments are tied to the very structuration of the ego via its relation with the other, they are likely to reinforce themselves in the processes of creating passification. They become more common, become, in fact, the basic assumptions that Bion identified in groups. Where I differ from Bion (if there is a difference) is that I hold that these affects are in the air as well as the individual psyche. We carry them in the earliest recesses of memory, but we also encounter them in the street. These affects are what threaten the discreteness of persons, the things that divert their psyches (or souls) from their distinct paths and ways of being. It becomes a question of how the psyche maintains its distinct path, how its striving to be itself, manifests despite the obstacles thrown up by the ego and its repressions. In this striving, the positive affects are evident, insofar as these are the means for unlocking draining fixations and directing energy away from the inversions that make for passification and illness.

Passifying constellations of affects persist in their internal effects regardless of present realities or relations. One does not free one's life drive simply by severing draining relations. One also frees it by unlocking the affective constellations of repressed images in which it is enmeshed in fantasy and memory, as well as projective judgment. As a practice, psychoanalysis aims at this unlocking and at reuniting ideas with the affects that were once attached to them. It aims at finding the means whereby a feeling can come to consciousness as a repression is unlocked and an energetic drive released. But this task is the more formidable when one considers that the affects are more likely to be split off from conscious thought as the self-contained individual comes to the fore. They are likely to be split, as self-containment presupposes that thinking can be clear of emotion and that affects can be studied as objective physiological states.

It remains to show that the process of reconnecting thought and affect is integral to discerning the transmission of affect, while noting that such discernment is harder to practice the more one is sealed off from the sensations and knowledge of any transmission taking place. By my argument, one is sealed off by the projective affective transfers that purchase the sense of self-containment. These transfers intensify in environments where anxiety also intensifies, as it is intensified in modern toxic environments. The process appears to be cumulative and to intensify as aggression and violence also intensify. But the gradual sealing of sensation and the knowledge of transmission is not absolute. As I shall demonstrate in the next chapter, the knowledge of how one discerns the other's affects is also coming into evidence. More accurately, perhaps, how that knowledge is being recovered. In this connection, the Judaic Studies scholar Henry Abramson's work on the transmission of affect and its relevance to understanding the "sealing of the heart" and the "decline of the generations," two tenets of Judaism, is especially pertinent.

Abramson connects the sealing of the heart with an imperviousness to communication by smell. First, he notes the significance of the heart in rabbinical findings on the transmission of affect, concluding, "When a person prepares his heart to love another, so too will the heart of the other respond." The heart is the critical organ in the circulation of the blood, and hence in communication by smell. Abramson adds, "This is true enough if transmission by pheromones is a fact, for these have to enter into circulation, so to speak, before they are registered as a communication by the other to which one does or does not respond.[44] Moreover, he continues, "In Rabbinic literature, the heart is the sense-organ not only of other people's affect, but of our own as well. All emotions . . . are circulated to the heart through the blood, and the heart thereby "knows" the entirety of a person's affect. . . . The heart can be plugged up, however—a sort of spiritual arteriosclerosis—and be prevented from receiving not only one's own affect, but the affects transmitted by others as well."[45] The sealing of the heart, in a reference that has to attract any Freudian, is tied to "the uncircumcised heart" of Deuteronomy 10:16 and Ezekiel 44:9. From Lacan's standpoint, the uncircumcised heart is the uncastrated heart, the heart that has not accepted its limitations. It is steeped in the ego's imaginary, in psychophysical territory where, convinced of its own entitlement, it refuses to acknowledge the existence of others. This refusal is the reason it cannot feel the feelings of others. It assumes those others do not feel. Abramson adds that he thinks (and I agree) that this is why the notion of the sealing of the heart is linked to another tenet of Judaism: the notion of the decline of the generations. The decline of the generation is understood in relation to what he calls the "defining moment of Sinai," when those in touch with the direct revelations of Moses understood them through the heart as well as sight and sound. The further we come from that revelation the less able we are to perceive it in the literal, physical terms in which it was intended, and which the Jews at some point understood. In Abramson's terms, "As we move further and further away from the defining moment of Sinai, our hearts have become more and more 'sealed'—and less and less 'communicative'—to apprehending the affect which others transmit to us. The heart as a receptor-organ is impaired because of our inability to understand ourselves, and it is weakened as a transmitter-organ because of the 'disturbed waters' that constitute the working area for the transmission of affect."[46]

But as we see our way through those disturbed waters, as we are less afraid, we are more able to approach the subject matter of demons in the right spirit, one which diminishes their importance. Demons have alarming supernatural connotations. After all, anything that increases fear (and fear of the supernatural, meaning intelligent forces beyond our comprehension or control) increases the purchase of the negative affective states. Understanding possession by demons as the transmission of material affective states diminishes the fear excited by notions of things beyond our comprehension. The thing about demons is that they move around, or can move around. To conceive of them as tied to sins, capable of moving from one person to another, is to do no more than describe the transmission of affect in a more anthropomorphic vocabulary. We have laid the basis here for analyzing the composition of these demons, in molecular and physical terms, from the standpoint of the knowledge we have now. Pursuing the research in hormonal interaction and olfactory entrainment, or the studies in rhythmic and other forms of identification, is understanding the aggression and anxiety out of which most spirits of deceit are composed. What is understood can be changed, whether it is through the understanding of its material nature or the changes wrought within that nature as it is understood.

CHAPTER SIX

The Education of the Senses

Paradoxically, feelings are sensory states produced by thought, while interruptive thoughts are produced by affects. Feelings are thoughtful, and affects are thoughtless. Feelings are meant to be information about whether a state is pleasurable or painful, whether one is attracted to something or averse to it. This is the classic and only basis for distinguishing feelings and affects. Feelings are meant to say, "I like it, it feels good to me," or "I don't like it" and to lead to action on this basis. But if feelings are tracing a logic in the flesh simultaneously with a logic in history, this means they feel good because they are living. The good feeling of living and the personal liking of the sensations that come with it coincide in what is termed "pleasure." But only up to a point. At that point, the point at which the organism would have to give up a distinct identity in order to go on feeling, it will generally choose the former even if it then feels bad. Thus a man gives into social pressure and chooses vanity (the need not to be ridiculous in the eyes of others) over happiness. The organism makes a similar choice, for instance, when it takes a new job far from those it loves because there is a "career advance." Biology, like Freud, falters when it comes to making sense of something that makes no sense for the living organism, only for the ego. Like Freud, it assimilates the ego drives to the life drive even when they are opposites (as I have shown). A real distinction would be drawn in terms of the difference between what is living and what is dead; the boundaries that matter, and the only ones that work, are those that shield the organism from dead matter by surrounding it with a field of living attention directed outward in a perpetual act of love.

In positing that people in the Western world were once aware of the transmission of affect, and that we have been sealed against this knowledge by the deadening, passifying affects of modern times, I have implied that knowledge of transmission was once conscious, although that knowledge is now repressed. Accordingly, the problem of how we discern becomes more acute in the modern context. To date, the only documented instances of modern discernment of the transmission of affect lie in literature and clinics. Despite this, I want to suggest that a faculty of discernment operates at various levels, and we can identify these readily if we admit that the practice of discernment long predates its application to matters of transmission. Those seventeenth-century philosophers that we turned our attention to earlier were not alone in turning their attention to the analysis of their states of passion. Similar forms of reflective or meditative analysis have been in practice since the origins of philosophy (and this practice originally constituted philosophy). Indeed, awareness of the struggle with affects or passions runs as long as the meditative tradition in which the faculty for concentration in the form of prayer has been pitched in battle against the sources of distraction. The Jesuit-trained Descartes and the Jewish-educated Spinoza were aware of meditative battle. It carries over to their own notions of a struggle with the passions. Both men were aware that the detachment necessary for self-observation is one thing, the energetic force needed to override a passion or affect another. Other pre-Cartesian instances of struggle with the passions are often recorded in the third person. While St. Augustine discusses his infantile antics in terms of *ego sum*, St. Teresa of Avila refers to herself as "a person." Meantime, the Jesuits' founder, St. Ignatius of Loyola, actually wrote (not well) *On the Discernment of Spirits* (meaning demons as well as angels, and hence meaning what we now term affects).[1] By the twentieth century, knowledge of internal psychological processes was relegated to the realm of depth psychology, itself dismissed for lack of objectivity. The psychology taught in universities today proceeds on the basis of holding as many factors constant—still, fixed—as possible. Similarly, all that is left of the meditative tradition in analytical philosophy is a tendency to focus on the examples of everyday life. The struggle with the passions has retreated to the unconscious; it has become the unconscious, or one form of it, as we have seen. But those in analysis, or engaging in the meditation rites that also resurrect the specter of self-detachment, do not call their opponents by the name of "demons," let alone "passions," or even "affects." They call it "the ego," if they are being analyzed properly, and even if they are not.

In the last chapter, I suggested that the ego was nothing more than a constellation of affects, grouped in clusters of associations (verbal and visual) around certain subjective fantasmatic positions, in turn the result of the subjective standpoint. I have also shown how the ego, as the named enemy, appears in the seventeenth century for Pascal and the authors of the *Port-Royal Logic*. The argument of this book goes further, suggesting that the ego replaces the affects because it is the affects in a more solid constellation. These egoic affects have become so predominant and organized (in the spreading of the foundational fantasy) that we now believe them when they tell us, "This is me." If, as we supposed in chapter 4, there is an alternative center for coherence in the mind, for bringing logic and reason to bear synthetically on diverse information, there is little evidence of its presence. That other I, the one who once struggled with demons, then fought the passions, and now negotiates with the ego, is less and less in evidence. This is especially apparent in the decline of religious practices and civil codes of courtesy. As we noted at the outset, civil and religious codes may be remnants of a conscious knowledge of transmission. In cultures where knowledge of transmission is unconscious, these codes have less meaning and are easily displaced by arguments that one should be "free to express one's feelings." As the stoically inclined realized long since, if freedom means anything, it is freedom from possession by the negative affects. Where such freedom holds sway, the other I of discernment and sensation gains a hearing. When possessed by an affect with which we are unfamiliar, it can seem entirely reasonable to do things that the unpossessed self would reject out of hand. Such things are readily rationalized at the time, but afterward the perpetrator marvels at how far he forgot himself. This, I think, is what Aristotle meant when he said that the doer of evil does not know at the time that he is doing evil. From the perspective of the affect in command of attention at the time, the action is entirely appropriate.

The point here, however, is that the significance of verbal, emotional restraint demanded by various declining codes is unclear when the transmission of affect is unacknowledged. We have established that when I judge the other, I simultaneously direct toward her that stream of negative affect that cuts off my feeling of kinship from her as a fellow living, suffering, joyful creature. I will expand on this notion briefly, before moving on. The act of directing negative affects to the other severs my kin tie with her by objectifying her. I make her into an object by directing these affects toward her, because that act marks her with affects that I reject in myself—"these affects do not exist in me, but in her." I assume that she does not feel as I do. At the personal level, the othering underpinned by judgmental projections is evident in the scapegoating that occurs in most familial or professional communities.[2] At the cultural level, these judgmental projections feature in othering by race or sex or sexual orientation. Here the other, collectively, becomes feminized, that is, styled untruthful by nature, too emotional, less logical, more superstitious than us reasoning beings.[3] When Rousseau in *Émile, or On Education* demands that Sophie be educated to lie, while Émile only speaks the truth, he is doing no more than putting the realities of modern affective projections into words. By encouraging attitudes of suspicion, by (worse) encouraging the idea that a privileged class, sex, race, or caste is free of dissembling, emotionality, or stupidity, one comes to overvalue one's own capacities.

By examining the affects experienced in judging another, one learns a great deal about how the illusion of self-containment is purchased at the price of dumping negative affects on that other. The dyadic and complex level of affective transmission is marked in terms of how it is that one party carries the other's negative affects; his aggression is experienced as her anxiety and so forth. By means of this projection, one believes oneself detached from him or her, when one is, in fact, propelling forward an affect that he will experience as rejection or hurt, unless he has shielded himself against these affects by a similar negative propulsion, a passionate judgment of his own.

When one judges, one is possessed by the affects. When one discerns, one is able to detach from them, to know where one stands, to be self-possessed. Hence the idea that the strong identification with—the living of—an actual ethical code is one basis for discerning the affects. Discernment, in the affective world, functions best when it is able to be alert to the moment of fear or anxiety or grief or other sense of loss that permits the negative affect to gain a hold. Discernment then is allied to a position in which one receives and processes without the intervention of anxiety or other fixed obstacles in the way of the thinking process.

On the face of it, any faculty of discernment must involve a process whereby affects pass from the state of sensory registration to a state of cognitive or intelligent reflection; this does not mean that the process of reflection is without affect, just that the affect is other than the affect that is being reflected upon. James shows that this was the case for Hobbes; nonetheless, reason and passion or affect and cognition keep reappearing as binaries despite the arguments against their separation in practice. Nevertheless, these binaries are attempts at approximating a real and necessary distinction between the ego and the faculty of discernment, between the passions and the "other I" who reflects on them. The use of the binaries, in short, may be an approximation of the palpable experience of being pulled in two directions. One of these directions feels more passionate (the desire to tick someone off); the other (to listen, to discuss) more reasonable; but the ticking off can present itself as coldly rational, while the reasonable discussion can be warm. Reason and passion, as a distinction, captures some of the elements at work here but misses the feeling or sensitive component in reason, just as it misses the calculating component in passion.[4]

However, the point is that discernment—by this argument—works by sensing (touching, hearing, smelling, listening, seeing) and the expression of the senses, particularly in words. It works by feeling (sometimes in the dark), and it works deductively, often with insufficient information; it makes mistakes when it is rushed to conclude before its time (it is rushed by the ego, which always needs a plan) or when it is delayed by the ego (which is always anxious about doing the wrong thing). Discernment, when it doubts the ego's judgment, registers as a feeling. Sometimes such feelings can be articulated with relative exactitude; they can be named, and reasons for their existence can be adduced. But this, precisely, requires a vocabulary; that is why we defined feelings as sensations that have found a match in words.

The naming of the feeling is one thing, but the ability to investigate its logic requires more. That investigation requires a conceptual vocabulary and a means for circumventing the affects' combined distractions. The notion that we are susceptible to transmitted affects makes more sense of Hindu, and related, recommendations for achieving peace,[5] just as it makes more sense of the meditative tradition Descartes inherited. In the Jesuit tradition, spirits or demons were and are discerned, much as affects are now discerned. There is a reason why Descartes's *Meditations* are called meditations. The pursuit of clear and distinct ideas may no longer mean what it once meant, but in the meditative context it means reasoned ideas that can be called upon when one is assailed by affects and modes in which one doubts one's faith.[6] These affects register as a series of apparently unconnected thoughts, in which one thought interrupts another thought's pathway without warning. By this means one is distracted and led to believe that one's feelings are other than they may be. Such feelings are recoverable in some cases via reflection, in others by analysis, but the procedure is essentially the same. It is that of historical recollection, the comparison of memories.

When a man realizes that there is grief behind his anger, and that what he felt when he heard this or that is not the passionate affect that possessed him at the time, but something finer, how does he do so? He remembers. Then he outwits the affects by comparing the state in which he was possessed by the othering affects with the state in which he discerned and felt. He may do so with an analyst or, occasionally, with the kind of friend who helps him see through the veil of affects rather than thickening the veil with misplaced sympathy—sympathy for the affects (as in the sharing of indignation) rather than love for the friend. He reviews the history of his own feelings and affects in the matter. He follows an essentially historical procedure in order to recover a truth, and he does so with loving intelligence rather than by wallowing in judgments of himself (guilt and shame) or others (fear and paranoia). The limits to this process are not only set by insight (the process whereby sensation and feeling connect) but by language and concept (the means whereby sensation and feeling connect). The process consists of the redirection of energy; the means lie in the comparative sensations of those redeployments, as well as the words into which we are born. Our man has to have a language for any matter involving historical review, and language is always cultural and traditional,[7] but that does not mean the development of language is over. In naming a sensation of which he may be aware (energy departing and returning) he may be limited by his current vocabulary, but he is pushed to expand it in accounting for sensations in sequence: the knowledge gleaned by comparison.

Comparison based on memory is critical in all practices of discernment. But unlike the instantaneous comparison of positions discussed in the last chapter, comparison based on memory does not depend on, but rather works against, the agitation of the affects.[8] The instantaneous comparison of positions effected by the egoic affects demands an immediate assessment and projection—or introjection—of one's position vis-à-vis the other. This unpleasant process of "placing" has no memory, no sense of historical indebtedness.[9] Historical comparison, by contrast, is fueled by living attention. It can only proceed by concentration. Yet in the maternal cases discussed previously, we saw that concentration can also be impaired when a constant stream of attention (the back of one's mind) is diverted toward an infant, leading to the conclusion that the thing that is marshaled in concentration is an attentive energy, without which concentration is powerless to defeat the affects and fantasies that interrupt it.[10] As we have also seen, the affects and concentration both draw on energy, but the affects have a direct relation to visual and auditory fantasy, while concentration and feelings have a direct relation to words (and that open form of vision and the "other ear," prevail when these hypothetical forms of vision and audition are not abducted by fantasy). As blocks in the way of feeling, vision and audition only serve the ego when one is wearing Freud's "cap of hearing on one side," and seeing with an offending eye.[11]

The battle between feelings and affects that has characterized this argument so far is plainly intensifying. So, in this chapter, will a battle between the notion of "spontaneous" emotions and educated feelings. The education, beginning with the discernment, of the affects relies on the feelings, which communicate with the sensations. But the sensations have a limited range of self-expression when no language for or practice in their recognition is available. This does not mean that the education of the senses has been altogether lacking. We shall look at how the education of the finer feelings was partially accomplished through religious codes and codes of courtesy. That is to say, codes of courtesy and ethical or religious conduct operate on a level similar to philosophical and psychological discernment insofar as they use the same means: comparison, detachment, and living attention. Following some reflections on religious and cultural codes, and a related discussion of the virtues embodied in those codes, I shall discuss the level of discernment that is reached by the various philosophical and analytic practices. From this discussion there follows more analysis of living attention and the life drive and of the role played by the theological virtues in transforming as well as resisting the affects. After that, we shall examine the mechanisms of discernment in relation to sensation.

Cultural Discernment

Civil codes are not understood, of course, as means for discerning and resisting the transmission of affect and responding to another's affective states in ways that would help dissipate negative and disabling affects (putting a person at ease).[12] But this is what they do. Codes of courtesy and religious codes compare the passionate impulse to act or cogitate in a certain way with a code of conduct and restraint. When the code is strong enough to override the impulse, whether its origins are internal or external or both, the impulse is refused. The ability to do this as a matter of course, or on occasion, was captured in the old expression, "finer feeling," something akin to fine sensory distinctions. The level of finer feeling is the level referred to in the Spanish *lo siento*: colloquially, "I'm sorry," and literally, "I feel it." On this level discernment and the social courtesies derived from it are manifest, insofar as one is open to others in a way that wishes them well and would dissipate their anxiety or sorrow if one could. It is an opening through which one feels the other's pain or joy as one's own. In describing friendship, Montaigne put it this way: "True friends feel each other's feelings."[13] They feel their joy or their sorrow. This taking on of the other's feeling, as a conscious thing, presupposes a different sense of self or boundary than the boundary the ego manufactures by projecting out—or by being swamped by negative affects. One is not open to the other through the ego's routes but through the deployment of sensation, meaning feeling. This is the equipment of the discerner, as distinct from the projector. Civil and spiritual codes that restrain affects that pass around as well as within could have been written with this difference in mind. For instance, a code of child rearing based on restraining anger does not only repress.[14] It also builds resistance to expressing a wave of passing angry affect. A code based on encouraging affective self-expression, on the other hand, could leave a person with no defense against invading affects, no means of telling whether they expressed the self or something other than the self. One suspects that some understanding of the need for discernment of the affects in child rearing is reflected in language suggesting that the affects and emotions are not something that originate sui generis. One is "beside oneself" or "out of one's mind" or "giving in to feelings." Conversely, one is "closed in", at best detached. There are implications here for ideas that have traditionally been dismissed as conservative. If affects wash through us, "giving in" to them or "losing it" in emotional display means that notions of emotional reserve, as a good thing, take on new meaning. In this respect, as in others, my account is only a mirror image of Rousseau's notion of being forced to be free.[15] When one does not adhere to the dictates of the general will, one is, for Rousseau, somehow estranged from an essential part of oneself, that part embodied in the collective. By this account, the ability to discern the transmission of affect may lead one to oppose the general will as an undesirable affective force. There is no automatic good in the general will. There is only automatic good in it when it embodies the direction of life.

There are codes that read like remnants of a knowledge of how to restrain the seven passifying affects, and which uphold or are based on virtues that do the same. For instance, envy is constrained when one prohibits manifestations of spite in general: "If you can't say something nice, say nothing at all"; or "qui accuse, s'accuse." These also constrain anger, as well as envy. Such prohibitions, together with injunctions to humility or kindness (read: injunctions to restrain pride and not to provoke envy or spite in the other), act as social constraints. What kindness is, I suggest, is the refusal to pass on or transmit negative affects and the attempt to prevent the pain they cause others—to really prevent it, not just be seen to do so. That very refusal carries an admixture of love that, when it predominates in the psyche, is also more than kindness; it is seeing the other in a good light, giving them the good image, streaming one's full attentive energy toward another and another's concerns, rather than one's own. Here it is enough to say that kindness is another way of describing the protective attitude that stands between another and the experience of negative affects. It is, then, also a practice of discernment to the extent that it encourages its would-be practitioners not to give in to common negative affects. Religions operate on similar principles. Buddha says to return a flower for the stone that is flung at you; Christ, like Isaiah before him, says to turn the other cheek. Both injunctions are also injunctions not to continue the transmission of negative affect; to stop it

before it can be passed on or back. They are injunctions, in fact, to ab-
sorb and transmute that affect, although as such they can give rise to a
conflict between mental health (do not allow yourself to be dumped
on) and spiritual health (do not dump back).

There are seven classical virtues, just as there are seven sins. Recent
tradition divides these virtues into four cardinal and three theological
virtues. I noted in the last chapter how the seven gifts of the Holy
Spirit, which match up more or less with the seven virtues, are coun-
terposed to the passifying passions. Consider how the four cardinal
virtues (fortitude, justice, temperance, and prudence) stand against
the affects. (I shall return to the theological virtues after the discussion
of discernment.) Strength is no more than the courage and ability to
refuse the negative affects under difficult circumstances. Temperance,
because dealing with another's excesses can often take the form of excesses of one's own. And I suppose prudence has to have something
to do with the conservation of energy or resources: Justice especially. I
submit that justice, and the process of being justified, means taking no
more affect than is appropriate for one's actions and thoughts, and
giving the affect that is also appropriate for what one receives as living attention from the other. Hence the Jewish understanding of the
"just man." One might consider here how the psychoanalytic and
meditative virtues of detachment, modesty, love of truth, and avoiding self-pity are also excellent benchmarks for behavior designed to
prevent the transmission of affect. These virtues are also means for
implementing the cardinal virtues. Detachment means attempting to
sort out affects from feelings. From their active yet receptive capacity,
I concluded earlier that feelings are also the means for sensing the
other's needs and dispositions. Kindness is referred to as thoughtfulness. This thoughtful process of itself may be the means for resisting
the other's negative affects; by thinking oneself into another's position, paradoxically, one meets all souls kindly, knowing that they too
are possessed by affects they would rather dispel than circulate. Modesty means not provoking envy or anger, which is prudent. Avoiding
self-pity is advisable because self-pity means enjoying the phenomenon of being hurt, and this means setting up a relation between hook
and fish; to dwell in the hurt is to accept the hook, to become the fish
on the line. I would like to say that negative affects only ever find their
mark if there is something within that accepts the hook. So that if I
blame myself for crimes unknown, I am more likely to attract aggres-

sive accusations of wrongdoing in relationships or others' spheres.[16] But one can also, as we have seen, be dumped upon *simpliciter*. This is the case in shock and trauma, and there is the constant and less tangible buffeting by everyday life. Buffeting can be discerned, just as the vaguely pleasurable process involved in masochistic complicity can be identified. But it takes an act of sustained consciousness, sustained because this resistance is precarious until or unless it becomes a habit.

Personal Discernment

The production of habits appropriate to discernment is a matter of personal practices involving comparison, recollection and memory, and detachment. These practices are held in common in the meditative tradition in philosophy, in psychoanalysis, and in meditation itself, or passive prayer, although the emphasis on one practice rather than another varies. Comparison for the religious works by comparing one's actual conduct with a religious ideal. For the religious and the early moderns alike, it also works by comparing and contrasting inner states. But such comparison of itself does not really explain the decision to embrace or reject a certain affect. If we conceive the moment of judgment as the moment in which we forcefully embrace or project an affect, then we can accept that the judgment itself is a deployment of energy directed toward an object, and as such, an affective force in itself.[17] But because the stream of judgments one makes in daily life takes place in the context of affective transmission, the lessons learned from the comparison of states of feeling are constantly interrupted by waves of affect. It is not only one's own inner states that are the objects of a meditative investigation by reflection and evaluation, as they were for Descartes and Hobbes. It is also a question of oneself and the other. But because of the other, we learn the difference between living attention and draining affects. One can experience directly the effects of receiving attention (once one knows to look) and the remarkable experience of being bored or drained. (Boredom, after all, is not explicable only on the basis of the bore's utterances. Another can say the same words and leave one vitalized and fascinated.)

The more one lives in the emotional world of judging or being judged the more the affects disrupt concentration or the process of sustaining attention. One can compare states of feeling as long as one remembers to note their passing, but one cannot attend to an inner progression when one is possessed; one forgets, one loses the thread. So much is evident when we turn to the scraps of writing on discernment in the clinic. To quote Bion:

> Now the experience of counter-transference [meaning the experience of the other's affect as discussed in chapter 2] appears to me to have quite a distinct quality that should enable the analyst to differentiate the occasion when he is the object of a projective identification from the occasion when he is not. The analyst feels he is being manipulated so as to be playing a part in someone else's fantasy, or he would do so if it were not for what in recollection I can only call a temporary loss of insight, a sense of experiencing strong feelings.[18]

In the clinic, the "temporary loss of insight" marks the interruption of one's chain of associations. Informally (as the question has not as yet been subject to a formal survey), clinicians who experience the transmission of affect say that they do so because the transmitted affect is at odds with what they understand of their own feelings, and the logic of those feelings, at the time of the transmission. The affects attached to ideas should make sense in a sequence. When certain affects seem disproportionate in terms of their alleged causes, one should take note. Similarly, when a new and strong affect comes out of the comparative blue, it is suspect. For example, when a woman was racked by remorse one morning, over the misdemeanor of having failed to thank her research assistant for fetching some books, she was aware that the extent of her self-reproach was too great for the offense. However, subsequently that same morning, she learned that her father, who was with her at the time, had also been remorseful over failing to thank her for a more significant service. As said earlier, rather than say the thought caused the affect, one might say that the affect caused the thought, especially when the thought it settles on is not weighty enough for its emotional burden.

Discerning if the affects are disproportionate requires being in a state to do so. In addition to comparing and contrasting historically, as well as noting when an affect has no apparent place in one's own historical sequence, one has to be either self-possessed (as distinct from self-contained) or away from the other (or both). As we dis-

cussed earlier, discerning insight is not achieved in a state of tempes-
tuous defense. It is achieved in that brief suspension of the state of
projection that leaves a refreshing inner silence by its absence, in
which one can detach from any possessing affect, and attend. To detach in accord with the procedure involved in comparing past and
present affective states is to marshal and move attention toward a
negative affect when one experiences it. The key to the nature of this
real detachment (as distinct from a sadodispassionate projection of
detachment) is that it is an exercise in feeling, but feeling of a calming
and discerning variety. When Kant advised telling an angry man to sit
down, and notes how that act already makes him calmer, he is advo-
cating an act of self-regulation that in our terms here could be recast
as an act of self-possession. One lets go of the affect by examining its
course or by allowing the course of other, calmer, feelings to assert itself.[19] This examination means exercising attention, which is literally
an aid to growth, whether given to oneself in the process of liberating
reflection (antithetical to narcissistic fantasy) or to those who need it.

For attention to be present one would have to be aware, rather than
focusing on an internal daydream or a preconception about the other.
In such a case we might say that attention is, as Freud had it when
talking of the best frame of mind to conduct analysis, "evenly suspended."[20] This state would then be one that is simultaneously active
and passive, actively aware yet undirected and receptive.[21] As the ego
is always focused on its own ends and judgmental structure, it cannot
attend in this receptive way. There has to be some agency that does
this attending, some other regulator of the powers of observation and
feeling aside from the ego. In addition, that regulator has to be capable of recollection when it is involved in historical comparison. To be
capable of recalling memories that seem to be lost, it has to be capable
of organizing and observing from a distinctive standpoint, a candidate for the "other I" whose existence has been inferred throughout
this study. "I" am nothing, as many a mystic and Lacanian has observed. But I am only nothing once I unpack the history out of which
I am composed, history gathered in affective clumps of memories.
And who unpacks this, if not the attentive other I, whose feeling perspective on events is not the same as the ego's, but blunted by the
ego's thuggish affects? This other I has to persist, or there is no one to
realize that I am an illusion, nothing to make the connecting links that
show this.

But we are getting ahead of the facts. All we can say is that what-ever embodies and directs attention away from fantasy or distraction, it is not the ego. It is whatever gathers attention together to discern the affects that disrupt concentration and reflection. This may be an-other center in the mind, a soul as distinct from an ego; and indeed, sometimes two selves do seem to be at work simultaneously. Con-sider how the mind-as-the-neurological-brain attends both to sublim-inal and routine matters while also focusing on a particular fantasy; hence, for instance, it can drive and daydream or converse at the same time, even if maintaining such activities simultaneously is hazardous. Its daydreams are the stuff of its identity maintenance, while its atten-tion keeps it and others alive. But consideration of another agency in the mind (a soul as opposed to the ego?) has to wait. The immediate concern is with the fact that attention obviously accords with what—pro forma—we are terming the life drive, at the same time as it pro-vides an alternative to the subject-centered focus.

The focusing of attention, as we have seen, requires both the logical and energetic ability to sustain attention; such energy is less available when the passions are monopolizing it. This undoubted fact may have led to Kant's conclusion that apathy—the state of no passion—is a goal to strive for, and such striving makes more sense when passion is un-derstood not as joy and pleasure but as waves of negative affect. Striv-ing for apathy—being without passions—makes more sense if the pas-sions one is striving to lose are: (a) acquired and redistributed via transmission, rather than one's own; and (b) unpleasant. But this does not mean striving to be without feeling or sensual enjoyment, espe-cially when feelings, hypothetically, mark out one's alternative bound-aries. The state of apathy, strictly, would be one in which one was sus-pended from the passions, but not bereft of feeling and sensual enjoyment. On the contrary, joy and enjoyment may intensify when feeling is not blunted by the affects. But drawing this out requires not-ing that, in the end, the personal discernment of the affects does not only require their resistance, it requires their transformation. More ac-curately, their resistance is their transformation, as we have already seen, and the key to it lies in the change in direction effected by a con-centrated change in thought. We can add here that the living attention that discerns and transforms the affects grows in climates of love and hope. That optimism also effects a biochemical shift (where different hormonal directions take over from others) is now a matter of record.

As we have established, the subject-centered ego has to project negative affects on or into the other in order to maintain its identity. Or the ego accepts familiar projections as depressions. These can be felt as judgments internalized with the anger that propelled them. Or they can be registered as inertia and rigidity, in order to maintain subjective identity by feminine means. Or both. These affective projections and introjections or judgments, as we saw at the beginning, can be discerned in the clinic and withstood in crowds. But it is obvious that the fewer of these affects there are, the easier it is to resist them. It is also now plain that such resistance is always the simultaneous deployment of living, energetic attention. What remains to be drawn out is the way the negative affects are transformed in the presence of other variants of living attention: love, optimism, logic. The next section turns to this. Personal discernment, in summary, involves evaluations of one's inner states and evaluations of the origin of the affects. These are effected by detaching from one's passionate judgments and affective depressions, and by observing their sequence. One discerns these things with attention.

The Theological Virtues

The cardinal virtues might be seen as preserving a kind of stasis of the self in relation to the affects. They protect the one from the affects of the other, but they do not in themselves change the climate in which the negative affects flourish. That transformation requires the presence of love (and other progenitors of living attention, such as hope, reason, and faith). To draw this out, we can begin by noting that passion, in its current connotations, is a very different animal from the passion refused by the advocates of apathy. The passion they refused is not sensual enjoyment, but more sinister. Kant's definition of passion as something like an obsession is a case in point. Passion for Kant was the perversion of the reasoning process, which is perverted when it is fixed on a self-absorbed direction. Psychoanalytically, the calculations characteristic of obsessionality derive from the ego's initial formation in a game of comparative advantage; only subsequently are these calculations given energy by the affects they help generate. One can think oneself detached from the passions and still be gripped by them, insofar as one calculates coldly. Regardless of whether this mistake was ever made by the ancients, it is made by those who think that coldness is equivalent to detachment, or worse, clear thinking. Being coldly detached is being much too preoccupied with one's own position, and it narrows one's focus. It forecloses the feeling intelligence at work in "evenly suspended attention" in which one is open to new ideas about the other. And as that feeling intelligence works by making connections between new and existing ideas, any constraint on it (such as a preoccupation with prestige) is a constraint on the soul's growth through knowledge. When I suggested above that there was something in attention that connected it with both love and the life drive as well as intelligence, I was thinking not only of the their shared processes of connection (documented in synaptic growth). I also had in mind their close links with sexuality, as did Freud when he conceived of a life drive. I have indicated why "life drive" is a needlessly homogenizing term, conjuring up a romantic animism when it should be shedding it. But for now I shall let it stand, with all its vitalist connotations, because it will remind the reader that Freud's original use of it connected life with the ego or self-preservative drives on the one hand (with thinking, action, and attention) and the libido or love and sexual drives on the other. Freud did not distinguish between the ego and the other I that thinks by making connections, but he did note that when too much libido is diverted inward in narcissism and fantasy, we fall ill. Moreover, such narcissistic diversion by the ego interrupts the process of logical connection in order to maintain its present array of judgmental attitudes (and hence its existing self-concept). Whether the libido is directed toward making connections in thought or making them erotically, it must make them whenever it directs its energy away from itself. That is its nature. Apathy in the sense of cold detachment does not fully resist the affects, for it has not completed turning its attention around, away from itself and toward the other. It has paused at the point where it notes what it receives from the other but not what it gives to the other. It detaches from the affect, but does not dissipate it. Dissipation, as we have indicated, is effected by the theological virtues: faith, hope, and love.

The relation of hope to combating the negative affects of transmission is obvious enough. It is similar to the "optimism that the future can be better" that Freud listed together with "the love of truth" (meaning honesty) as positive factors in prognosis.[22] Optimism—or hope—repels rather than attracts anger and depression. Faith is a superb shield insofar as it presupposes that one is the focus of a divine loving intelligence, but the trusting ability it also presupposes is at odds with the modern existential temperament, which views faith as symptomatic of a childlike dependence (which it is), an alternative to the courage to look aloneness full in the face.[23] On the other hand, if the modern person truly wants to grow up, he or she will have the courage to follow through on reason when its exercise leads to the recognition of the existence of God, and not deny this conclusion because of an emotional dependence on the other's social approval. For my own part, I think faith depends on reason, insofar as sustaining a faith hangs on reason rather than the ego's credulousness.[24] But reason is also tied to love. Love, as we have argued throughout, cannot really be divorced from attention and, therefore, from thinking. In short, thinking and loving are closely related in themselves. They are also—both of them—forms of resistance in the nonperpetuation of the negative affects, as it seems is any process of making or sustaining connections consistent with the known facts or the needs of others and psychical and physical health. In short, the tendency to bind and bring together, to make things cohere, follows the logic of the life drive. Without it, the psyche is in pieces. This erotic and cohering energy is absent especially in psychosis, whose schizophrenic versions are marked by the inability to make logical connections and by lack of sexual affect and/or loving ties to others.[25] (Milder forms of these inabilities also characterize the hysterias, not to mention the disorders of attention and hyperactivity (see chapter 1). At the same time, while one may gauge a thinker a cold fish, that does not mean he is without love; it may be that he is merely channeling all of his ability to connect with his thoughts rather than siphoning it off by interaction.

But the main point is about the relation between the virtues and the practice of discernment. It is perhaps plain now that the internalization of religious codes, and the religious observance of codes or courtesy, are also linked (potentially at least) to an inner process of discernment, discernment at a more private level. This is the case insofar as these internalizations function as an ethical sense. That deep ethical sense is a means for differentiating between one's position (oneself) and the legitimacy or conviction an invading affect lends to thoughts that were hitherto kept in their place. Consider an example: I am toying with a fantasy of revenge that I have examined ethically and spurned for what it is. Then I am possessed by a fury, a combination of anger and the wish that the other should cease to harm me by disappearing, a kind of hate. The thought I had hitherto spurned now takes over consciousness. Let us also say that this hostile thought is levered into place by a hostile act on the part of the party I want to be gone and to feel in his going the affects he has made me feel. Let us say, too, that this hostile act causes me anxiety, perhaps based on financial insecurity if my enemy is in the workplace.

As long as my religious or secular ethics can counter this anxiety and force back this invading affect, I am myself, and moreover, in a position to discern the workings of the affect within me. But I cannot discern it when I am driven by anger to act against my provocateur. Instead, I experience this drive as an inner propulsion. My ego has been engaged in a manner that permits the affect entry. This is the place of my fear and anxiety, which are the hooks for aggression, just as depression is for anger. But the negative affects, as have often been noted, have a function in self-preservation. As the (good) ego they literally keep us alive, in that reality-based anxieties remove us from situations of peril, while aggression can save one's life when deployed in defense. But the arousal of anxiety, as we have seen, may make me party to an unjust idea, whose injustice is evident in the wave of aggression my ill wishes direct toward my enemy. These ill wishes, this judging wave of affect, also reinforce the fear and anxiety in my foe, for he too feels the threat from my animus, just as his animosity produced a corresponding fear in me.

Both of us have directed passionate judgments toward the other, judgments that convey the revengeful constellation across space by their energetic force. What I can mobilize against this force is the strength of my identification with the principle of forgiveness—and the discerning other I who may emerge if I have a strong identification with that principle. When we love, the other feels it. When we love those who are not like us, even though they don't think like us or read the same books or read at all, those others feel it. Sometimes the other even listens, because the love allows them to lower their own shield (of projected affects or judgments) and permit entry to a new idea.[26] To love or forgive is to remove oneself from the loop. This is why the act of real forgiveness can be entirely selfish. The forgiver is the beneficiary, insofar as he or she is then free of transmitting a negative affect, and so free from attracting more of the same. Moreover, if there is a negative affect directed toward one in reality, refusing it may irritate the projector unmercifully, insofar as he or she counts on an aggressive response. Really love those that hate you; do good to them that persecute you. There is no better escape, no clearer path to freedom. There is also no better revenge.

But if one is to be free of the negative affects, one has to give over an identity based on projected judgments. In the introduction, I proposed that an identity based on discernment was not the same as an identity based on the ego's status-bound boundaries. Enough has been said about the latter. We can now add that proceeding by discernment and proceeding by judgmental projections are different, but we can only see this because we have situated both processes in the context of affective transmission. If one maintains the sense of a distinct identity by discernment, one does so best by meditative practices and an openness to the distinct being who is sheltering behind the common ego, in oneself and others alike. Only then can one attend to one's own sensations and feeling for the other, by sensing what is not oneself, and noting, as well as feeling, when one falls back on the negative affects. But we have been stretching a point by continuing to use the language of an other I, when all we have really shown so far is that the claims of the feelings and senses can be at war with those of the affects and ego. But we have also shown, a little at least, that a sense of self anchored in discernment is possible and desirable, and that it is more likely to take hold where the negative affects, as a social phenomenon, are diminished.

If a social context is one that reinforces the means for struggling against the negative affects through religious and cultural codes, then the practice of personal discernment becomes easier and the resistance to the ego—with its world of appearances and things—stronger. In this late-modern context, in which affects thicken, discernment is so weak that people no longer know that there is anything to be discerned. In such a context, the sense of self does depend on boundaries formed by projecting and introjecting affects, it depends on knowing who one is by depositing alien affects in the other. The urge to do this—and maintain boundaries by these aggressive means—intensify as the affects one wants to live without, anxiety especially, thicken socially. The affects are thickened, the heart sealed better, when there are real threats to living, such as hunger, homelessness, and grief. These threats give rise to anxieties that undermine any attempt at peace of mind, as do related demands for unpurposeful work, which leave the body unrested and prey to passing affects. Attitudes of discernment are more easily adopted and reinforced where there is enjoyment and where there is plenty; the bodily changes in rage and pain are indissolubly tied to those in hunger;[27] and too much hunger for too long can drive a people mad. Yet discernment can also be communicated in appalling physical circumstances, otherwise a form of resistance like Gandhi's satyagraha[28] could never have taken hold.

The negative affects are brought to a stop when a dyadic or binary loop is broken because the response to aggression is to resist it without violence. They are transformed when love or its variants (wit, reason, affection) reorder aggression. They can be deconstructed (the images and energies trapped in them taken apart) and turned around. For oneself, this can be done in solitude. But the transformation of the affects at large requires being in the world, rather than living the life of the mind. It requires subjecting oneself to eddies or even torrents of affects, while somehow maintaining equilibrium. Such is the practice of souls who, when assailed by envy or contempt or rage do not take it personally, for they know that these are forces that possess even the finest souls, whose discerning agencies sometimes cower in the corners of their possessed minds, waiting for it to be over.

The other feels it when we love or give generous attention, and benefits from it. The benefits may not be conscious, but they are real as long as love is really love, that is to say, the gift is one of attention to the other's needs rather than an obsession or a demand to be loved. I hypothesized earlier that light might be cast on some of the unknowns in embryology if the living logic of the mother's flesh constituted a shield against the negative affects, in the same way that her energetic attention constitutes a shield after birth. But the nature of this postnatal shield is different. Loving attention does not provide the absolute shield that partaking in the living logic does, but it is its best approximation.

Feelings

Proceeding further means encountering the subjective standpoint that stymies us each time we turn to a given area for the state of its research. The active yet receptive capacities of discernment and attention cry out to be named "the soul." But these capacities, by the definition of feelings employed here, are linked to the unimpeded senses—the sensitive and vegetative capacities, such as smell, rather than the higher ones, such as thought, the traditional abode of the soul. Setting aside further discussion of the investigation of the other I or soul for now, we can look at feelings as such, which takes us back to the idea of the senses as "the seneschals of attention."

The difficulties in understanding that the senses and the flesh embody a logic that moves far faster than thought are tied to Western schemas that degrade the body and bodily intelligence. This is because the schemas invariably rank the soul in terms of intellect first, followed by the capacity to sense, followed by the fleshly passions and/or vegetative soul. The fleshly category is assumed to be the least intelligent and to have the maximum disorder. It is prime matter without form, or the successor of form, thinking intelligence. Yet it is through the blood that hormones dance their dance of communication, while the senses try to make sense of them in a vocabulary that does not provide them with an appropriate nomenclature.[29] More to the point, all the senses, as vehicles of attention, connect the supposedly higher cognitive faculty of linguistic thought with the fleshly knowledge or codes of the body.

By the logic of this argument so far, it would be a grave mistake to perpetuate the association between the higher aims in human endeavor and the higher brain functions. For instance, smell may appear more primitive than the "higher" development of language, but it is, nonetheless, incapable of lying. It can be deceived, just as hearing and vision can be deceived, but one cannot consciously decide to emit a smell that is at odds with one's affects. Above all, smell precisely discerns. It does not content itself with wallowing in the primitive affective responses with which it is so often associated. It also works with great rapidity, processing much in a millisecond, whereas language takes its time.

Yet the intelligence of such rapidly moving olfactory knowledge is regarded as inferior, something like a reflex, rather than a faster moving mind within. Why is this? I suggest that there is one reason and one reason only, and it is named the foundational fantasy. That fantasy results in the disposition to see activity as mindless when it is not directed from the standpoint of self-interest. (In turn, this leads to the difficulties in conceiving of the activity of nature—or pregnancy, or matter—as passive.) Even when the senses are actively palpating, they are classified as subordinate to thinking in words and pictures because they are not directed from the standpoint of self-interest.

In truth or reality, sensory registration bypasses perceptions structured from the subject standpoint in a search for language that works with the living logic and circumvents the ego. When the senses succeed in producing conscious awareness of this or that, they produce knowledge that can be communicated either to oneself or another in language (when the words exist or can be learned), but the conscious awareness it produces precedes that expression, and may stumble for words, although it will run after the words when it sees or hears them. Information is gleaned by the senses, but then it is interpreted or transliterated by something split from the senses. It may be interpreted by something aligned with the logic of the senses or by something opposed to them, something interested in constructing a world view based on its own whims. Such interpretations are made by the ego, and the ego's interpretations are tendentious, based on censorship. In the interpretation lies room for suggestibility, for paranoia, for fundamental misreading. For instance, if I smell of fear, you may discern this and try to put me at my ease. Or you may miscalibrate my nervousness. You smell something offensive, but you also misread my apprehensive expression. In consequence, you interpret me as aggressive in my intentions toward you.

In the example just given, my olfactory senses would work more subtly than the visual perception that shapes my response. Sensory registration and perception would not be the same thing.[30] The information from the senses conflicts; one is accurate, the other sees through a darkened eye, but when they are interpreted in concert, even the accurate information supports a misinterpretation. The information it attempts to communicate is suborned to the service of the ego, which has censored what it sees and hears as it seeks reasons to agree with social opinion. The senses, as I have stressed, are not the emotions; they are the vehicles for their discernment, just as they are for alerting us to other aspects (the weather, the traffic) of the environment and circumstances in which we exist. But they work by communicating along various neural pathways. Before they come or return to the brain, they have to negotiate various synaptic censors and the translations from chemical to electrical impulses, and vice versa.

These chains of communication are inseparable from the impulse they communicate. Their matter is their form. Yet *what* they communicate also changes in the transliteration to language and concept at the same time as the impulse *to* communicate persists. It persists in that it seeks to circumvent the censorship effected by the ego.

The conscious ego forecloses knowledge and assumptions that challenge its sense of intellectual superiority in its body; the unconscious ego censors similar knowledge by repressing it and keeping it unconscious. By this censorship and this foreclosure, the ego creates gaps in conscious understanding. These gaps mean that ego-consciousness knows less than the senses whose multiple communications battle with the ego's censorship and denial. It means that the senses and the informational channels of the flesh (whose matter is intrinsic to their form) are intelligent, aware, and struggling either to overcome or get through to a slower, thicker person who calls itself I, or worse, me. It also means that the extent of one's intelligence depends on a struggle between different ideas, different chains of information, a struggle mediated by the available concepts as well as the ego's clinging to its own standpoint.

Now whether the ego speaks its empty speech or the soft voice of reason prevails, both speak. One is speaking the passionate, heartless language of the affects. The other is relying on logic (in part) and its sensing and feeling of the empirical state of things.[31] The outcome of this struggle depends on how far love or living attention prevails over the force of affects directed by the ego. To some degree, it also depends on the education of the senses, which improves their chances of discerning and resisting those affects. The education of these senses gives us joy. It is the "arousal from below" that is so significant in rabbinical literature.[32] Yet as the ego loses standing when the fleshly senses win through to consciousness and direct the body's government, we also find them terrible as an army, leaving nothing of us in its wake.

CHAPTER SEVEN

Interpreting the Flesh

Freedom from the affects means freedom for the feelings to be known to consciousness. Feelings can be sifted from affects, and better known to consciousness, through the deployment of living attention or love. But such attention encounters a formidable opposing force. Affects (via hormones and other means of projection and reception) are carried in the blood, and with them is carried the presence of the other and the social in the system. (To find an utterly pure soul within, something untouched by human error, one would have to sustain living attention through a process of complete exsanguination.) As a rule, affects can be sifted from feelings in everyday life through discernment, or through practicing cultural codes that suppress the affects, or through analysis. These embody living attention directed toward the other within and without. But feelings are less likely to be known when the heart is sealed, for the reason that the more the affects thicken and harden the more difficult discernment becomes. The hardening of the affects is a social affair, so their transformation requires political as well as personal attention. In political as well as personal cases, changing the disposition of the affects (from passivity-inducing and raging judgments of the other to love or affection) requires practice and knowledge. The understanding and deployment of feelings is critical in both endeavors as the means for discerning affects and reconnecting with the original knowledge of the senses.

Lo siento, it was noted, means, literally, "I feel it." The verb here, *sentir*, also means to smell in the French languages. I mention this now

139

because this particular verb illustrates more than a putative historical knowledge of the transmission of affect. It may also be an instance of the body's intelligence finding an accurate match in the choice of word, which reveals some of how it feels and knows by feeling means.

Throughout, I have depended on a definition of feelings as sensations that have found a match in words. In part, this definition was based on the clinical belief that relief and energetic release comes with the words to say it. Language releases us from the affects (through genuine psychoanalysis or other practices of discernment) via words that express something occluded and thereby releases the energy deployed in this occlusion. The right words dislodge the misperceptions generated by the foundational fantasy. But words do not do this of themselves. They are pushed by the life drive, that is, the senses and the informational channels of the flesh that, I have argued, are intelligent, aware, and struggling either to subdue or communicate with a slower, thicker person who calls itself I.

The difference between the slow "I" and the faster "I" is the difference between the self who knew but did not know it knew and the I who presents itself as the knowing subject. This other, this more comprehensive and more accurate awareness, may not be acknowledged in the sense of becoming the focus of one's attention if words are unavailable to it (it has never been linked to words because the words for it do not—now, or yet—exist) or it may be censored. Either way, it presses for the attention only words and energetic focus together can give it, and that is the point. Insofar as people attend actively, listen to what they are feeling, they can identify sensations, sounds, and images they can name or, after struggle, can find words for. We do this all the time. It is called thinking. It may be most recognizable to us as the struggle for a word already known, but it may also exist as a struggle for a new concept that can lead to new words. People's vocabularies can expand. What one cannot now say, another can or has or will, and one can learn. One can learn rapidly, in fact, when new words release sensations that had hitherto strained for linguistic expression.

The last chapters have identified how the place of self-interest, or the subject-centered standpoint, is at the bottom of the prejudice against the intelligence of the flesh. We have seen (chapter 4) how subjective self-interest fabricates links between mind, activity, and agency and how it objectifies the means for connecting and communicating affects and feelings (closing consciousness off to olfactory knowledge). We have also analyzed (chapter 6) how this bears on the notion that sensory communication is less intelligent or knowledgeable than conscious linguistic thought. It remains here to argue why the reverse is the case. First, I will draw out the grounds for thinking that there is a preexisting synchrony or homology between the structure of language and that of other bodily codes. Then we can turn to the question of this homology via Lacan's critique of the idea. The contradictions in his critique help make the case for the homology, because they pinpoint how other codes are structured like a language in the flesh—the DNA codes, for instance, and the signaling and receipt of hormones. We shall see, moreover, that the only reason for rejecting the notion that these fleshly codes work as language does is that they do not pause to witness or record the fact that a communication is taking place. But there is nothing here that tells us that the other bodily languages are less intelligent. All we can reasonably conclude is that conscious linguistic thought is slower than communication that is unimpeded by reflection.[1]

Finally, we look at how understanding and communication are slowed down by the blocks in the way of communication, blocks occasioned by the foundational fantasy. These make us slower, logically, by impeding the connections necessary for rapid thought and learning.[2] The foundational fantasy removes us from the sphere of more rapid understanding, just as it slows us down in relation to the freely mobile energy into which we are born. In *Exhausting Modernity* I proposed that humans slow down natural, energetic time by constructing inertia—an artificial time of fantasies and fixed commodities.[3] This notion is here linked to language and the severance of thought and feeling by the affects of self-interest, which make us pause to take stock of how a given situation does or does not advantage us. This calculation severs links with the other, including the other that is one's flesh, links that can be reestablished by a different kind of reflection that identifies sensations with words. The difference between reflection as a means for reconnection and reflection as the calculation of advantage is tied, in the concluding section, to the two forms of science or knowledge (logical, and that based on subject/object thought). Understanding fleshly languages as languages—structured systems of intelligent communication whose matter is intrinsic to their form—enhances the likelihood that science will identify more of them.[4]

Language

When Ferdinand Saussure established that language takes its meaning from the difference between signifiers, rather than from (or as well as) a relation between word and referent, he showed that the linguistic code was structured as a self-referential code.[5] As a logical process, it makes sense in its own terms, regardless of whether a subject is present or not. This is true at two levels. Subject or no subject, the linguistic chain exists as a taxonomy of tonal values (sea/see/seer/see ya/ and so forth). Not only this, but meaning, in the sense of signification, is structured by the relation between terms in language as an internally consistent chain of differences. "Tree" as a signifier takes its meaning from "branch" and "trunk," in the same way that Venus takes its meaning from Mars and the Sun, from its position in a solar system. Such logics exist independently, as do the logics of other systems living in the flesh and the environs that sustain the flesh. Not only this, but, as Claude Lévi-Strauss discerned, the models of kinship and exchange, like the common elements of myth, also embody structures that reflect those of language.[6] Lacan went further, arguing that when a child takes up its place in a family or kin group, a place that is always tied to sexual identity, it frees itself from the imaginary by sacrificing its immediate desire (to possess the mother) in favor of its actual and symbolic place in another ongoing structure or chain, that of exogamy. This sacrifice also works in the interests of life overall, for incest and inbreeding degrade the organism's living potential and genetic stock. When it concentrates on its immediate desires, the subject is less likely to be psychically or organically healthy than when it gives up those desires and accepts its place. When one acknowledges one is a child who will grow one day to be a man, one postpones one's desire for the mother, and in doing so, one becomes healthier, more intelligent, all those things that do not result from repression in any naturalistic philosophy of human potential. Contra Wilhelm Reich, the lifting of sexual repression is not always tantamount to making us healthy. It depends on the nature of the repression being lifted. This, then, is the other reason, apart from a structural disjunction, why the signifier is important for Lacan. It is not only that the signifying chain is structured in relation to its own terms rather than ours. It is also that when we adhere to a structure parallel to the order of signification in terms of how we conduct kin ties, we fare better. To put it briefly: Language functions by giving us a place in relation to others, so enabling us to overcome the subject-centered illusions that plague each of us, and it also gives a voice to the affective blocks and feelings that otherwise stand in the way of rejoining enough of the flow of life to survive.[7] Language channels desire away from its oedipal objects and dismantles the misperception that fuels imaginary aggression.

The great insight about the structural nature both of kinship and of the linguistic chain, as the philosophy and social science of a century have noted, is that it removes the subjective generation of meaning from the picture in favor of the system or structure. The order of signification does not begin, and it does not end. Because of its infinite nature, as Lacan argued so well, the structure of the linguistic chain is at odds with the finite concerns of human beings.[8] Human concerns are focused on life and death and the meaning of it all. But, in Lacan's words, "the world . . . in which we orient ourselves . . . doesn't only imply the existence of meanings, but the order of the signifier as well."[9] What Lacan implies is that neurotic and finite concerns sit ill with the structure of signification, which can give no solution to the meaningful questions of life and death because its nature is antithetical to them.[10] (The debt to Kierkegaard's belief that finiteness is simply wrong is clear.) The realization that language, that pivot of the human capacity to convey meaning, also has an independent logic and system of reference might have meant for Lacan—and the structuralists—that the subject's place in the scheme of things had been overrated. Here we were, imagining that our subject/object view of things was the God's-eye view, only to discover that the language we used and world in which we were oriented has a different logic altogether. But despite the blow to the subject's narcissism occasioned by the fact that it is not the source of meaning, the belief in the subject's importance persisted. It persists for instance in the Derridean notion that without the subject, there is no meaning, as opposed to the idea that if the subject does not have a monopoly on meaning, the subject, not meaning, is in question. (These opposing points have been conflated in twentieth-century work on signification.)[11] In his own way,

Lacan, too, was clinging to the importance of the subject. He was clinging insofar as he was reluctant to let go of the idea that the subject has a monopoly on intelligent communication. This reluctance is evident in the way Lacan calls on language, "the thing that makes us human," and enables us to communicate, as the only agency of our redemption. Lacan was lyrical on how language manages to get us out of the soup, not only by providing the words to say it but by modeling as the template for kinship. Yet how and why language releases us remains mysterious.

I suggest that the releasing power of language only makes sense if the release is actually a *re*-alignment of language with the intelligent bodily logic from which it was split at birth. At least, I am arguing that in certain circumstances there is a realignment between erotic energy (which is otherwise directed inward in repression, or—better—toward objects, animate and inanimate) and the linguistic faculty for making logical connections. Given that there are biological codes that appear to function in the same way as languages, why then cannot language be efficacious when it is aligned with these other codes, able to express them and the sensory information informing them by putting their concerns and communications into words? In such a case, communication from these other fleshly languages would not be impeded by the blocks thrown up by way of repression. Lacan, however, was insistent that these fleshly codes are not languages in the sense of intelligent systems of communication.[12] His first argument against this idea was that the order of signification, unlike biological communication, records or witnesses. Without witnessing, there is no self-consciousness or reflexiveness concerning the communication from one's own standpoint.[13] Without that function, in turn, there is no communication as we know it, because there is no acknowledgement of receipt. This is why those who claim that biological systems are languages are wrong, said Lacan. These biological systems do not involve pausing to acknowledge the communication. Yet Lacan was also troubled by this formulation of the originality of the signifier, as he scrupulously dealt with the next objection to it, which is that hormones *do* appear to acknowledge the communication.[14] But they do not pause. In other words, signaling receipt need not be tied to pausing. Then again, if signaling receipt can be divorced from pausing, then pausing is not necessary to witnessing or acknowledging, and hence not necessary for communication. By acknowledging this, in effect, Lacan undercut his own argument. For all that seems to distinguish these bodily languages from the language of conscious communication is the matter of pausing. If one pauses to note a communication, one does, in that pause, reorient oneself to take account of it. But if one is not thinking of oneself or one's standpoint, the requisite reorientation demands no time.

From here on, I shall argue that the linguistic chain is split from the other chains of meaning and logic—hormones, genetic codes, solar systems—by the insertion of the subject position where it does not belong. Finiteness is wrong because it does not belong in an order whose logic is at right angles to that of the human perspective, as if the codes of the living logic, together with the chemical senses, communicate on a horizontal axis, while those of the human historical perspective function on an vertical one. But the vertical subject's perspective on meaning has material effects and produces its own network of material communications; certain direction-giving pheromones and hormones, for instance, are locked into a cycle of over-production that exacerbates aging while confirming the subject's own standpoint. I am arguing that without the insertion of the subject position into the original codes of the flesh, the structure of the linguistic chain is homologous with that of other living chains, living sequences whose interaction determines the extent of the life drive. With the insertion, the structures are more or less right angles. This argument entails that the life drive is not a single animistic force but the result of interweaving—yet diverse— chains, capable of transformation from one order of living symbolism to another. As noted earlier, for Freud and Walter Benjamin, language at some point was split from the stuff out of which affects also came. I have foreshadowed a tentative agreement here, but that agreement depends on understanding the life drive as the proportionate and rhythmic intersection of numbers of vast and small internally consistent chains that are all communicative and, in this respect, like languages.

If the erotic energy, or the life drive, is composed of fleshly codes that parallel those of language, this could explain why it is that the body seems to do its own thinking. As Lacan said of the id, "It thinks." But the thinking "it" is more than the slumbering but relentless amalgam of energies and affects that constitute Freud's *das Es*. In reality "it" is part of something that thinks infinitely more rapidly than the secondary process that follows on behind, putting everything into words, like a middle-aged lady puffing to keep up with a train she is trying to catch. How "it" thinks is logical, even though the ego presents this thinking as nonsensical. It is logical insofar as life is composed of interweaving logical chains that are self-referential and exist independently of the subject, but which sustain the life of the subject's kind through their interaction (such as the logical chain that maintains the biosphere). It is the living or reasoning chain that is the source of energy in the myriad intersections that are homogenized in the concept of the life drive. For I am assuming, as I said earlier, that logic has to be embodied. It is precisely a living logic.[15] When Heracleitus described the logos as proportionate matter, he highlighted the fact that the logic is material and that its intelligence (its proportions) is inseparable from and intrinsic to the nature of its living materiality. The logos then is in and of the flesh, but it is not all there is to the flesh. There are also the subjective, affective, and driven paths embedded in flesh and blood, as well as the living logic that presses our subject to follow paths that preserve life around and beyond it. Both the pathways of the negative affects and those of the living logic serve intentions beyond those of the conscious self, although the conscious self works hard to convince itself that its actions are done for its own ends. Like the negative affects, this directional force—the life drive and/or some of the living chains out of which it is composed—operates with intentionality, intending to reproduce more life or organization. As shown above, the slower linguistic consciousness, which formulates the reasons for our actions, claims intentionality after the fact, but it is not the only intentional force within us.

When the human being is on a lively or life path it is less slow in its thinking and responses. The alignment or realignment of fleshly codes and language lends the faculty for making conscious connections a force and speed lacking when laboring in the face of passions and desires fixed to objects. Realignment lends the conscious mind the force and speed of the body's consummate intelligence, which makes connections more rapidly—in the unconscious codes structured like languages—when unconstrained by whether or not a particular action will be good for an individual as distinct from the body in its environment at large: that is to say, whether it will also be good for the life drive, for the living purpose which transcends any individual desire to preserve oneself in comfort, or what feels like comfort from the stunted, limited temporal perspective one has on things *right now*.[16]

The mystery of how and why language redeems is resolved once the homology between the structure of the order of signification and that of other living chains becomes salient. The problem has been that these structures are at odds; there is the disjunction between the endless, infinite structure of the signifying chain and the finite concerns of neurotic subjects, who are worried about birth and death and their meaning in the scheme of things. But there is an alternative explanation, other than linguistic mysteries, for this disjunction. The alternative is the notion that something went wrong in the scheme of things, something that split the order of signification from the orders of the flesh. The orders of the flesh became mortal, whereas those of signification remained infinite. The orders of the flesh, in this scenario, have become mortal because they are obstructed by something that slows them down. This, it will be recalled, is what the foundational fantasy appears to do.

Blocks in the Way of Feeling

The self-conscious standpoint, through the foundational fantasy, is tied to the erection of self-contained barriers against feeling the other's affects and/or feelings. It is also tied to the construction of the inertia that slows the subject down energetically relative to the energetic and intelligent (or unsplit) chemical communication of which it had hitherto been part in utero. Within this account of constructed inertia, there lies a theory of temporal causality that I tried to draw out above, and also at more length in chapter 4 of *Exhausting Modernity*. The essence of that theory is this: When we repress that first hallucination, we remove ourselves from the timeless state in which needs and their meeting coincide, just as we remove ourselves from the delusional state induced by hallucination. By taking stock of what is and is not real, we also remove ourselves from a situation of unpleasure or pain. The cessation of unpleasure is one yardstick of reality. But reality is also distorted from the outset by the imposition of one's imaginings, whose illusory status is only acknowledged when they cause distress. Were it not for the carryover of megalomania from the time before birth, when the organism did not distinguish its own capacities from those of the other, there would be no directed hallucination, hence no repression, hence no subjective standpoint. From this perspective, constructed inertia is the foundation of a subjective temporality, born of a fantasy and its repression. This constructed inertia is also the occasion of the splitting of an order of signification from an order of affective meaning. The signifier is split from the affect (the mental representation is split from the physiological experience) by the repression of a visual fantasy in the first instance, although auditory as well as other visual hallucinations and fantasies later follow suit.

Just as the subject overlays the (retroactively) faster world of chemical and hormonal communication—in which it first stored memories—with the slower world contingent on seeing things from its own standpoint, so too does he lose the means for rapid interpretation of the logics of the flesh. One can put it in terms of energy or in terms of linguistic communication. Either way, the subject-to-be loses touch with the pathways that connect him without impediment when he has to pause in the face of an image and learn to ask whether the image is real or illusory. Hence, by this account, what stands in the way of the reconnection, or transliteration, of sensations and feelings are affects: memories and fantasies that trap energy in their repressions and fixations in visual images. It is these that make us pause. The energy that escapes service in the name of fixation is misdirected in the affected drives: it is directed away from the living paths it otherwise follows naturally toward the constructed pathways of subjectivity, pathways built around inertia and lack. While living pathways have a structure and, especially, a logic that is akin to language, points of captation interrupt and divert their flows away from the logical, connecting processes common to sustaining life and reasoning. Life operates according to a certain logical sequence. It arranges matter in systems that release energy through their sequencing. It does not release this energy, or release as much of it, when it is diverted to the service of the repressions and fixations that maintain images, beginning with a self-image.

The Interpretation of the Flesh

It then behooves us, as a species, to reconnect language and understanding with the fleshly and environmental codes from which our consciousness has been split by fantasy and illusion. Those natural pathways do their best in the dark, but bump into each other without the regulating force of living attention. Even so, bodily physiological and chemical processes themselves push for admission to consciousness past blocks of self-absorption via a slow linguistic gateway. Language may echo the facts of transmission; *sentir* may mean smell either because we once knew that we felt the other's feelings by smell or because the body knows it still and seeks the word that will best describe its operations. But whether the affinity between the operation of certain physical processes and their linguistic signification was previously conscious, more conscious, or unconscious, it is, as we have tried to show, evident. Yet, for us as speaking beings, this consciousness has already been changed into parallel systems of signification: the linguistic, the sensitive, and the affective. That this splitting involves sundering a unity is plain when affect and the right word come together. When a hitherto nameless feeling succeeds in identifying itself, consciousness feels release. Conversely, when the problem has no name, consciousness feels constricted. But the point here is that both release and constriction are not brought about coincidentally if word and affect were once joined. They belong in a certain configuration, a certain lining up with one another, and the correct alignment appears necessary for the unimpeded or less-impeded flow of energy. The more one can signify one's sensations and feeling the more, presumably, one can identify their origin, whether within or without. But one can only signify them correctly if one assumes immortality as a starting point, meaning that the logic of the flesh lies on the same axis as that of language. The process of correct alignment might better be described as symbolic transformation, meaning that the different alphabets of the flesh could be aligned in such a way that life was released from one order into another, transforming inert blocks of matter in the system and yielding more freedom, more intelligence, and more energy. Symbolization is the means for transformation as the process whereby energy locked up in an alphabet in which it cannot speak (such as traumatic grief) is released back into the flow of life by words, or by the strange chemistry of tears.[17] Symbolization, as the act whereby information is transferred from one register or alphabet to another, is simultaneously an act of transformation. We see it when a word releases an old injury, but we also see it when the physical infusion of love or living attention unblocks sclerotic matter, releasing it back into the flow of life, as when an injury is healed by the laying on of attentive hands.

Aside from the implications for a personal practice of discernment, the notion of aligned codes, like that of the transmission of affect, is at odds with subject/object thought and the visualization basic to objectification.[18] As chapter 5 discussed, the gateway between (linguistic) consciousness and the codes of bodily sensation is manned by visual images. That is to say, to make itself conscious, a bodily process has to be imagined—given an image. The images it can be given are determined by signification, but different images can be conjured up by the same sound. Dream censorship is effected by substituting a misleading image for the signifier (hence, as I noted earlier, I dream of a "seabed," rather than seeing a bed, when it is actually a bed my energetic health needs to consider). This visual censorship in dreams is not to be underestimated. It blocks needed information surfacing to consciousness, deploying the visual perceptual categories and the stored images over which it has charge, images stored from the three-dimensional standpoint of a subject arrayed against an object. Freud understood how the ego (hand in glove with the superego) works as a censor but not why it was a visual censor. It is a visual censor because it identifies objects from the standpoint of the subject. But Freud, and especially Lacan, also understood that language has a structural affinity with the life drive in that it seeks to get the truth through despite the opposition of the subjective ego. If we listen to the letter ("See, bed!") we learn the truth the living being needs to heed. It is only when we depend on visual perception that we are led astray into the subjective thought that takes the human standpoint as central. Such thought requires that one stand apart to observe the other and reduce it to predictable motions and reactions, the better to study it as an object. It also requires that the intention embodied in the logic of the life drive be prevented from connecting with that embodied in the reasoning process.

But together with the two forms of knowledge (that of the living logic and that framed in subject/object terms) there are two forms of science, and only one is really science. The other traces things from the subjective standpoint, rather than a living or reasoning chain existing independently of that standpoint.[19] Reasoning as a process also follows the logic of life, of which it is part. It is the conscious exercise of living attention; while living attention itself is evident in synaptic growth, which marks out the pathways of learning. Insofar as these pathways coincide with the direction of the organism's ongoing well being, its life and living energy are enhanced.

In this account love ceases to be a metaphysical concept and becomes a matter of energy. It was always a matter of energy for Freud. Freud associated both love and energy with sexual energies, personified by Eros. But he associated love with coherence. The erotic is not only a matter of the senses; it is a matter of how life coheres or comes together in those forms of organization that enable life to persist. But the pathways constructed from the organism's own standpoint do not do this; they diminish its chances of living and accelerate its aging. In this respect they are irrational, or at least illogical. At the same time, they appear to be essential to the sense of self. The difference in direction between these pathways, and those of the living logic, is paralleled by "science" constructed from the subject's standpoint (science that cooperates with the direction toward death) and (true) science that traces out logical (rather than functional) systems in which the subject's place is incidental. Poststructuralism, when it cast its eye back over the pathways the subject had traversed in attempting to make meaning a human affair, rightly found them absurd. But it balked at its own conclusion, which was that meaning reappeared once we subtract the subject's concerns with living and dying from the relevant equations. When it strives to preserve its own life at the expense of the perpetuation of the life around it, it contributes to the anxiety that corrodes living pathways within itself as well as in others. It draws to itself more of the same, and more of the same leads to more drastic moves of self-preservation, although these moves cost its life in the longer run. We live when we forget about own lives and die when we do not.

Nature is good, as the body is, but it is slowed down as it contends with the negative affects generated by aggression, fear, and anxiety, affects that accelerate aging and decay. The identification of the means for transmitting these affects, through further research on hormones, is also the beginning of their reduction and eventual elimination. For such things are possible. The Gnostic heresy denied that matter is good, claiming that the creation of the earth was the work of a demiurge. By contrast, this argument, and the notion of the arousal from below, are premised on the good in matter and the flesh, while seeing death as the product of an unnatural and unintended slowdown of the energy that is only permanently divorced from matter when matter is no longer biodegradable, no longer able to obey the laws of symbolic transformation at even the simplest vegetative level. Recovering those laws scientifically, as well as practically, is part of that symbolic transformation.

Some sciences, such as physics, progress each time they take a step away from a subject-centered standpoint, each time they allow for the distortions imposed by its common-sense perspective ("the earth is flat") or measure a factor such as observer interference. The life sciences have not made the same progress, being evidently more concerned with delaying death or the point at which the subject ceases to be distinct in relation to its surrounding environment. However, not all the life sciences are conducted in relation to a subject-centered standpoint. As indicated already, the environmental sciences, for instance, consider life in terms of chains that are the necessary condition of existence for species and kinds and habitats. These chains may not preserve a particular subject's life, but they do preserve and continue life as such. In the same way, truth from the unconscious may embarrass the conscious subject when the ego is in the ascendancy but may preserve its life by changing its path in a way that releases energy. In this respect, any thinking being is involved in an ongoing struggle in which the intellect is aligned with the life drive against a subjective worldview framed by a fantasy.

The intellect is that thing then that thinks in terms of logic, and logic itself does not begin and end with the subject but belongs to atemporal orders of signification, including mathematics as well as verbal language. In social or material reality, however, the subject has to negotiate between its subject position and the directions toward which it is pulled by the drives as they seek to reconnect with signifiers.[20] For drives do seek to be known to consciousness; they press against their repression, as Freud observed. We do not know the nature of the life drive before the split, or what reasoning, loving, and desiring feel like from a non-split place. We do know that the ability to love and work, or think, are the conditions of health. By this argument, both involve the reconnection of the order of signification with the life drive, or living chains of logic. This reconnection has to overcome the subjective affects or meanings focused on the subject's own beginning and end. That is why thinking is hard. It is turning the attention and capacity to conceptualize deployed in ego maintenance in the same direction as the life drive (or will) from which it has been split. By turning attention toward the paths of life overall, it becomes free of the affects that have possessed its attentive energy and distracted its concentration. The faculties for concentration as well as discernment ensure that the fantasy is not uniform in its effects, otherwise the colorless world of numbers would never have prevailed over the common senses (meaning common sensory perceptions) that perceive the earth as flat and matter as passive. Famously, those who have faith in reason over observation constitute the rationalist as opposed to the empirical tradition in science. We might also say they constitute the opposition to foundational thinking, insofar as they reason or think logically and insofar as logic flies in the face of common sensory perception. The more logic and language push on regardless of what they objectively see or behold with common sense the more likely it is that we will extend the range for imagining and conceptualizing bodily processes. To extend the range of visualization beyond what the visual senses behold means following the path of logic even when it conflicts with common sense. Thus we can readily imagine a heliocentric solar system today, as the range of imaginary visualization was extended (beyond its own standpoint) in the wake of the logic that defied the common sense view that the earth was flat. I am proposing that we will understand more of the workings of the body if we defy common sense in another respect, by hypothesizing that death (via the affects of aggression and anxiety) is a force that comes to the living body from without as well as within and does battle with the life drive in all its derivatives.

At present we only have a rudimentary language for connecting sensations, affects, and words, for connecting bodily processes and the conceptual understanding of them. The development of that language requires an attention to the pathways of sensation in the body, an attention that is more concentrated and sustained than the attention received by the body hitherto. This is the precondition of beginning to formulate bodily knowledge more accurately and to pass it on by the verbal means that increases the rapidity of human understanding. Extending knowledge in this way is the reverse of gathering it by objectification, or studying bodily processes disconnected from living attention. This living attention is distracted from living ends when it is captured by fantasies that represent the force of death even while conjuring images of life in greener grass. They do this because they obstruct the extension of living attention. Extending knowledge of sensation, following it farther along its pathways, means extending consciousness into the body, infusing it with the conscious understanding from which it has been split hitherto. That split has hardened with the sealing of the heart, but it has also come under examination in all the practices and knowledges that, taken together, presage the resurrection of the body. Some of these systems of knowledge already nestle in the objective arms of science, especially those focused on the complex systems of body and brain rather than more isolated organs or processes. Others are found in the schools of Chinese and other holistic health systems that are attracting increasing numbers of adherents. What these systems of healing have in common (despite uneven levels of rigor) with the study of the body in its complexity is precisely the notion of systems—of language and communication that seems to be modeled on language, insofar as a biochemical chain or a DNA sequence can be structured like a language in another medium.

The distinctions may be immaculately fine, but at the human level, they would be more easily made if our vocabularies more than our brains (which evidently have room for extra storage) were extended. These can be extended through science or study, combined with practice in differentiating sensations by attending to them. At present we have only limited linguistic categories for perceiving fine distinctions and are subsuming similar, but distinct, data under one heading. This suggests not that there is less precise information to be gathered by olfaction but rather that this is the sense of which we have become most unconscious. What olfaction (and the "lizard brain" in general) communicate can barely be named in the crudest terms—confronted with odors, informed human response does not extend much beyond ooh, pooh, yum, and Proust.[21] This crudity is matched only by that of the pleasure principle, which interprets internal bodily sensations as either pleasure or pain (and it makes mistakes even with these). We differentiate finely neither in respect of our interior sensations nor in relation to the messages emitted by others. The notoriously sharp-smelling sweat of fear, while it is a term bequeathed to us by detective novelists, is nonetheless distinct from the clean sweat of sport. In these rudimentary distinctions lies room for more research. Most smells and the fine distinctions between them are missed by human consciousness. We do not know how conscious they are in infancy, but they appear powerful. In later life it appears that at an unconscious level they are received and partially processed, and that in some instances they can penetrate consciousness as a "feeling." Thus Arlie Hochschild notes that women who avoid rape in dangerous areas at key times differ from victims in their "trust of feelings."[22] What we call smell may be merely input, but like all information, there is a limit to what can be placed in storage and processed without driving the organism mad. But the information registered via smell can only be conveyed to consciousness when it can be named and translated into conceptual, linguistic information. In this conveyance lies the hit-or-miss origins of affects as well as feelings.

The need for transliteration is downgraded in a psychical economy that blinds itself to information from the other by any such connecting means. In this same economy, the ego moreover has no control over what it gives off by way of information, anymore than it has control over what it receives. But the more conscious we become of what we repress (remembering here that primary repression is the repression of unprocessed sensory information) or ignore, the less we think in projected and judgmental terms, the less consciousness is drowned in the swamp of affects. But such conscious consciousness is only possible when we invent or reinvent the words to say it. The transliteration into language from the minutia of sensory knowledge and its sifting may be processes entirely unknown to consciousness at present; the lifting of affective and projected judgments may be felt only as a sense of openness to others and a renewed ability to learn, but it marks the beginning of something more. Extending conscious sensation, finding the words or images, means grasping the nuances of fleshly grammar and alphabets. It means describing and accounting for those sensations, which entails translating them into the everyday currencies of speech and so extending the range of their visualization. What is repressed is not available to consciousness. It is withheld knowledge, something that is only available to whatever it is that represses it. This thing and its repressions present themselves as the disordered flesh, when it fact the thing and its repressions are the occasion of that disorder. Disorder is not inherent in the body or the flesh, which loves regulation. The body thrives in health when its real needs are respected, as distinct from the ego's imaginary anxieties.

When the mystic St. Bernard of Clairvaux talks of love, he talks of it as a regulating force for the body's relation with the soul and the mind.[23] Regulation by love means working with the interweaving logical, living chains of association, which, taken together, ensure continuity of life. Regulation is the negotiation within and between the individual organisms that thrive in those chains, but its negotiations are disrupted when any one organism takes more than its due. Ultimately, only human beings have the free will to do this in any way that seriously distorts the living logic.[24] That is what free will is: the ability not to go with the flow. But it is also the means for coming to consciousness of that divine will, the living logic that interweaves. How does one align oneself with the will that interweaves? As Spinoza said, by studying it. By extending environmental knowledge of the chains of life supporting the human body. By extending awareness of and capacity to translate or transliterate information of the body's codes. Analysts say that all things are known in the unconscious, and they are right. Furthermore, they have given us the clues as to what it is that makes us unconscious of all things, not as a necessary adjunct to our distinct survival but as something withheld rather than preconscious. What is repressed is precisely not available to consciousness. It is withheld knowledge.

It is not the body that produces disorder. It is the inclinations and the moods. It is, in short, the affects. But why are their consuming desires seen as desires of the flesh, *tout court*, when they only serve the psyche? The psyche is, of course, also a physical or embodied thing. This has to be so if one accepts the premise that the psychical actually gets into the flesh, whether it is manifest as the inertia of depression, or as an actual psychosomatic illness, or in other ways, such as anger. It is these embodied psychical urges, these constellations of affects, that lead us to eat the wrong way, do the wrong things, push ourselves for the wrong reason, and so forth. My point is twofold. These urges while material, intentional, psychical, and physical, are in conflict with the body's own real interests insofar as we may define reality as health (all that is real is rational, and what is rational is the furtherance of the body's good, which means necessarily the good of its environment). The body or the flesh as such is not the uniform opponent of the spirit. The body has divided interests. Its subject-centered psychical urges take it away from its good health and toward dissolution. Other urges nudge it toward that which increases its sense of long-term well-being, well-being that can also be felt in the short term. On the face of it, the psychical urges conflicting with the environmental body's real interests can be traced to the negative affects. Chief among these, perhaps, is anxiety, a key stressor and prompter of the desire for things that are bad for us or others (including all the components of the biosphere whose regulations are linked indissolubly to the regulations governing our own bodies' well-being).

When one has knowledge of what is good and bad for the body, the wholesale denigration of the flesh becomes an obstacle in the way of uniting mind and physical being. It makes sense only when accompanied by a cultural ignorance of the body's—that is, the embodied mind's—requirements. Learning to distinguish between what is good and bad for the body in its environmental context, learning to have pleasure in foods that increase its health and joy in activities that do the same—these things are also part of the modern way in the West now. They mark out how, once again, practice marches ahead of theory. Once again, the body is there before the slower ego consciousness gets it, in this as in other respects.

The ego, in turn, at least in part is a vehicle for distorting our place in the scheme of things, and it does this most effectively when we have no idea any longer of what that place is. It does this through comparison, which in turn predisposes the ego to collect other negative affects. As we have also seen, these affects stem from and embody the principle of fixation, which institutes and maintains the arrangement of energy from one's own standpoint, an arrangement that interrupts, severs, and diverts the energy arranged by the creative laws of life. Moreover, arranging energy from one's own standpoint splits the experience of cognition from its physical correlates. Henceforth, our thinking seems immaterial. Extending attention into the body reverses this as it unlocks the energy fixed in diverting images and other visual associations and realigns it with the logical pathways connecting reason and feeling. Here again it is the very opposite of subject/object thought. The "object" becomes actively involved in the sensing process of pursuing alignments between codes, while the "subject" seeks to link thinking to sensation, to have it vibrate with energy, to pursue a logical path wherever it leads, undiverted by self-interest and its associated anxieties. If in the end this means recognizing that the body and its actions have always been ahead of the slow calculations of reflective consciousness, then may we concede with grace. If it means realizing that the flesh our veiled consciousness has learned to despise is faster, more intelligent, and more alive than the "consciousness" that claims credit for its inspiration, even as it gropes around for words, then may we be delighted at what we have in store to learn.

What has occluded this recognition of the body's primary intelligence (the logics embedded in systems such as the DNA code, as distinct from the embedded affects that intensify disorder) are the affects. They do this both through the stumbling blocks they place in the way of reasoning and through the foundational fantasy's hallucinatory understanding of form as something distinct and imposed from above, which fantasy also has effects on intellectual work.[25] When the imposition was recognized for what it is, when the idea of a suprasensible and subject-centered God was deconstructed for the fiction it is, the deconstruction accepted the terms resulting from the splitting of mind and body, individual and environment. Deconstruction, poststructuralism, and Lacanianism alike accept these terms insofar as they deny the embodied logic of the flesh. They deny it whenever they claim—however tacitly—that humans are nonetheless more intelligent than the hand that interweaves the life drive. Their intellects are already bowed down by the affects that cut them off from the feeling, discerning apparatus that otherwise links language with sensation. But in consequence of their narcissistic denial (itself a product of an ego thickening with negative affects), they have been unable to conceive of a source of meaning independent of the subject, and misunderstand the atemporal logic of signification—divorced from the logic of other living chains—as arbitrary. Just as intelligence was considered supraordinate to flesh, so was form conceived of as an external addition or imposition. Form is not considered inherent to matter, except as a potentiality at best. One of the descendents of this predilection to view matter as a mess is the trend to objectification in psychology and biology, which have proceeded on the basis that it is best to make people as much like objects as possible in order to be able to study them in controlled and replicable ways. We know more about human capacities at their most mechanistic than we do about those capacities at their most refined.[26]

It is plain from this study of the affects that anything that takes account of systems and codes is to be preferred to biological studies that isolate entities from their context and place. Knowledge that uncovers even a small strand of the logic of life is more likely to aid consciousness in attending to and learning to work with sensation, learning how to realign word and affect in the process, increasing the precision of its feelings, and uncovering the true joys of the flesh. This is what the resurrection of the body means. There is no waving a magic wand, however strong the wish for a magical religion. There is much research and the invention of new practices for regulating the relation between the body and the physical mind.

In *Globalization and Its Terrors* I have discussed bioregulation, an idea that presupposes that the body has its own natural cycles of regulation—sleep, eating, and so forth—and bio-deregulation, the notion that interfering with these cycles by pushing too hard on any one system in oneself or others means abusing free will. The health-conscious middle-class knows that when the body is fed certain things and given exercise, even though the exercise and the healthy food may go against one's inclination, the whole being does better in body and mood. One also knows that the inclination to consume often gains control of whatever faculty it is that governs ingestion and activity. The fact that we want what is not good for us as bodies suggests that the body has been mistakenly cast as the enemy in the received understanding of Christian ascetic thought, although mystics of Christian and other faiths discern that the opposite is true. Nothing is more material than mysticism. Through sustaining living attention by concentration, the mystic enters into a timeless state that eventually yields an experience that is evidently sensual and spiritual.[27] It seems in this experience that the soul attains its desire of union with the body, and it does so through the regulation of its passions, thoughts, and feelings. The descriptions of this union can be read as forms of hysteria. But they are rather attempts at putting an extraordinary experience—capturing some part of the union of spirit and sensuality that was lost with the fall into a divided mind and body—into the feeble form of recollected words. Inevitably, humans will understand what is new by trying to gather it back into the categories informed by their own experience. If we have not experienced the union of sense and soul, we will read the descriptions of it as somewhat hysterical, when in fact these writings are describing something yet to come to us or be found by us. The uninterrupted harmony of mind and flesh is the reverse of hysterical disorder but may easily be mistaken for it by those who have experienced neither.[28]

The mistake is made readily in a world where psyches (or souls) are seen as self-contained entities rather than known as expressions of intentions that struggle within them. But that eventual understanding may be the gift of the Age of Reason to the resurrection of the body. As the philosopher Quentin Skinner shows, the founding philosopher of individualism, Thomas Hobbes, at first believed that reason could assert itself against the claims of self-interest. Hobbes also knew that true wisdom is the reasoned link between sense "and the proper use [deductive ordering] of names in Language," and he believed in the strength of the process in the face of the passions.[29] When he lost faith in wisdom, it was because he believed that the succession of passions that pass through us are entirely endogenous. Creatures who conjure up all the negative affects within themselves are as dislikable as Hobbes assumes them to be. Yet Hobbes also knew that these distorting affects could be conjured up by the art of *amplificatio*, which leads "a man . . . [to] sensibly feeleth smart and damage, when he feeleth none."[30] The thing that fractures individual reason, by this account, is no more individual than the living attention that supplies the soul with the means to make deductions, deductions modeled—in method—on the logic of the flesh of which the soul, as the principle of organization, is part. Crowds may be swayed against their reason by indignation and pity but only when individual self-interest captures their intentionality, directing them to condemn or uphold without thought. Both emotions invite us to judge, to pour scorn, or to identify. In doing so, they assert the claims of short-term material concerns against the conclusions of reason or loving intelligence. Against this, in the Hobbesian world where only force will restrain self-interest, reason is all that constrains affect, apart from fear. If one concludes, as Hobbes did for a time, that reason is a weak force because its voice is soft, this is due to the drowning of reason and deduction in the isolation of a psyche (or soul) that believes its affects are self-contained.[31] In such a psyche, where we hold ourselves responsible for all the intentions that claim us in thought, even when we halt their mobility in deed, the strength of organization and loving intelligence are underestimated. But once it is known that this reasoned logic lives still, independently of the subjects whose individualism led them to claim it as their own, then its strength grows in argument. From the burden of individual self-absorption comes the interest in directing attention around and through the very structures that produce that self-absorption in the first place, releasing affects via the conscious exploration of their sedimentation. Extending attention into the flesh is simultaneously an exploration of the affects that have captured both individual souls as well as crowds of souls, and in this exploration there is an acknowledgement and a coming to terms with what the ages of reason and individualism have excluded from consciousness. This is the connection, affectively and energetically, to other living and dead things, the connection to the living logos and to the thing that misdirects affects and energies toward destruction.

The few deep breaths taken by Kant's angry man represent the rudiments and the beginning of a vastly more extensive and conscious knowledge of bodily processes. For instance, it is known that interference with parasympathetic regulation by anxiety or other negative affects (for instance anger, or the inverted anger and anxiety of depression) can be lessened by the attempt at conscious regulation involved in attentive breathing. It is also known that the most advanced practitioners of some forms of yoga are capable of regulating areas traditionally under the control of the autonomic or parasympathetic nervous system, such as the regulation of heart rate. As these practices are brought into alignment with their simultaneous intellectual exploration, we may yet understand what Spinoza meant by knowledge as the pathway to becoming one again with God. Such knowledge rushes ahead when it has the unimpeded strength of the life drive, also known as love, aiding it. That strength is dissipated by splits that divert its energies into negative affects, sometimes briefly energetic, more often turned inward, blocking concentration and motion.

As and when the extension of conscious understanding comes to be known as the resurrection of the body, it will be because of its relation to the purgative environmental judgment we are inflicting on ourselves at present. As the biosphere and species are destroyed, and human quality of life is degraded, the owl of Minerva points to the natural laws governing and regulating the survival of what has been or is being destroyed. One learns what a necessary condition of life was as that condition ceases to exist. This diabolic experiment with the earth and its creatures reveals how individual human organisms depend like other organic life on the diversity of the whole biosphere. The nascent learning of human bodily codes takes place in this context and should extend to a knowledge of how those codes intersect with those of other living things in a mutually sustaining endeavor. If we reverse course in the face of the judgment we bring on ourselves and start to work with rather than against the natural cycles of regulation, that work can coincide with and build on the exploration of bodily processes hitherto cut off from conscious regulation. That exploration needs to begin at the youngest possible age. We are not taught our bodily codes at the age we most need to learn them (childhood) but only stumble on them if we are fortunate in later life: too late to open up the whole brain to the translation into consciousness of all that bodily information, coded in languages we have yet to understand.

This distinction between the living and the dead, and the idea that humankind is following a direction that works against life rather than for it, does not only depend on a few erratic hormones. In fact, evidence from alterations wrought environmentally for economic gain gives a clearer picture of this anti-life direction than that which can be gleaned through knowledge of the human body (at this point). But where such economic actions evidently work against the reproduction of the living by increasing the percentage of dead matter in relation to living energy, the decay of the body is supposed to be an entirely natural thing, although it is recognized that aging can be exacerbated by anxiety and its derivatives. Now I have argued that, just as economically generated entropy overlays a process of physically determined inertia, so too does a socially and psychically constructed inertia accelerate the natural wearing down of the human body. The difficulties in perceiving the actions of this deathly force within result from the assumption that human beings are biologically impervious to direction from without. We have established that insofar as human beings are affected by entrainment, and insofar as such entrainment is a material, chemical, and electrical affair, we do not follow our own intentional paths as a matter of course. We are interrupted by other intentions, affects that seek their aim in ends to which we are often incidental. An affect of anger can attach itself (in theory) to a thought whose entertainment by conscious attention gives the affect a new home, cuddled up with old angers nursed in repressed knots of self-interest. When this occurs, our paths are interrupted to greater or lesser degrees, just as they were interrupted by the initial hallucinations that caused the first repressions. To this, I have objected that without those repressions, we would not exist. In which case, talk of one's own path, whether it is shaped by the genes or the soul, is irrelevant. Against this, I have supposed that the ability to dissect the ego is indicative of another organizational center in the mind. The nature of that center (and whether it is anything other than the life drive's organizational impulse) remains to be discussed, together with the relation (if any) between the organism's distinctive path and that of living nature overall. But it may be that we will find out more about this center as we cease to live in the unreal but three-dimensional world of the negative affects, and live instead in the energy of life.

In this book I have concentrated on the transmission and formation of the negative affects rather than the nature of the organizing soul or "other I" consciousness, assuming that the education of the precisely proprioceptive senses, and the practice of discernment will reveal more of their nature as they cease to labor under the weight of the ego's direction. But even without an understanding of that other consciousness, this analysis of the negative affects enables us to begin to slough off the skins that stand in the way of its emergence, leading it in the wrong direction. This direction, the common direction of the ego, presents itself to us as "me" and "my interests." It stakes its claims on our attention on the grounds of personal threat, and by this means leads us to act in ways that threaten others. The affects that accomplish this are negative, and they are transmitted from one to another whenever they are not resisted. They foster short-term self-interest but lead to death in the long run.

The significance of these findings on affects is that they bring the devil down to earth. He is nothing, a hollow core, an inert lump. But this hollow core attracts and gathers wells of negative affect around it. The idea of wells of negative affect is material, and because it is material, it can be countered materially as well. It can be countered without reference to the hysteria that is the stock-in-trade of those who spread the contagion of negative affects, expressed as affects often are in the phenomena of persecution and judgment. It can be countered by a shift from a metaphysical paradigm downward into the physical, which would lead us back naturally to the point where philosophy began. Then we will know how the form-giving capacity inheres in the very nature of energetic matter, now as it always has done. We will feel it and know in a united body and soul that the matrix was never, and is never, passive; it is simultaneously active and receptive, intelligent and substantial, as giver of life.

If it yet seems that with the resurrection of the body, I have resurrected the specter of demons to be struggled against and overthrown, this is also true. But once it is recognized that these demons are familiar affective patterns that can be undone, that these affects can be countered whenever we refuse them entry, once, in short, that they are understood as forces in human affairs that can be cleaned up and transformed, converted back into living energy as they are released from distorting blocks of inertia and repression, then they have no power to whip up the superstition, anger, and anxiety that prevail when their capabilities are inflated. They have power only when we see them, hear them, think them, as well as smell and touch and taste them—and then grant them admission. Their power to torment us exists only as long as we permit it to exist. It is our living energy these demons thrive on, and it is only theirs when diverted through ignorance from the drive to love and create into the pathways of conquest, war, exploitation, and death. Of that we cannot speak, thereof we must learn.

Notes

1. Introduction

1. In many cases the clues to transmission are multisensorial, as we read affects in others by multisensorial means. For instance, one is aware of stress in the other because its onset produces contraction in the skeletal muscles. At the same time as the muscles contract, the hypothalamus sends chemical messengers to the pituitary gland to release hormones into the bloodstream (and these may be released into the atmosphere via connections with other hormones). As muscles tense, breathing becomes faster and deeper, the heartbeat quickens, blood pressure rises, throat and nostril muscles expand these passages, perspiration increases, and the pupils of the eyes dilate involuntarily. Certainly, many of these acute reactions can be seen by the eye. But there are also unseen actions with potential effects on the other, in terms of smell and touch and voice tones, as multitudinous chemical responses are unleashed throughout the brain and body.

2. Lynn Smith-Lovin's historical review of the study of affects in sociology sums up: "The sociology of affect and emotion is theoretically rich but short on empirical evidence. Most of our knowledge about affect and emotion comes from research in other disciplines or substantive areas. Much of this research developed independently of the sociological theories of emotion and takes on new relevance when viewed in this perspective." Lynn Smith-Lovin, "The Sociology of Affect and Emotion" in *Sociological Perspectives on Social Psychology*, ed. Karen Cook, Gary Alan Fine, and James Hanse (Boston: Allyn and Bacon, 1995), 135. Just how much "new relevance" is only now beginning to emerge.

3. See the discussion of countertransference in chapter 2.

4. "Emotions do not form a natural class. A set of distinctions that has generally haunted the philosophy of mind stands in the way of giving good

descriptions of the phenomena. We have inherited distinctions between being active and being passive; between psychological states that are primarily explained by physical processes and psychological states not reducible to nor adequately explained by physical processes; distinctions between states that are primarily nonrational and those that are either rational or irrational; between voluntary and nonvoluntary states. Once these distinctions were drawn, types of psychological activities were then parceled out en bloc to one or another side of the dichotomies. That having been done, the next step was to argue reclassification: to claim that perception is not passive but active, or that the imagination has objective as well as subjective rules of association. Historically, the list of emotions has expanded as a result of these controversies. For instance, the opponents of Hobbes, wanting to secure benevolence, sympathy, and other disinterested attitudes as counterbalances of self-interest, introduced them as sentiments with motivational power. Passions became emotions and were classified as activities. When the intentionality of emotions was discussed, the list expanded still further: ressentiment, aesthetic and religious awe, anxiety and dread were included. Emotions became affects or attitudes." Amélie Rorty, "Explaining Emotions," in *Explaining Emotions*, ed. Amélie Oksenberg Rorty (Berkeley: University of California Press, 1980), 104–5. Rorty goes on to describe the historical logic that produced the gradations from the overarching category of emotions and/or affects to "motives," "feelings," "moods," and "traits."

5. Aristotle, *On Rhetoric*. As Susan James shows in *Passion and Action: The Emotions in Seventeenth-Century Philosophy* (Oxford: Clarendon, 1997), these categories persist. Early modern writers are divided between those who follow the Aristotelian enumeration, and those who adopt Cicero's structuring of four fundamental passions: distress (*aegritudo*), pleasure (*laetitia*), fear (*metus*), and desire (*libido*). Like the desire for a supposed good (*libido*), apprehension (*metus*) refers to the future or the past, not the present. By contrast, *laetitia* and *aegritudo* are responses to present joy or evil.

6. As James R. Averill writes, "Emotions can be treated as actions . . . [as they] are directed toward some goal (i.e., have objects), occur in concrete situations, are normatively regulated, and involve some expenditure of energy (physiologically speaking). . . . The emotions consist of related but semiautonomous elements—cognitive, behavioral, and physiological. . . . On the biological level, for example, the focus might be on physiological elements and their relationship to other subsystems of the organism, such as the cardiovascular system. On the social level, one might focus on those aspects of emotional responses which involve the interaction among individuals and their relationship to certain institutions. . . . Similar considerations apply to the personality and cultural levels of analysis" (James R. Averill, "Emotion and Anxiety: Determinants," in *Explaining Emotions*, 50).

7. Smith-Lovin, "Sociology of Affect," 135–36.

8. Amélie Rorty notes that some but not all emotions can be described as "feelings, associated with proprioceptive states" ("Explaining Emotions,"

106–8). See also Magda B. Arnold, *Emotion and Personality*, 2 vols. (New York: Columbia, 1960).

9. Rorty, "Explaining Emotions." See also Smith-Lovin, 135–36.

10. Thus Averill's remark (note 6 above) that emotions involve the "expenditure of [physiological] energy."

11. Using Freud's postulate that depression is anger turned inward as a jumping off point, the scientific research shows a correlation between clinical depression (particularly in women) and chronic exposure to the anger of others, that is, abusive and/or alcoholic partners. See chapter 2.

12. In a related disorder, fibromyalgia syndrome, "compared with patients with rheumatoid arthritis, those with fibromyalgia had significantly higher lifetime prevalence rates of all forms of victimization, both adult and childhood, as well as a combination of adult and childhood trauma. . . . Sexual, physical, and emotional traumas may be important factors in the development and maintenance of this disorder (FMS) and its associated disability in patients." E. A. Walker, D. Keegan, and G. Gardner, et al., "Psychosocial Factors in Fibromyalgia Compared with Rheumatoid Arthritis: II. Sexual, Physical and Emotional Abuse and Neglect," *Psychosomatic Medicine* 59 (1997): 572–77.

13. The relation between endogenous and transitory, historically acquired and transmitted affects will concern us again in chapters 4 and 6.

14. I was going to add "private in our experience of pain," but then realized that despite the emphasis on the privacy of pain, from Wittgenstein's account of the "beetle" onward, this was deeply misleading. I would hazard that people are never more alike than when they are in the grip of pain, just as, and for the same reason, they are never more similar than when their egos, rather than whatever makes them distinctive, is foregrounded. Whatever makes them distinctive, it is certainly not the ego. By my argument, we are never more alike than when we are in the grip of an affect of the ego. But why should pain be a common thing, just as the ego's dynamics of triumph and humiliation (and, as Lacan puts it, "posturing, ostentation, negation, and lying") are also similar? (Only the content differs, and there is usually not much difference in that.) Pain is a response of the sympathetic nervous system, and, after all, each body has its own. Nonetheless, as we shall see, the phenomenon of entrainment encroaches directly on perceptual registration, through sight and hearing and the modulated frequencies involved in both. Perception in turn impinges directly on, and to a large degree is, the sympathetic nervous system. If entrainment means that certain responses are transmitted from person to person, or from the social order and social pressure to all people, then it would be fair to assert that the experience of pain, like anxiety, can be at least inflected if not produced in the same way. It is well known that anxiety "increases" pain, which leads me to wonder if pain and anxiety are not in some way of the same genus, both composed of the same nerve-racking stuff. It is also fairly well known that the registration of pain in humans is dramatically dysfunctional. The registration and intensity of pain continues beyond that necessary to alert the nervous system

about the risk to life or limb. We might consider here that the ego, as the agency of perception, and as the conscious registration of the surface of the body (as Freud insisted it was) is also tied to, and to some degree is, the central nervous system. If socially produced and transmitted anxiety, and hypothetically, socially exacerbated pain, affect the ego in similar ways in the same social formation, then they must also affect the central nervous system. This in turn would mean that pain in some social formations is a more intense experience than it is in others. It should also mean that pain will be strongest wherever the ego is strongest. And in case it appears that I have wandered too far down the road of speculation, we might consider how these speculations bear on a range of facts, from the inexplicable way in which pain in childbirth seems more intense for Englishwomen than Scandinavians (obviously female) in a well-known study, to why it is that Americans, inhabiting the heartland of the ego, often seem to those from other cultures to be hypochondriacal in their experience and fear of pain.

15. Amélie Rorty explains: "Sometimes our emotions change straightaway when we learn that what we believed is not true. The grieving husband recovers when he learns that, because she missed her plane, his wife did not die in the fatal plane crash. But often changes in emotions do not appropriately follow changes in belief. Their tenacity, their inertia, suggest that there is akrasia [a state of mind in which one acts against one's better judgment] of the emotions; it reveals the complex structure of their intentionality. . . . [These are] cases of unexpected conservation of emotions: those that seem to conflict with a person's judgment and those that appear to have distorted our perceptions and beliefs, making them uncharacteristically resistant to change or correction" (Rorty, "Explaining Emotions," 103).

16. But whether this results in a continuity of affective disposition is uncertain. People change, as many a divorce appellant has argued, and where the "affections are alienated" the flesh has at the most significant level been split asunder. In certain circumstances, such changes are the result, perhaps, of the severance of a hitherto connecting affective thread: this could be attentive or loving, hence protective or life enhancing, or depleting.

17. The case against reductionism (and for physical changes in the brain effected by the environment) is developed in Colin Blakemore, "How the Environment Helps to Build the Brain," in *Mind, Brain, and Environment: The Linacre Lectures*, ed. Bryan Cartledge (Oxford: Oxford University Press, 1980), 51–54.

18. This may be mob mentality, workplace morale, or Durkheim's "ritual arousal of ecstasy." See Émile Durkheim, *The Elementary Forms of Religious Life*, trans. Karen E. Fields (New York: Free Press, 1995).

19. It has now been established that menstrual synchrony is the result of pheromonal factors. (See the discussion in chapter 3.) Pheromones are also used in the marking of territory and delineating of hierarchical structures.

20. The term "responsiveness" might be better than "entrainment" where responses are opposed or complementary.

21. Just in the area of stress alone there are many hormones. The adrenal

glands release two, epinephrine and norepinephrine; the pituitary gland secretes thyroid-stimulating hormone (TSH) and adrenocorticotropic hormone (ACTH), which between them signal the body to produce about thirty (and still counting) more. There are hundreds of hormones altogether, and more are being discovered.

22. D. Chen and J. Haviland-Jones, "Rapid Mood Change and Human Odours," *Physiology and Behaviour* 68 (Dec. 1–15, 1999): 241–50. This is a particularly clear-cut example of how the social environment shapes the affects.

23. "Smell is the most direct of all our senses. . . . Each day we breathe about 23,040 times and move around 438 cubic feet of air. It takes us about five seconds to breathe—two seconds to inhale and three to exhale—and in that time, molecules of odor flood through our systems. . . . Unlike the other senses, smell needs no interpreter. The effect is immediate and undiluted by language, thought, or translation." Diane Ackerman, *A Natural History of the Senses* (New York: Vintage, 1991), 6–11.

24. There is a difference between an open, receptive vision and the gaze by which one projects. This open or receptive vision is also at the heart of John Drury's *Painting the Word: Christian Pictures and Their Meanings* (New Haven: Yale University Press, 1999). One sees one way, open to what there is; the other way, one's seeing accords with the dictates of social pressure, which closes one's eyes.

25. This example is based on James Gilligan's outstanding analysis of the causes of violence, in turn based on his psychiatric work with prisoners. Gilligan identifies being "dissed" or "disrespected" as the most common factor provoking violence; that is to say, violence (this is also true of social violence or "rudeness") is a response to insulted pride or wounded ego. James Gilligan, *Violence: Our Deadly Epidemic and Its Causes* (New York: G. P. Putnam, 1996).

26. The expectation that the mother should be available to the infant day and night is historically specific and recent. For instance, in France after the Revolution, there were new expectations of "republican motherhood." Mothers are meant to breastfeed and to care for their infants with loving attention. Putting a less attractive gloss on this, one might say that the mother is now meant to be available full time for dumping. I suspect that the famous guilt of motherhood is also historically specific, and that guilt is the experience of the other's projected judgment as well as an invitation to be judged. See Joan Copjec, "Vampires, Breastfeeding, and Anxiety," in *Read My Desire: Lacan against the Historicists* (Cambridge: MIT Press, 1994).

27. Jane Caputi writes, "Violence is both the paradigmatic means of 'proving manhood' and the last resort of those without other forms of social power to accomplish that end. As [James] Gilligan understands it, men who suffer shame due to a recurring loss of manhood—a loss occasioned by a variety of factors, including social insignificance, failure at work, inability to control the women in their lives, depression, poverty, racism, personal victimization by other men—tend to act out violently, transferring their shame and sense of insignificance to their victims, most frequently women or men

who are made to serve as women." Jane Caputi, " 'Take Back What Doesn't Belong to Me': Sexual Violence, Resistance, and the 'Transmission of Affect,' " *Women's Studies International Forum* 929, no. 1 (2002): 1–14.

28. See introduction and chapter 1 in my *Interpretation of the Flesh: Freud and Femininity* (London: Routledge, 1992).

29. R. D. Laing, *Self and Others* (New York: Pantheon, 1969).

30. Daniel Stern, *The Motherhood Constellation* (New York: Basic Books, 1995).

31. "The full body without organs is produced as antiproduction, that is to say it intervenes within the process as such for the sole purpose of rejecting any attempt to impose on it any sort of triangulation implying that it was produced by parents. How could this body have been produced by parents, when by its very nature it is such eloquent witness of its own self-production, of its own engendering of itself? And it is precisely here on this body, right where it is, that the Numen is distributed and disjunctions are established, independent of any sort of projection. Yes, I have been my father and I have been my son." Gilles Deleuze and Felix Guattari, *Anti-Oedipus: Capitalism and Schizophrenia*, trans. Robert Hurley, Mark Seem, and Helen R. Lane (London: Athlone Press, 1984), 15.

32. ". . . 18.8 million adult Americans (or about 9.5% of the U.S. population age 18 and older) have a depressive disorder. Depression is also the leading cause of disability in the US and established market economies worldwide." National Institute of Mental Health, "The Numbers Count" (Bethesda, Md.: NIMH, Jan. 2001).

33. "Living in a piecemeal and accelerated space and time, he often has trouble acknowledging his own physiognomy; left without a sexual, subjective, or moral identity, this amphibian is a being of boundaries, a borderline, or a 'false self'—a body that acts often, without even the joys of such performative drunkenness." Julia Kristeva, *New Maladies of the Soul* (New York: Columbia University Press, 1995), 7.

34. I am curious here as to whether antidepressants work by a kind of redirection, a shifting away from the self, of the molecules embodying depression. But no one appears to know precisely how antidepressants work, although it is known that neurotransmitters such as serotonin are involved in depression and its relief. Currently, these are studied in terms of levels rather than directions, as per the discussion in chapter 4.

35. "More than just a commodity or a new variant of the 'opium of the people,' the current transformation of psychic life may foreshadow a new humanity, one whose psychological conveniences will be able to overcome metaphysical anxiety and the need for meaning. Wouldn't it be great to be satisfied with just a pill and a television screen? The problem is that the path of such a superman is strewn with traps. A wide variety of troubles can bring new patients to the analyst's couch: sexual and relationship difficulties, somatic symptoms, a difficulty in expressing oneself, and a general malaise caused by a language experienced as 'artificial,' 'empty,' or 'mechanical.' These patients often resemble 'traditional' analysands, but 'mal-

adies of the soul' soon break through their hysterical and obsessional al-
lure—'maladies of the soul' that are not necessarily psychoses, but that
evoke the psychotic patient's ability to symbolize his unbearable trauma"
(Kristeva, *New Maladies*, 8–9).

36. For a more detailed discussion, see my *Exhausting Modernity: Grounds
for a New Economy* (London: Routledge, 2000).

37. James, *Passion and Action*, 119.

38. Michel de Montaigne, *Essays*, trans. J. M. Cohen (London: Penguin,
1958), 36.

39. Michel de Montaigne: "Il lui dit que c'en était l'un [de] me donner occasion de me plaire en sa compagnie, et que fichant ses yeux sur la fraîcheur
de mon visage et sa pensée sur cette [ga]ie allégresse et vigueur qui re-
gorgeait de mon adolescence, et remplissant tous ses sens se cet état fleuris-
sant en quoi j'étais, son habitude s'en pourrait amender. Mais il oubliait à
dire que la mienne s'en pourrait empirer aussi." Michel de Montaigne, *Es-
sais 1*, ed. André Tournon (Paris: Nationale Edition, 1998), 180.

40. If we inquire into how the idea that we are self-contained came about,
then ontologically as well as phylogenetically, we find that vision is critical.
At the individual level, it is the priority given to hallucination in the formation of the individual that is significant. In infancy, hallucination and fantasy are the key tools for inventing a world that is other than the dependent
world of reality. In adult life, such fantasies are aided by visual media.

41. Anthony Smith, *The Body* (London: George Allen and Unwin, 1970), 387.

42. Although this status remains questionable. "People who think they
have perfect vision should think again. From blind spots to smearing of images, human sight is flawed to a great extent, according to research [pre-
sented by J. Kevin O'Regan, director of research for the National Center for
Scientific Research in France] at the fourth 'Toward a Science of Consciousness' conference [in April 2000]." In light of the discoveries, O'Regan com-
mented on the potential veracity of Plato's comment that "vision was not as
reliable as the sense of touch." Blake Smith, "Great Vision? Think Again,"
Arizona Daily Wildcat, April 11, 2000.

43. This is a paradox, as the one most susceptible to the transmission of affect fulfills a social function by bearing the unwanted affects. Consider the
concept of the scapegoat. Originally, this was an actual goat that carried the
sins of the city upon itself and was placed beyond the city walls. One could
also invoke an issue of justice here. If the one who is susceptible to the transmission of affects is susceptible to negative affects, he or she is the likely victim of dumping. The one who is stigmatized is the one who maintains the
"boundaries" of the other.

44. This conceptualization means denying the common-sense experience of
affects and emotions as personal and particular. So powerful are our convictions in this respect, so real does our experience of ourselves as emotionally
distinct subjects seem, that one form of thought (here termed cognition), as
well as perception, is structured in terms of subject and object. The object
does not feel. We do.

45. These experiments are mentioned in the notes to chapter 4.

46. This is both right and not right. It is right in that the complex or cognitive affects mentioned so far have elements of simple violence as well as the complex selection of an object. But these more simple elements, which Freud more or less called drives, may well be affects in search of an object. On the other hand, the complex affects, as Aristotle noted, all presuppose an object, insofar as they all express an attitude or inclination toward that object. The Kantian notion of an inclination is the key to the distinctive origin of the cognitive affects, but it does not of itself preclude their gathering in simple affects, such as rage or fear or nameless anxiety.

47. See *Exhausting Modernity*; see also Teresa Brennan, "Social Pressure," *American Imago* (September 1997): 210–34.

48. See my *Globalization and Its Terrors: Everyday Life in the West* (London: Routledge, 2002).

2. The Transmission of Affect in the Clinic

1. Brennan, *Exhausting Modernity*.

2. Teresa Brennan, *The Interpretation of the Flesh: Freud and Femininity* (London: Routledge 1992).

3. Emil Kraepelin (1856–1926), *Memoirs* (New York: Springer-Verlag, 1987), 7. The impressions were so strong that Kraepelin thought of leaving the practice of psychiatry.

4. Richard M. Restak, "Possible Neurophysiological Correlates of Empathy," in *Empathy*, ed. Joseph Lichtenberg, vol. 1 (New Jersey: Analytic Press, 1984).

5. Paula Heimann, "On Counter-Transference," *International Journal of Psychoanalysis* 31 (1950): 81–4.

6. Phyllis Grosskurth, *Melanie Klein: Her World and Her Work* (New York: Knopf, 1986).

7. Mabel Cohen, *Advances in Psychiatry: Recent Developments in Interpersonal Relations* (New York: Norton, 1959), 77.

8. Darlene Bregman Ehrenberg, *The Intimate Edge: Extending the Reach of Psychoanalytic Interaction* (New York: Norton, 1992).

9. Christopher Bollas, *The Shadow of the Object: The Psychoanalysis of the Unthought Known* (New York: Columbia University Press, 1989), 58–59.

10. Ibid., 189.

11. Ibid., 214.

12. Harold Searles, *Countertransference and Related Subjects: Selected Papers* (Madison, Conn.: Psychosocial Press, 1999), 210–11.

13. Projective identification did not mean this when Klein introduced the term in her great 1946 paper on splitting. It meant, strictly, the identification (in the sense of the lodgment) of a split-off part of oneself in the other, effected by the force of projection. It did not entail a simultaneous identification with the other's projection (which is what it has come to mean). As we

have already seen, Klein disliked the new conceptualization of counter-transference. While I think her idea of projective identification was about one aspect of countertransference, the transmission of affect is also the crude and transitory picking up of an "idea in the air," the communication that we find in groups.

14. See Caputi, "Sexual Violence."

15. See Lawrence DiStasi, *Mal Occhio, the Underside of Vision* (San Francisco: North Point Press, 1981).

16. See R. D. Laing, *Self and Others* (New York: Pantheon Books, 1969).

17. It is the abstract cast of Bion's argument that makes much of his work difficult to process. Lacan can be difficult for the same reason. For instance, in Lacan's theory we are told that language severs the imaginary dyad be-tween child and mother and marks the entry into recognition of the state of lack that clinging to the imaginary avoids. If we suppose that the imaginary dyad consists of sensory connections such as those that convey knowledge by smell, then the idea that these connections are "severed" by language be-comes more concrete. I would even hazard that further research on the brain will reveal a decrease in the sense of smell coinciding with the advent of lan-guage.

18. Bion quoted in León Grinberg, Dario Sor, and Elizabeth Tabak de Bianchedi, *Introduction to the Work of Bion: Groups, Knowledge, Psychosis, Thought, Transformations, Psychoanalytic Practice* (New York: J. Aronson, 1977), 188.

19. For an argument that love and living attention are the same thing, see my *Interpretation of the Flesh*, and below, chapters 4 and 7.

20. The difference between Laplanche's argument and mine (which was de-veloped contemporaneously) is that I have located the transmission of the "unconscious" of the other within an intersubjective economy of affects and energy, in which transmission occurs as a matter of course. In addition, I see transmission as pertaining primarily to energetic affects (for which I have reserved the term "imprint") and, moreover, working within an interactive dynamic in which the infant resists that imprint because it is felt as restric-tive, and in which the living attention of the other also alleviates the sense of restriction.

21. And it is a theory of the transmission of affect that is demanded, for fan-tasies cannot be divorced from affects.

22. Daniel Stern addresses the relation of the object and the affect in ener-getic terms in *The Motherhood Constellation*.

23. Brennan, *Interpretation of Flesh*, 68.

24. Raymond Fink, "Bioenergetic Foundations of Consciousness," in *Toward a Science of Consciousness: The First Tucson Discussions and Debates*, ed. Stuart R. Hammerhoff, A. W. Kaszniak, and A. C. Scott (Cambridge: MIT Press, 1996).

25. Robert M. Sapolsky, *Why Zebras Don't Get Ulcers* (New York: W. H. Free-man, 1994), 85–86.

26. *Harvard University Gazette*, June 11, 1998, 1.

27. Sapolsky also raises the question of the material effects of missing love and attention (and hence the transmission of the affect of love). See Sapolsky, *Zebras*.

28. *Nature Neuroscience*, August 2001.

29. Ibid.

30. Sigmund Freud, *An Outline of Psychoanalysis*, vol. 23 of *The Standard Edition of the Complete Psychological Works of Sigmund Freud*, ed. James Strachey (London: Hogarth Press, 1940): 148.

31. See my *Exhausting Modernity*.

32. In the light of this split, Freud was more or less right to hold Eros responsible for all human action, but only right if we take the nature of the life drive and force of love combined, before the split, as a spiritual as well as a sensual thing. It is the lot of humans not to know the union of spirit and sensuality in this life unless they take the arduous mystic path toward it, a path that psychoanalysis begins, according to Kristeva, but does not complete.

33. The idea that living attention fuels all the affects is why passionate love can quickly transform itself into its opposite. The libido and the living attention in entails are used to being attached to a certain object, and can maintain the relationship with it while changing the affect.

34. See Daniel Stern, *Motherhood Constellation*.

35. Lacan's attention to mathematical "knots" and equations raises similar issues.

36. The feminine party colludes in this process because even if the attention she receives is negative at least it gives her an image: it gives her borders or boundaries that, even though they are restricting, are welcome insofar as they give her an identity. However, this has been argued in another volume. See my *Interpretation of the Flesh*.

37. Cindy L. Brody, David A. Haaga, and Lindsey Kirk, and A. Solomon, "Experiences in Anger in People Who Have Recovered from Depression and Never-Depressed People," *Journal of Nervous and Mental Diseases* 187 (1999): 400–5.

38. G. Parker, K. Roy, K. Wilhelm, and P. Mitchell, "'Acting Out' and 'Acting In' as Behavioral Responses to Stress: A Qualitative and Quantitative Study," *Journal of Personality Disorders* 12 (1998): 338–50.

39. R. L. Cautin, J. C. Overholser, and P. Goetz, "Assessment of Mode of Anger Expression in Adolescent Psychiatric Inpatients," *Adolescence* 36 (2001): 163–70.

40. J. K. Moreno, M. J. Selby, A. Fuhriman, and G. D. Laver, "Hostility in Depression," *Psychological Reports* 75 (1994): 1391–401.

41. W. P. Sacco, S. Milana, and V. K. Dunn, "Effect of Depression Level and Length of Acquaintance on Reactions of Others to a Request for Help," *Journal of Personal Social Psychology* 49(1985): 1728–37.

42. National Center for Environmental Health, "Attention-Deficit/Hyperactivity Disorder: A Public Health Perspective," NCEH Pub. No. 99–0362, Centers for Disease Control, Atlanta, Ga., Sept. 1999.

43. Joseph Biederman, Sharon Milberger, et al., "Impact of Adversity on

Functioning and Comorbidity in Children with Attention-Deficit Hyperactivity Disorder," *Journal of the American Academy of Child and Adolescent Psychiatry* 34 (1995): 1495–503.

44. Researchers attempted to measure mother-adolescent interactions along with family beliefs and conflicts. Using a group of eighty-three adolescents with ADHD, they subdivided the teens into those with ADHD alone (n=27) and those with oppositional defiant disorder (ODD) as well (n=56). The results showed that *both* ADHD groups had "more topics on which there was conflict and more angry conflicts at home than control adolescents." Russell A. Barkley, Arthur D. Anastopoulos, David C. Guevremont, and Kenneth E. Fletcher, "Adolescents with Attention Deficit Hyperactivity Disorder: Mother-Adolescent Interactions, Family Beliefs and Conflicts, and Maternal Psychopathology," *Journal of Abnormal Child Psychology* 20 (1992): 263–88.

45. N. J. Roizen, T. A. Blondis, M. Irwin, A. Rubinoff, J. Kieffer, and M. A. Stein, "Psychiatric and Developmental Disorders in Families of Children with Attention-Deficit Hyperactivity Disorder," *Archives of Pediatrics and Adolescent Medicine* 150 (1996): 203–8.

46. Gilligan, *Violence.*

47. A. Farmer, I. Jones, J. Hillier, and M. Llewelyn, "Neuraesthenia Revisited: ICD-10 and DSM-111-R Psychiatric Syndromes in Chronic Fatigue Patients and Comparison Subjects," *British Journal of Psychiatry* 167 (1995): 503–6.

48. J. G. Dobbins, B. H. Natelson, and I. Brassloff, et al., "Physical, Behavioral, and Psychological Factors for Chronic Fatigue Syndrome: A Central Role for Stress?" *Journal of Chronic Fatigue* 1 (1995): 43–58.

49. The survey included 12,730 subjects age 16–64. The result: Out of a total of 10,108 subjects who agreed to cooperate, 9 percent reported symptoms of chronic fatigue. P. Skapinskis, G. Lewis, and H. Meltzer, "Clarifying the Relationship between Unexplained Chronic Fatigue and Psychiatric Morbidity: Results from a Community Survey in Great Britain," *American Journal of Psychiatry* 157, no. 9 (2000): 1492–98.

50. Sing Lee, Hong Yu, and Yunkwok Wing, et al., "Psychiatric Morbidity and Illness Experience of Primary Care Patients with Chronic Fatigue in Hong Kong," *American Journal of Psychiatry* 157, no. 3 (2000): 380–4.

51. Leslie A. Aaron, Laurence A. Bradley, Graciela Alarcon, et al., "Perceived Physical and Emotional Trauma as Precipitating Elements in Fibromyalgia," *Arthritis and Rheumatism* 40 (1997): 453–60.

52. Edward A. Walker, David Keegan, Gregory Gardner, Mark Sullivan, David Bernstein, and Yayne J. Katon, "Psychosocial Factors in Fibromyalgia Compared with Rheumatoid Arthritis: II. Sexual, Physical, and Emotional Abuse and Neglect," *Psychosomatic Medicine* 59 (1997): 572–77.

3. Transmission in Groups

1. Gustave Le Bon, *The Crowd: A Study of the Popular Mind* (London: Ernest Benn, 1952), 27.

2. Gregory R. McGuire, "Pathological Subconscious and Irrational Determinism in the Social Psychology of the Crowd: The Legacy of Gustave Le Bon," in *Current Issues in Theoretical Psychology*, ed. William J. Baker, Michael E. Hyland, Hans Van Rappard, and Arthur W. Staats (Amsterdam: Elsevier, 1987), 206.

3. Le Bon, *The Crowd*, 126.

4. Ibid., 31.

5. Ibid., 32.

6. Freud, *Group Psychology and the Analysis of the Ego*, in *Standard Edition*, vol. 18, 76–77.

7. Le Bon, *The Crowd*, 102–3.

8. Margot-Duclos, "Les Phénomenènes des foules," *Bulletin de Psychologie* 14 (1961): 857.

9. Le Bon, *The Crowd*, 58.

10. I disagree that individuals' distinctiveness lies in their conscious rather than their unconscious personas: the reverse is often the case. Social pressure can often compel people to a similarity of conscious opinions when they are engaged in what, for Le Bon, is the most individual of acts: writing and thinking. See my "Social Pressure."

11. Freud, *Group Psychology*, 119.

12. Wilfred Trotter, *Instincts of the Herd in Peace and War* (New York: Macmillan Company, 1916), 33.

13. While Trotter is friendly to the herd instinct, seeing it as the origin of the guilt and duty that makes social life possible, he is also criticized (by, for instance, McGuire) for implicitly keeping company with those who would pathologize groups and crowds on the basis that "gregarious suggestions are still primarily carried out at a subconscious level, effectively precluding a rational understanding of their influence by those who are affected these instincts" (McGuire, "Irrational Determinism," 209). The automatic tie here between the pathological and the not rational is dubious. Some of the best things we do are not rational. Trotter is also criticized by McGuire (210), but earlier by Freud, for the racist slant he gave to herds, using the herd instinct tendentiously in favor of Britain to explain the outbreak of World War I.

14. William McDougall, *The Group Mind: A Sketch of the Principles of Collective Psychology with Some Attempt to Apply Them to the Interpretation of National Life and Character* (New York: G. P. Putnam's Sons, 1920), 37. One is reminded here of Galen and why he termed the sympathetic nervous system "sympathetic." That is to say, Galen located sympathy for the emotions close to the skin, far from the brain with its capacity for reflecting on them.

15. McDougall, *Group Mind*, 42.

16. Ibid., 59–60.

17. Freud, *Group Psychology*, 84.

18. Herbert George Blumer, "Collective Behavior," in *Principles of Sociology*, ed. Robert E. Park (New York: Barnes and Noble, 1939), 170–71.

19. Ibid., 174.

20. Floyd H. Allport, "The Group Fallacy in Relation to Social Science," *Journal of Abnormal and Social Psychology* 19 (1920): 62.

21. Floyd H. Allport, *Social Psychology* (Boston: Houghton Mifflin, 1924), 294.

22. Ibid., 300.

23. Ibid., 295.

24. Ibid., 292.

25. Despite his individualist premise, Allport offers evidence against it when he observes that "the social stimulations present in the co-acting group brought about an increase in the speed and quantity of work produced by individuals" (*Social Psychology*, 284). For the purposes of our later argument on how aging and expertise alike increase the dominance of ego-consciousness over the "consciousness-held-in-common" it is worth adding that Allport's empirical work also showed that this increase was more pronounced in explicitly physical efforts rather than intellectual ones; younger rather than older persons; and in less trained rather than more trained personnel. Allport here was drawing on Norman Triplett ("The Dynomogenic Factors in Peacemaking and Competition," *American Journal of Psychology* 9 [1898]: 507–33) and A. Mayer ("Über Einzel und Gesamtleistung des Shulkindes," *Arch. ges. Psychol.* 1 [1903]: 276–416). The work is extended in E. C. Simmel, R. A. Hoppe, and G. A. Milton, *Social Facilitation and Imitative Behavior* (Boston: Allyn and Bacon, 1968), in terms of familiar and unfamiliar tasks. See also Robert Zajonc, "Social Facilitation," in *Science* 149 (1965): 269–74. The extraordinary thing about this research is the way it tries to explain how a group carrying out an unfamiliar task can do it better than a group of people who are familiar with the same task. The explanation they offer is that those who are doing something new try harder. I think that understanding this phenomenon in terms of how it is that ego-consciousness is fundamentally slower than the consciousness-held-in-common (a conclusion happily buttressed by those who claim the unconscious is smart rather than dumb) takes us farther here.

26. Allport, *Social Psychology*, 317.

27. A similar approach is found in the work of Miller and Dollard who, like Allport, conceded that a crowd could indeed be mad; it could cease to be rational, but it does so because the baser drives of individuals are reinforced. In Miller and Dollard's development of Allport's individualized approach, the drives are more defined. There are innate or primary drives: pain, nutrition (thirst, hunger), fatigue, cold, sex (these are reminiscent of McDougall); there are secondary drives based on the primary drives such as money and approval. ("Emotions" figure in this account as the learned responses to the primary drives.) The key to Miller and Dollard's approach is that crowds provide opportunities for overcoming the frustration of these drives. Frustration, as a concept, is critical. Essentially, Miller and Dollard are learning-response theorists, thorough behaviorists both of them. People learn by rewards. Rewards strengthen a connection between drives, which recognize certain cues, and responses. If the response is reinforced by a reward, it will recur the next time the same drive and the same cues are present. Neal Miller and John Dollard, *Social Learning and Imitation* (New Haven: Yale University Press, 1941), 20.

28. Ibid., 222.

29. Alexander Mintz, "A Re-Examination of Correlations between Lynchings and Economic Indices," *Journal of Abnormal and Social Psychology* 41 (1946): 154–60.

30. Stanley Lieberson and Arnold R. Silverman, "The Precipitants and Underlying Conditions of Race Riots," *American Sociological Review* 30 (1965): 887–98.

31. McDougall, *Group Mind*, 35.

32. Erving Goffman, *Behavior in Public Places: Notes on the Organization of Social Gatherings* (New York: Free Press, 1963); Clark McPhail, *The Myth of the Maddening Crowd* (New York: Aldine de Gruyter, 1991). For the purposes of this analysis overall, three terms suffice: the group, the gathering, and the crowd. The distinction between the group and the gathering is that a group need not meet to exist, although it must have some means of association. These means of association can be passive, as when a group is constituted through an external definition given to it, or active, as when the group actively constitutes itself; the gathering is a meeting of the group. The crowd is something that exceeds the self-understanding of a gathering in one, or both, of two ways. The gathering may spontaneously do something that is not in its initial purview, as when a group of sports viewers attacks the spectators supporting the opposing team. Or a crowd may exceed a gathering in that people who would not normally belong to the group do so on a particular occasion: a gathering that congregates to admire Christo's wrapping of the Reichstag may become a crowd when joined by others with no interest in art but some in famous people. I was debating whether to add a fourth term: the mob (as in lynch mob), to signify the violent or sadistic group, but decided that the terms "violent group" and "violent crowd" do the job.

33. McPhail, *Maddening Crowd*, 210. What we have here is a cognitive theory that relies, just as much as McDougall and Freud relied, on sight as well as sound for how it is that individuals have the same response. But whereas McDougall saw it in terms of individuals conjuring up the same affect within themselves, McPhail attempts to break out of the circularity by positing a third term, the "reference signal" (one's team scores a goal), which leads to a display of approval (applause) and sometimes to more complex responses. Symbolization is critical in this account, as is an awareness of circularity, but it is symbolization that has its effects through cognition rather than, or as well as, through affect. But the awareness of the problem with earlier explanations in McPhail is phrased very much in the context that Le Bon's legacy has been a conservative one, a disparagement of the collective action whose political success in the 1970s helped form the rational crowd theorists, giving birth to a social movement scholarship that rejects the "spontaneous emotional images of crowds" (McPhail, *Maddening Crowd*,

xiii), leaving us with a picture of the organized "crowd"—the gathering in cognitive control. Any notion of affect largely disappears in this work.

34. Bion used this theory to contribute to, and develop, group psychoanalysis as a method of treatment, basing himself on the idea that the psychotic parts of an individual, while normally most intractable to individual analysis, emerged more plainly in a group.

35. Wilfred R. Bion, *Experiences in Groups and Other Papers* (Basic Books: New York, 1961), 166.

36. Bion calls this last the "pairing group," because such a group often has an explicit idea that a sexual relation is taking place between two of its leading members. However, the explicit idea is not necessary for the group to be focused on the idea of "what is to come." In sum, of the three basic-assumption groups the dependent group depends on a strong leader or a deity; the pairing group on the hoped for birth of a messiah; the flight/fight group on avoidance or aggression toward a real or imaginary threat.

37. One depends on the parents, one believes that through pairing new birth comes, one is angry at those who threaten one's security, or especially those who make one think (presumably one's existing ideas are sources of security), and wishes to fight them, or flee. This last basic assumption fits least easily into the oedipal schema, and in trying to insert it, Bion is at his most Kleinian.

38. Bion, *Experiences in Groups*, 164.

39. Ibid., 172.

40. Ibid., 158.

41. Ibid., 143.

42. At the simplest level, it can also be the case that isolation makes us mad.

43. Bion only discusses the theorists that Freud discusses, which can leave one with the impression that not much has happened in the interval between those theories and his own.

44. Like Freud, Bion did not find it necessary to postulate a herd instinct, but he did look to a form of group bondage that does not require a leader, and this again is the basic assumption.

45. Bion, *Experiences in Groups*, 153.

46. Ibid., 175.

47. Ibid., 170.

48. Ibid., 185–86.

49. What is clear is that spectator violence is prompted by or at least preceded by the evident enjoyment of violence among the players, violence that is in turn roundly exploited by the media. The enjoyment is attributed, in a psychoanalytically resonant argument, to an association between violence and dominance. When the "power forward" takes the "opponent out of the play . . . violence may serve to indicate or emphasize the degree of dominance." This could bring pleasure to "the spectator who fits the Adlerian scheme of motivation and who is capable of sharing power vicariously. This view is often expressed in terms of 'identifying with the hero' (a sports hero or heroic team)." Jennings Bryant and Dolf Zillman, "Sports Violence

and the Media," *Sports Violence*, ed. Jeffrey H. Goldstein (New York: Springer-Verlag, 1983), 199.

50. Power from my standpoint is never the neutral force it is for Foucault. Power may be diffuse, but it is unevenly distributed, precisely because some are energetically empowered, and some depleted, by what they project into others.

51. Dolf Zillmann, *Hostility and Aggression* (Hillsdale, N.J.: Lawrence Erlbaum, 1979).

52. R. P. Michael and Eric B. Keverne, "Pheromones in the Communication of Status in Primates," *Nature* 218 (1968): 746.

53. Piet Vroon, *Smell: The Secret Seducer* (New York: Farrar, Straus and Giroux, 1997). Vroon's definition is very close to that of Kathleen Stern and Martha McClintock in 1998: "Pheromones are airborne chemical signals that are released by an individual into the environment and which affect the physiology or behavior of other members of the same species." Kathleen Stern and Martha McClintock, "Regulation of Ovulation by Human Pheromones," *Nature* 392 (March 12, 1998): 177.

54. For instance, in her study of menstrual and ovarian synchrony, Martha McClintock observed that the phenomenon of ovarian synchrony has been documented in human beings as well as hamsters. Martha McClintock, "Pheromonal Regulation of the Ovarian Cycle," in *Pheromones and Reproduction in Mammals*, ed. John G. Vandenbergh (New York: Academic Press, 1983). Although "the female social signals that generate the phenomenon are less well understood" it is clear that male hamsters and rats promote the sexual development of nearby females by the use of pheromones. One recent study has confirmed earlier findings to the effect that women have more regular periods when they are exposed routinely to male perspiration, even if there is no male attached to the sweat in question. I have said "something like" pheromones because research on humans has concentrated on androstenes and copulines contained in perspiration and mucous products, which do have effects like pheromones, and which have been highlighted in the studies mentioned so far. Vroon, *Smell*, 130; See also Jane L. Veith et al., "Exposure to Men Influences the Occurrence of Ovulation in Women," *Physiology and Behavior* 31 (1983), 314. In other words, the operation of something like pheromones seems to be the best candidate for explaining the otherwise inexplicable phenomenon of "female cycling," a term for when women in regular close proximity menstruate on the same timetable: recent studies have shown that women's menstrual cycles can be synchronized with those of women they have not met and are not in proximity to, through exposure to extracts from one another's perspiration. See Winnifred B. Cutler et al., "Human Axillary Secretions Influence Women's Menstrual Cycles: The Role of Donor Extract from Men," *Hormones and Behavior* 20 (1986): 463–73. Lower down the evolutionary ladder, it is the queen bee's pheromones that are the mechanism for forestalling sexual development in other female bees, although John Free shows that touch appears to be necessary for this inhibition to take place: "odor alone is insufficient." John B.

Free, *Pheromones of Social Bees* (Ithaca, N.Y.: Comstock, 1987), 47–48. In bees, the senses of touch and smell are interrelated (Karl von Frisch, *Bees: Their Vision, Chemical Senses, and Language* [Ithaca: Cornell University Press, 1987], 39ff.). In general, the more complex mammals have been shown to effect sexual or reproductive changes in others of their species solely by smell, hypothesized as pheromonal contact. Prior to the recent upsurge of interest in human pheromones in the late 1990s, research had concentrated on animals and sexual reproduction because "the few studies that have been made on the behavioral effects of olfactory stimuli . . . derive[d] chiefly from the breeding of farm animals" (Michael and Keverne, "Pheromones in Communication," 747).

55. Vroon, *Smell*, 126.

56. E. O. Wilson and William H. Bossert, "Chemical Communication among Animals," in *Recent Progress in Hormone Research*, ed. Gregory Pincus (New York: Academic Press, 1963).

57. Restak, "Empathy," 67.

58. Ibid.

59. Ibid., 68.

60. It is also the case that auditory cues give us more information as to whether we are being deceived, whereas facial expressions do not (although other visual bodily gestures may do so) Miron Zuckerman, et al., "Verbal and Nonverbal Communication of Deception," *Advances in Experimental Social Psychology* 14 (1981): 1–59.

61. If I am not nervous but smell panic around me, I too may become frantic; my individual psychology is secondary to that of the group, unless there is that rare quality of imperviousness (an interesting word) in me that means I stay focused differently. This quality can be the secure conviction concerning an interpretation as to what is occurring, an interpretation that persists even in the face of a group response leading to a contrary interpretation.

62. The effect of rhythm in crowds has received some attention. Turner and Killian mention it in connection with "expressive symbolizing tendencies" in a crowd type they classify as both expressive and "solidaristic" (a religious congregation is the preeminent example here). In line with the tendency toward taxonomy that has dominated recent scholarship of the crowd and the gathering, these authors are mainly concerned with the typology of crowds. Their work was the first, nonetheless, to stress just how much classification of types had been neglected in work on crowds. Ralph H. Turner and Lewis M. Killian, *Collective Behavior* (Englewood Cliffs, N. J.: Prentice-Hall, 1987).

63. J. van Honk, A. Tuiten, R. Verbaten, M. van den Hout, H. Koppeschaar, J. Thijsen, and E. de Haan, "Correlations among Salivary Testosterone, Mood, and Selective Attention to Threat in Humans," *Hormones and Behaviour* 36, no. 1 (August 1999): 17–24.

64. D. H. Hellhammer, W. Huert, and T. Schurmeyer, "Changes in Saliva Testosterone after Psychological Stimulation in Men," *Psychoneuroendocrinology* 10, no. 1 (1985): 77–81.

65. In this case, the image does cause the physiological response, which in turn suggests that the images one has in one's mind—"ideas"—cause physiological responses as well as the other way around.

66. Testosterone is an androgenic (masculinizing) hormone linked to other chemicals that emit odors. R. L. Doty points out that "complex relations exist between odor-guided behaviors, hormonal states, and experiential factors." Such factors are discussed in the next chapter. R. L. Doty, "Odor-guided Behavior in Mammals," *Experientia* 42 (1986): 257–71.

67. B. I. Grosser, L. Monti-Bloch, C. Jennings-White, and D. L. Berliner, "Behavioral and Electrophysiological Effects of Androstedienone, a Human Pheromone," *Psychoneuroendocrinology* 25, no.3 (April 2000): 289–99.

4. The New Paradigm

1. Ted Benton, "Social Causes and Natural Relations," in *Alas, Poor Darwin: Arguments against Evolutionary Psychology*, ed. Hilary Rose, Steven Rose, and Charles Jencks (New York: Harmony Books, 2000), 249–71.

2. Mary Midgely, "Why Memes?" in *Alas, Poor Darwin*.

3. It remains to be explored how the intersection of the horizontal line of the protesting heart and the linear line of history shapes the perceived thought of the time.

4. L. Monti-Bloch, V. Diaz-Sanchez, C. Jennings-White, and D. L. Berliner. "Modulation of Serum Testosterone and Autonomic Function through Stimulation of the Male Human Vomeronasal Organ (VNO) with Pregna-4,20–diene-3,6–dione," in *Journal of Steroid Biochemistry and Molecular Biology* 65 (April 1998): 237–42. The authors sum up: "In mammals, external chemosensory signals from conspecifics of the opposite sex acting on vomeronasal organ receptors can modulate the release of gonadotropins. There is developmental, anatomical and functional evidence showing that the human vomeronasal organ (VNO) has the characteristics of a chemosensory organ. We have been using naturally occurring human pheromones to serve as models for designing novel synthetic compounds that we call vomeropherins. In previous publications we reported that vomeropherin pregna-4,20–diene-3,6–dione (PDD) delivered to the VNO of normal female and male human volunteers significantly affected male subjects only, decreasing respiration and cardiac frequency, augmenting alpha brain waves, and significantly decreasing serum luteinizing hormone (LH) and follicle stimulating hormone (FSH). Results of the present work confirm that PDD produces a local dose-dependent effect in the male human VNO. This is followed by a mild parasympathomimetic effect characterized by 10% increase of vagal tone, together with decreased frequency of electrodermal activity events. Furthermore, PDD locally delivered to the male human VNO significantly decreases serum LH and testosterone ($p<0.01$). The present results contribute additional evidence supporting the functionality of the human VNO and its repercussions in autonomic and psychophysiological functions, as well as in neuroen-docrine secretions."

5. Moreover, such sensitive capacities, when educated or given a language, constitute feelings as distinct from affects. The linguistic and conceptual education of feelings presupposes that they are given means for identifying or naming, synthesizing, and interpreting information from the various senses. By this definition, they are connected with the capacities for reflection or cognition as well as with the senses, which means that feelings, as discussed above, are linked to proprioception and language. By language they are linked to history. Some of what they have learned may be conscious, some repressed. Similarly, the affects are both conscious and unconscious. They are conscious when they are felt and interpreted, and subjective causes attached to them. They are also conscious as changes in thought and behavioral patterns, which can be barely conscious, more something we find ourselves doing than something we intended to do. The measure of agency in an action is its degree of conscious intentionality. As we shall see, there is a difference between actions linked in a logical progression and intentions leading to actions at odds with one. That is what a pheromone is: an intention. Not one's own, but the other's. Yet intentions by this definition are linked to both the voluntary and autonomic nervous systems. As a first approximation, we might say that feelings are tied to voluntary intention. They are, therefore, conscious and thoughtful. Affects are conscious as states discerned by feelings, but their production is involuntary and unconscious. Affects are thoughtless. This does not mean they go unaccompanied by cognition. What alerts the thoughtful to the presence of an affect is precisely a change in thought tone: say, from the calm and scholarly to irritation at lack of recognition. In the first case attention is engaged and contented in its reflections on a subject other than itself. In the second, it is interested in nothing but itself. I am drawing these preliminary distinctions to illustrate that a particular kind of thought—a connective thought that is reflective in relation to ideas and others—leads to feeling insofar as it approximates a parallel path in the flesh. It traces a path of linkage historically, in that its reflections go over ground in retrospect; such reflections can lead to the activation of its sympathetic nervous system, enabling it to understand the other or itself (why it does things that harm itself) while disengaging with the affects that "blocks in feeling" attract. Such neuronal blockages, I have hypothesized, are produced by primary repression, which then attracts similar (secondary) repressions toward it.

6. Walter J. Freeman, *Societies of Brains: A Study in the Neuroscience of Love and Hate* (Mahwah, N. J.: Lawrence Erlbaum, 1995). See also Charles Luther Herrick, *The Brain of the Tiger Salamander* (Chicago: University of Chicago Press, 1948).

7. In this connection it is worth reconsidering the sociological discussion of the unintended consequences of action. But, for the time being, I intend to sidestep these debates and the related question of an unconscious intention, because they are framed by assumptions of self-containment.

8. Hippolyte Bernheim, *De la suggestion et de ses applications à la therapeutic*, 2d ed. (Paris 1887).

9. I would add that electrical entrainment and hypnosis are probably the same thing.

10. Hobbes was insistent that our desires motivate our actions and yet convinced that reason would somehow prevail over the claims of rhetoric, whose task was to outwit reason by manipulating the emotions.

11. Jurgen Habermas, *Legitimation Crisis*, trans. Thomas McCarthy (Cambridge: Polity), 1988.

12. As I have argued, the complex of views associating intentionality with individuality, agency with activity (and so forth), originates in a fantasy rather than an intellectual history. Intellectual history is, of course, deeply implicated, but the point is that the fantasy arises in each of us independently of that history. Hence, real philosophical work is infected by the foundational fantasy, but it is not equivalent to it. There is too much thinking or struggling with the fantasy, evident even in the philosophers who perpetuate assumptions that split mind and body. The act of thinking and the act of struggling to follow the laws of reason (logical deduction) through the maze of fantasy-imbued sensible perception are the same. The foundational fantasy also lies at the base of the distinction between the biological and the social, insofar as these are supposed to have impermeable domains. Impermeability is presupposed at the level of intentionality, which is how we understand agency and intelligence from the standpoint of the fantasy.

13. Richard Dawkins, *The Selfish Gene* (New York: Oxford University Press, 1976).

14. "It is clear that emotional states affect . . . the functioning of the entire reproductive system, implicating the hypothalmus, the releasing factors for LH and FSH, the pituitary, its hormones, the functioning of the ovaries (perhaps less so the testes), and the automatic nervous system and its links with the sex organs. We can see this clearly from such facts as that fear of pregnancy can, alone and unaided, bring about a cessation of the menstrual cycle and several of the physiological manifestations of pregnacy itself." Vernon Reynolds, *The Biology of Human Action* (Reading, England: W. H. Freeman, 1976), 144.

15. Tim Ingold, "An Anthropologist Looks at Biology," *Man* 25 (1989): 208–29.

16. Colin Blakemore, "How the Environment Helps to Build the Brain," in *Mind, Brain, and the Environment: The Linacre Lectures*, ed. Bryan Cartledge (Oxford: Oxford University Press, 1998).

17. The term "sympathetic" goes back at least to Galen, who believed that the brain "was responsible for rational thought and the peripheral viscera for the emotions." Sapolsky, following Levine, suggests that Galen called the sympathetic nervous system "sympathetic" because the collection of neural pathways linking the two allowed the brain to sympathize with the viscera, or the viscera to sympathize with the brain. Alternatively, the sympathetic nervous system allows a person to sense the affects of others and to

direct a response toward them. The sympathetic system releases adrenalin at two locations, at the adrenal glands and at the sympathetic system's nerve endings. While adrenalin (epinephrine) is secreted by both the adrenal glands and the peripheral nerve endings alike, noradrenalin (norepineph-rine) is secreted only by the sympathetic nerve endings. Very hypothetically, let us suppose for a moment that noradrenalin may be a means for register-ing intakes of information from the other; adrenalin may be the endogenous response.

18. Sapolsky, *Zebras*, 24.

19. Are the similarities in structure within this class of hormones (the ste-roids) explained in the way that the similar differences in adrenalin and nor-adrenalin might be explained: as differences related to direction, or the pro-cess of projection and that of introjection? In other words, are certain steroids imbibed in some way, so that what for the one was a pheromone (the projection of a hormone) attaches itself to a similar receptor hormone in the other?

20. "It is now recognized that the base of the brain, the hypothalamus, con-tains a huge array of those releasing and inhibiting hormones which instruct the pituitary, which in turn regulates the secretions of the peripheral glands." Sapolsky, *Zebras*, 30.

21. Ibid., 34.

22. Ibid., 35.

23. Ibid., 35.

24. Ibid., 236.

25. B. I. Grosser, L. Monti-Bloch, C. Jennings-White, and D. L. Berliner, "Be-havioral and Electrophysiological Effects of Androstedienone, a Human Pheromone," *Psychoneoroendocrinology* 25, no. 3 (April 2000): 289–99.

26. One of the reasons I queried whether these hormones are not best de-scribed as feminine or masculine ones is that they tend to exist in smaller or larger concentrations in both sexes. The experiments discussed in the last chapter showed that testosterone increases in men and women when per-forming visual tasks in the selection of angry faces. Anne Fausto-Sterling's work on the social distribution of the various sex hormones, meaning the social—possibly historical—range of hormonal compositions that arbitrar-ily designate male or female, is fertile ground for exploring these questions further. "Evolutionary explanations of human sex differences usually ignore an entire literature on norms of reaction and phenotypic plasticity." Anne Fausto-Sterling, "Beyond Difference," in *Alas, Poor Darwin*, 223. Of addi-tional interest here is that androgen is a significant variable in utero and one that moreover has effects on intelligence in the form of spatial perception.

27. A. E. Storey, C. J. Walsh, R. L. Quinton, and K. E. Wynne-Edwards, "Hor-monal Correlates of Paternal Responsiveness in New and Expectant Fa-thers," *Evolution and Human Behavior* 21, no. 2 (March 2000): 79–95.

28. The assumptions about interpersonal depression do not justify projec-tion onto the innocent (as in "But I'm not angry; it's your anger I'm feel-ing"). This projective application of this theory flies in the face of its first

tenet, which is that any negative projection onto another is an act of transmission rather than reception. That is to say, an identification made in anger of another as the source of an angry projection merely perpetuates the process.

29. H.G. Pope Jr., E.M. Kouri, and J.I. Hudson, "Effects of Supraphysiologic Doses of Testosterone on Mood and Aggression in Normal Men: A Randomized Controlled Trial," *Archives of General Psychiatry* 58, no. 4 (April 2001): 403–4.

30. *Archives of General Psychiatry* 57, no. 2 (February 2000): 133–40; discussion 155–56.

31. Here, a longitudinal study (controlling for normal age decline in testosterone levels) on the impact of occupation as well as environment on hormonal levels would be especially interesting.

32. Sapolksy, *Zebras*, 36.

33. M. Dorakovova, R. Kvetnansky, Z. Oprsalova, and D. Jezova, "Specificity of the Effect of Repeated Handling on Sympathetic-Adrenomedullary and Pituitary-Adrenocortical Activity in Rats," *Psychoneuroendocrinology* 18, no. 3 (1993), 163.

34. At least in part, what is unconscious through primary repression may be owing to the atrophy of means for detecting pheromonal intentions at odds with the organism's immunal assessment of its needs.

35. Blakemore, "How the Environment Helps to Build the Brain," 29.

36. Ingold, "An Anthropologist Looks at Biology," 208–29.

37. See Aristotle, *De Anima*, trans. with an introduction and notes by Hugh Lawson-Tancred (London: Penguin Books, 1986).

38. The pervasive and often irreversible effects of fetal alcohol syndrome have been documented in the scientific literature for over two decades. We are told that the consequences of acute ethanol exposure to the fetus include a range of teratogenetic effects, including intellectual and motoric retardation. See also F. Schmid, "Alcohol Embryo-Fetopathies" (article in German) *Fortschr. Med.* 95 (1977): 2003–5; J. F. Brien and G. N. Smith, "Effects of Alcohol (Ethanol) on the Fetus" *Journal of Developmental Physiology* 15 (1991): 21–32; M. Kirchner, "Embryonal Alcohol Syndrome" (article in German), *Kinderarztl. Prax.* 47 (1979): 574–84; H. Loser, "Alcohol and Pregnancy: Embryopathy and Alcohol Effects" (article in German), *Ther. Umsch.* 57 (2000): 246–62.

39. J. P. Relier, "Influence of Maternal Stress on Fetal Behavior and Brain Development," *Biology of the Neonate* 79 (2001): 168–71.

40. J. P. Relier, "Importance of Fetal Sensorial Capacity in the Establishment of Mother-Child Exchange during Pregnancy" (article in French), *Archives de Pédiatrie* 31 (1996): 272–82.

41. Carlos A. Bedate and Robert C. Cefalo, "The Zygote: To Be or Not to Be a Person," *Journal of Medicine and Philosophy* 14 (1989): 641–45.

42. In 1979, four of my students and I attempted a synthesis of the findings available at that point on the influence of the maternal environment on the embryo. As mentioned at the outset, our conclusion was that if RNA mem

ory protein was embedded in the endometrium, then the moment of the blastocyst's implantation in the endometrium (which appears a cannibalistic moment in that the blastocyst needs whatever is in that endometrial blood to move to its next stage) is the moment when the memory of the mother's blood intersects with that of the new union of forty-six chromosomes. Our interest at the time was in demonstrating that potential paths of inheritance through maternal influence had not been explored with the same thoroughness as those of the genes and that gender identities, as we know them, are not immune from history. If such things could be inherited through memory, we reasoned, then they would also change as the flesh acquired new memories over time. But as such fleshly changes come about more slowly than those of language, there are grounds for optimism of the intellect. It is not that they will not change. It is just that they take time and persistence. But they cannot change through human agency and the simple will to follow a new direction, if all our fates are given in the genes. As we were reasoning, a book was published called *The Inevitability of Patriarchy* by Steven Goldberg, arguing that "endocrinology" showed that men had superior intelligence to women. The response to arguments such as these has been to show that the statistical claims do not have the universality suggested by proponents of white supremacy or sexism, to show that there are far too many exceptions to make a rule, and to show that the study of endocrinology has been conceptually flawed. The truths of these counterclaims are most certainly not disputed here; what is at issue, rather, is that these scientists' arguments on the social influences on endocrinology do not go far enough. If pheromones change moods, and moods change hormones, then the investigation of the social construction of sex and gender has barely begun. Research will speed up the more researchers think around and past the prejudice imposed on their thought by a fantasy that makes the mother a passive garden in which an active embryo disports itself. The directions they should follow in thinking around the existing blocks in thought are manifold. But if the regulation of form is affected by alterations in heart rate and minute (or substantial) pulsations in the flow of blood, such alterations are significant in themselves.

43. In this model, the heart circulates blood, and blood carries oxygen that it meets in the lungs. Changes in the rate of pulsation are measured as changes in heart rate linked to blood pressure: low heart rate equals low blood pressure. Blood pressure is the force of blood against the walls of arteries, determined by the force of the heartbeat, in turn determined by how hard the heart has to work against gravity (hence weight is a factor in blood pressure). Heart rate accelerates pressure, but pressure is also to some degree independent of this acceleration.

44. "Chains" constructed from the subject's own standpoint have the appearance of reasoning and may in the physical world have the appearance of causality. It may indeed appear that cutting this tree here causes global warming there, and the action indeed does have this effect. But they are not chains of life. The exercise of the subject's free will when it diverges from

that of creation is the infliction of death via the construction of a chain of material causality that imposes the subject's perspective on the life world, and in so doing diminishes the substance of life.

45. Appreciation of the physical facts here gives an additional and material dimension to the notion that psychical reality *is* real in the unconscious.

5. The Sealing of the Heart

1. E. R. Dodds, *The Greeks and the Irrational* (Berkeley: University of California Press, 1951), 15.

2. Henry Abramson, " 'Like Water, the Face to the Face': Transmission of Affect in Rabbinic Literature," unpublished paper, 2000. The only matter on which I take issue with Professor Abramson (on whom I otherwise rely in the following discussion of the sealing of the heart) is the notion that the ability to discern by smell in finely graded circumstances is always a gift rather than an achievement. Specifically, Professor Abramson notes that women who are uncertain as to whether blood flow indicates menstruation or some other hormonal response should take a sample of the blood in question to a rabbi. One early rabbi was able to tell a woman that her bleeding was the result of desire, not menstrual blood (Abramson, "Like Water," 8). This presupposes an olfactory ability so acute that it seems a God-given gift. In a sense, it is. Nonetheless, if my general argument is right, the sense of smell is more developed when the ego's "sealing of the heart" is less powerful.

3. Sloth is most commonly translated as *accidie*, although the original term was *acedia*, which meant "religious tedium." Tedium of any kind belongs to the same psychical constellation as inertia and general joylessness. On the relation of acedia to accidie, see especially Siegfried Wenzel, *The Sin of Sloth: Acedia in Medieval Thought and Literature* (Chapel Hill: University of North Carolina Press, 1967), 206, n. 1. Before Gregory formalized the list of the seven deadly sins, sometimes sadness (*tristitia*)and sometimes vainglory (*vanitas*) is listed as an eighth sin. Gregory amalgamated sadness and sloth into one sin. He also amalgamated pride and vainglory, on the grounds that they were meant to be alike. Finally, he added envy to the first Christian list, formulated by Evagrius.

4. Wenzel cites this text despite his insistence on a fundamentally Christian origin for the seven deadly sins (Wenzel, *Sin of Sloth*, 13.)

5. The chief historian of the seven deadly sins, Morton Bloomfield, tells us that the concept of seven chief sins comes most directly from Gnostic ideas of the "soul journey," based on an ancient pre-Hellenistic idea that the soul journeyed past the guardians of the seven planets after death. Each of the planets was identified with a particular vice (the term "sin" comes later, with Christianity). While Gnosticism had the most developed account of the soul journey, it was prefigured in the Zoroastrian, Mithraic, Babylonian, and Egyptian religions. In the Mithraic mysteries, for instance, there was a

seven-step journey through the seven heavenly spheres, and seven related degrees of initiation. See Morton W. Bloomfield, *The Seven Deadly Sins* (East Lansing: Michigan State College Press, 1952), 22–23. The *Corpus Hermeticum*, that ancient Greco-Egyptian text that was once believed to have been written at the time of Moses, but which is now believed to have been composed in the second century A.D., also refers to the soul drama. The reference in Libellus is most interesting: the soul mounted through seven *zones* of heaven, ruled by specific planets with different evil qualities (see Libellus 1, 25–26, in Bloomfield, 47). Before the Gnostics, the planets were also identified with virtues, as if they had two sides, a vice and its corresponding virtue. As Frances Yates shows, a text supposedly by Hermes (mythical author of the *Corpus Hermeticum*) "describes how to treat illnesses caused by bad stellar influences by building up links with the methods of sympathetic magic and talismans to draw down, either by an increase of good virtue from the star which has been causing the trouble or bringing in influences from another star" (Frances Yates, *Giordano Bruno and the Hermetic Tradition* [Chicago: University of Chicago, 1964], 47). It is only with the Gnostic distaste for matter in any form that the planets become purely evil. (Nonetheless this association between the vices and the planets is a common one in the pre-Christian world. Servius speaks of torpor for Saturn (*torporem Saturni*), anger for Mars (*Maris iracundiam*), lust for Venus (*libidinem Veneris*), envy or cupidity for Mercury (*Mercurii lucri cupiditatem*), and grandiosity for Jupiter (*Iovis regni desiderium*): Servius (1881: 718, 21, 98). What is common throughout all the pre-Christian planetary accounts is the idea that, in the soul journey, a particular soul had to be permitted to pass by the guardians of each planet before it could rejoin God. After the soul had traversed the seven heavenly spheres with their evil guardians, it arrived at the eighth and blessed sphere. For a time, this tie between the sins and the planets is preserved in the Christian tradition. In their planetary order: pride, the chief vice, is associated with the sun; avarice with Saturn; lust with Venus; envy with Mercury; gluttony with Jupiter; anger with Mars; and sloth with the Moon. (Martin Lings, "The Seven Deadly Sins in the Light of the Symbolism of Number," in Jacob Needleman, *The Sword of Gnosis* [London: Routledge & Kegan Paul, 1986], 220). In Gregory the Great's official list of the seven deadly sins, the sins are opposed to seven virtues, the "gifts of the Holy Ghost." (Jean Delumeau, *Sin and Fear: The Emergence of a Western Guilt Culture, Thirteenth-Eighteenth Centuries* [New York: St. Martin's, 1990], 193). This idea, that a vice was the mirror of a virtue and capable of being transmuted into that virtue, appears to some scholars to be Christian in origin. (Aquinas dismissed this idea; he believed that sin did not mean turning from virtue, but rather loving a transitory good [see Delumeau, 193]). But the apparent contradiction is resolved if we note that transitory goods as such only come into being with the Fall. Transitoriness is a temporal phenomenon, and the Fall produced time as we know it. And it is through the same Fall that the planets take on their dual function (of marking vice and virtue). Indeed, the convergence of the two ideas—that sin is the love of a transitory good and that sin and virtue alike are related through the axis of a particular planet—is evident in the Gnostic idea that to be bound by the laws of the planets is to be bound by the laws of time and space, except that, as noted in the texts, the Gnostics for the main part only saw vices in the material tie to the cosmos. Theologian Martin Lings interprets the transmutation from vice to virtue in terms of a beautiful passage from the New Testament, where it is said that "stone which the builders have rejected has become the keystone of the arch." See Lings, "Seven Deadly Sins," in Needleman, *Sword of Gnosis*. If the rejected stone is pride or vanity, it could become the personal keystone if it is transmuted into strength, the virtue that is pride's opposite. If the rejected stone is lust, it could become the keystone of love. If avarice, the turnaround could lead to generosity; if it is sloth, the result could be peace.

6. Bloomfield, *Seven Deadly Sins*, 44–45.

7. Another account of the sins ascribes their origin to the lists made by pre-Christian moral philosophers of what to avoid, such as the lists made by the Stoics and Servius and Horace. Then again, there are those who see the main origin of the sins as Christian, with the Egyptian desert monk Evagrius playing a critical role in formulating the initial list. Those who believe in a Christian origin for the sins do so because the earliest record we have of the idea of capital or deadly *sins* (as opposed to vices or spirits of deceit) comes from Evagrius, writing in the fourth century. Evagrius listed eight sins. Sadness and vainglory were on his list before Gregory removed them, and Evagrius did not mention envy; but basically, his list is the same as the later official one. Evagrius was probably drawing on existing accounts when he made his list, but his is the name associated with the "invention" of the sins today. Some scholars minimize the idea of earlier influences, thinking the monk's experience in the desert was largely enough in itself to give rise to a list of sins. Wenzel sees the probable origin of the sins as the formalization, in early Christian Egypt, of the vices the desert monks had to combat. Wenzel also argues against Bloomfield on the grounds that no full list of the seven sins existed in pre-Christian times. Also, Evagrius, the monk so critical in formulating the original list of sins, wrote of *eight*, rather than seven, evil thoughts. See Wenzel, *Sin of Sloth*, 15.

8. Before he went to the desert, Evagrius was influenced by the East; he lived in Constantinople. And according to Bloomfield, Evagrius had the early Church father Macarius as a master, and Macarius, like the Gnostics, spoke of *Telonia*, a term the Gnostics used to mean "tax-collectors," or guardians of the planets, and which the early Church fathers used to mean heavenly spheres. See Bloomfield, *Seven Deadly Sins*, 56–59.

9. Wenzel, *Sin of Sloth*, 12.

10. For instance, in the *Corpus Hermeticum*, which existed well before the monks had their say, there were different demons or gods for the different hours of the day. The *Corpus Hermeticum* notes this, and then enjoins us to "Pay attention to this: since the decans [divine or demonic forces] command over the planets and we are under the dominion of the seven [decans guarding seven planets], do you not see how there comes to us a certain in-

fluence of the decans, whether through the children of the decans, or through the intermediary of the planets?" (*Corpus Hermeticum* 3 [an excerpt from Stobeus 6]. One way of understanding this is that each hour carries with it different physical effects. A given demon, and its corresponding angel, is at its height when the angle is right, because that demon or that angel is the physical embodiment of certain energetic relations, affected, as all energy is affected, by the passage of time through space. There is an excellent discussion of the hours and their decans (and the sons of the decans, the demons) in Yates, *Giordano Bruno*. We should also remember that the word "demon" has changed in meaning since Christian times. There were evil demons and benign daemons, at least for Socrates, although we have lost sight of this.

11. See Wenzel, *Sin of Sloth*, 109. The idea here seems to be that the idleness and inertia of sloth give the devil a home from which the more volatile sins could always eject him. The very force of the passion of these sins might propel the sinners from a state of sin to one of virtue. This notion that sloth is the devil's resting place takes on extra meaning, as we see in the text. There is some warrant for the use of *inertia* in later medieval writing on the sin of sloth, where *inertia* is sometimes used in preference to *acedia* (religious tedium). Thus Adam Scot, a twelfth-century Carthusian monk, wrote that "oftentimes, when you are alone in your cell, a certain inertia, a dullness of the mind and disgust of the heart seize you. You feel an enormous loathing in yourself. You are a burden to yourself" (see Scot, [c. 1190], quoted in Wenzel, *Sin of Sloth*, 34).

12. See Lings, "Seven Deadly Sins," 220.

13. See Wenzel, *Sin of Sloth*, 54–55. But here we happen upon, as Wenzel points out, a more complex, if ultimately more simplified, genealogy of the sins and the passions that are tied to them. For Aquinas, building on Aristotle, there are two basic affects (joy and sorrow, or pleasure and pain: *gaudium* and *tristitia*). These are at the root of all passions.

14. See Horace, *Epistles*, ed. Roland Mayer (Cambridge: Cambridge University Press, 1994), 21. Horace's list of the vices and directions to their antidotes is worth recording in full: "Invidia, iracundus, iners, vinosus, amator, nemo adeo ferus est ut non mitescere possit, si modo culturae patientem commodet aurem." *Epistulae*, bk. I, 1, 38.

15. Servius, *Servii Grammatici qui ferunter in Vergilii carmina commentarii: recensuerunt* [Commentaries on Virgil] ed. by George Thilo and Hermann Hagen (Leipzig 1881–1902; reprint, Hildesheim: Olms, 1986), 714, 98. See also Bloomfield, *Seven Deadly Sins*, 45–50. Servius also reveals that the tie between the vices and the planets was a common one in the pre-Christian world.

16. One of the advantages of this account of the Fall is that, because of its emphasis on the physicality of the event, the original words used by the saints and prophets become more explicable. In particular, I am thinking of the Magnificat of the Virgin. Mary's famous declaration, "My soul doth magnify the Lord," has been cleaned up in the post-Vatican II translations of

the New Testament—"magnify" has been removed, lest we think Mary was being too grandiose (and indeed, she was criticized for vanity by the early Church fathers; see Marina Warner, *Alone of All Her Sex: The Myth and Cult of the Virgin Mary* [New York: Knopf, 1976]). But if we accept that an inert soul magnifies evil, just by virtue of its inaction and its fixity, then a soul free of inertia might have the opposite effect—it would do so by virtue of its movement, rather than any claims on priority in relation to the divine (which would be absurd).

17. Wenzel, *Sin of Sloth*, 108.

18. Ibid.

19. The more exact symbol for *acedia* is the foot, which frequently represents the emotions or affects in medieval writing. Or sometimes, both feet are referred to (in an image evoking Plato's black and white horses, the twin charioteers of the soul); one foot stands for *intellectus* and the other for *affectus*. "Our spirit has two feet—one of the intellect and the other of the affect, or of cognition and of love—and we must move both so that we might walk the right way" (see Philippe de Vitry, cited in Wenzel, *Sin of Sloth*, 108). The person who suffers from acedia moves the *pes intellectus*, but the *pes affectus* (otherwise known, significantly, as the *pes operis*, or "working foot") lags behind. This is an almost exact description of the concept of obsessional neurosis found in Freud. For Freud, the essence of obsessional neurosis, and by implication of the inertia to which it gives rise, is the splitting of word and affect. The affect is separated from the idea, which follows its own path, while the affect is buried and struggles on unconnected with the words that might, by naming the affliction, give us release. In this era, the problem is precisely finding the right word for what ails us; "sloth" does not quite fit, but "inertia" may well. Compare Freud's case study of the Ratman (Freud, "Notes on a Case of Obsessional Neurosis," *Standard Edition*, vol. 9, 152–318).

What is attractive about the second description of sloth—the noonday devil—is the idea that not only are demons related to the affects, they are also related to times and temperatures, which in turn influence chemical-pheromonal interactions.

20. Susan James, *Passion and Action*, 7.

21. Benedictus de Spinoza, *Ethics*, in *Collected Works of Spinoza*, vol. 1, trans. Edwin Curley (Princeton: Princeton University Press, 1985), 84–85. Anticipating a later argument, I hazard that one way of understanding this is to say that when we are affected by the other's affect, we are moved by something that is partially outside of us. We are not an adequate cause for our actions in that the drive or motion toward that action in part derives from affects in the environment, those of others toward whom we are sympathetic or who are our antagonists. But this way of understanding Spinoza does not pertain to the status of an interpretation; it is merely a concrete situation that the philosopher's more abstract words may encompass. It is, however, a concretization of Spinoza's difficult notion of adequate and inadequate causes and their corresponding ideas. Consider his definition of the affects:

"By affect (*affectus*) I understand the modifications of the body by which the power of action of the body is increased or diminished, aided, or restrained, and at the same time the ideas of these modifications" (Spinoza, *Ethics*, 84–85).

22. James, *Passion and Action*, 146.

23. "Spinoza's definitions of particular passions are grounded on the claim that our striving for power is manifested in our responses to the world around us. Love, for example, is what we feel when an external cause increases our power and is consequently a kind of joy—joy with the accompanying idea of an external cause. Hatred is sadness accompanied by the idea of objects that diminish our power. Envy is hatred of other people whose happiness makes us sad because it lessens our power. These definitions retain the familiar notion that the passions are functional, and are ideas of things as beneficial or harmful to us. But instead of simply asserting that we are disposed to preserve ourselves, Spinoza interprets the function of the passions as an expression in humans of a more general disposition—the disposition of all natural things to persevere in their being" (James, *Passion and Action*, 147).

24. James, *Passion and Action*, 38. Despite the insistence on the passivity of the maternal organism in relation to the germinating seed implanted in the womb (see chapter 4), Aristotle classifies the nutritive power that transforms one kind of matter into another as active, and contrasts it with sensation, which he sees as passive. Sensing, for him, is receiving the sensory forms of other things. But this passive process is not affective. It is "like bare asserting or thinking" (Aristotle, *De Anima*, trans. by Hugh Lawson-Tancred [London: Penguin Books, 1986], 431/a). Subsequently we will return to whether this sensing process is not simultaneously an active thing when it is deployed in the process of discernment, for we can only surely be conscious of the sensory forms of other things when we are simultaneously aware of our own sensory form, and by this awareness, maintain that form.

25. James, *Passion and Action*, 41.

26. Aristotle, *On Rhetoric*, Book 2, 121.

27. James, *Passion and Action*, 53.

28. Aquinas, *Summa Theologica* 1a, xiv, 10 *ad* 4. This definition, as we shall see, is close to Lacan's definition of the ego.

29. Together with Aquinas's attempt at generating a typology of the passions that explains them in terms of action and conflict between passions directed to that which is proximate, existing in the present and the present tense, and that which is difficult to reach (geographically, and in the future. There is, then, in Aquinas a move toward the distinction between affect and desire, insofar as desire too is for that which is not present.

30. Aquinas also makes a useful distinction between the passions and a calmer version of them. He calls these calmer versions "the affects," but they are close to what I mean by loving intelligence.

31. James, *Passion and Action*, 78.

32. Ibid., 87.

33. Rorty, "Explaining Emotions," 49.

34. Following Amélie Rorty from an anthropological perspective, R. C. Solomon notes that "the primary emotions, those of the greatest concern, vary considerably from culture to culture. Indian classifications and distinctions between emotions, passions, and afflictions display a very different structure from our own common taxonomies. And even when certain emotions remain superficially the same, they may have very different status and play very different roles in social interactions. *Angeris* is considered merely 'fear' in Utku culture, and fear is inevitably mixed with humiliation in a warrior society. Family affections, which would seem essential to virtually every society, are very different depending on the conception of family, the conception of family roles, and so forth. And these conceptions, needless to say, undergo change, both gradual and violent, as in the several social revolutions of the past few decades." R. C. Solomon, "Some Notes on Emotion, 'East and West'", *Philosophy East and West* 45, no. 2 (April 1995): 171–202.

35. Alisdair MacIntyre, *After Virtue: A Study in Moral Theory* (Indiana: University of Notre Dame Press, 1981).

36. James, *Passion and Action*, 174.

37. Ibid., 179.

38. Ibid., 159.

39. Teresa Brennan, *History after Lacan* (London: Routledge, 1993), part 1.

40. Similarly, this too was foreshadowed by seventeenth-century philosophers. Our passions, when warped by grandeur, make us restless and even mad. Madness and knowledge are opposed here, for, "by making us restless, our passions undermine the steadiness and concentration that the pursuit of knowledge requires." James, *Passion and Action*, 181. I return to this below in the discussion of discernment.

41. See Freud, "Negation," *Standard Edition*, vol. 19, 235–39.

42. Nor can one measure time and distance without a fixed reference mark.

43. Augustine, *City of God*, 14.6.

44. Abramson, "Like Water," 15.

45. Ibid., 19.

46. Ibid., 19–20.

6. The Education of the Senses

1. The Oxford University classics professor Christopher Rowland points out to me that there is a world of difference between reading the *Spiritual Exercises* of St. Ignatius and practicing them. He is right to see St. Ignatius's writing style as irrelevant. The fact of practice must also be borne in mind when reading *On the Discernment of Spirits*.

2. I have not explored the relationship between this account and Emmanuel Levinas's understanding of alterity in his *Alterity and Transcendence*. However, the notion of othering is derived from Levinas, which in itself is

enough to indicate some recognition of the resonances between Levinas's philosophy and this one.

3. As various writers on "othering" from E. M. Forster to Norma Fuller have shown, othering at the personal and the cultural level comes together in the stereotypic representations of the parvenu as the woman or man of another culture or class than that of the colonial rulers—one who is not to be trusted.

4. Although feelings are calm, affects are experienced as immediate, as a pressure seeking instant release or expression. This immediacy feels like a form of possession. One can even know one is possessed and yet be unable to silence the voice fueled by the negative affect, whose power or energetic force overrides the affect attached to the power to say no to that voice. One hopes that it is only temporarily, but it has grabbed hold of the reins of action and language, vehicles of the life drives. It is this living energy that needs to be reappropriated and redirected through the lively examination of one's passions, which can lead gradually to the overcoming of those passions. When the intelligent energy that is the means for this examination is free of the waves of anger and anxiety that otherwise impede its path, it rapidly finds words that suit it.

5. The individualist context surrounding the new popularity of meditation in the West obscures the extent to which the exercise of meditation is an exercise in concentration. Some of its Hindu theorists argue that meditation *is* concentration, most especially when it is the form of meditation whose aim and method is to cease having thoughts of any kind. At a certain point, they continue, such concentration ceases to be arduous and becomes a state in which affects cease to bat around fretfully in boredom and also stop following the impassioned directions of the judgments. When concentration has truly found its resting place in this way, it knows an energetic peace that fosters loving and logical ideas and right actions consistent with one's purpose. When prayer or mantra meditation takes one to a place close to this, it also does so by focusing attention on a single strand of words or an image, whose constancy enables one to reduce the number of distractions to a single one, which is why images are both good and bad in worship. At the last, they stand in the way of a complete release from the prison of affects.

6. C. S. Lewis made the same point when he argued that what one depends on in maintaining a faith is not the emotions but one's reason.

7. See Hans-Georg Gadamer, *Warheit und Method: Grundzüge einer Philosophischen Hermeneutik* (Tübingen: Mohr, 1975).

8. It may be worth reiterating that the energetic deployments consequent to this positional interaction with the other are what distinguish this account from the investigation of phenomenological space begun by Husserl.

9. This historical process has the great virtue that, if it persists hard enough and long enough, it can wind back the scattered threads to the knot where energy was misdirected toward affects. But as the knot was tied through memory contrasting and comparing the unsatisfactory experience of hallucination and fantasy, so it is that only history can unravel it.

10. This is why psychoanalysis and similar interlocutions directed toward this discovery are distinct from so-called therapies based on making the other feel good by sympathizing with their affects. This is also the difference between good conversations and those that are collaborative agreements to expel the negative affects somewhere else (gossip), where what is said matters less than the pleasures of trashing, a pleasure that comes from locating the affect in another person, somewhere else. One can always tell the difference between a good analyst and a bad therapist because the latter dwells in sympathy with the affects, while the former tries to unravel them.

11. Freud discusses the ego's one-sided cap of hearing in "The Ego and the Id" in *Standard Edition*, vol. 19, 19–27.

12. Norbert Elias, *The Civilizing Process*, trans. Edmund Jephcott (Oxford: Blackwell, 1992).

13. Michel de Montaigne, "On Friendship," in *Essays*, trans. J. M. Cohen (London: Penguin, 1958).

14. Post-Winnicott child rearing is ruled by the idea that if a child feels absolutely loved, it will be capable of loving others. But love is misunderstood when it means the free expression of all feelings. If a child is washed by a torrent of rage against which it has no defenses, it needs to learn to erect those defenses by understanding that rage is not something to give in to. The more practice one has at this, the more one fortifies one's defenses against a rage that is not one's own. It is different when the rage *is* one's own, however, just as it is different when one carries the other's rage as one's own depression.

15. For Rousseau also has Émile's tutor remark that "one is *more free* under the social pact than in the state of nature." Jean-Jacques Rousseau, *Émile, or On Education*, trans. Allan Bloom (New York: Basic Books, 1979), book 5, part 4, 841. But in Rousseau's case, there is something missing that is only supplied by the general will: "Our true *self* is not whole entirely inside of us" (*Émile*, 461). By contrast, if one is discerning affects, discerning what is not ours but inside of us is the aim of the exercise.

16. For Freud this crime was the imaginary murder of the father, a murder committed every time the father was surpassed by the son. See Freud, "Those Who Are Wrecked by Success," *Standard Edition*, vol. 14. There is always an interlock in any relationship between two in which the energy and capacities of the one are enhanced at the expense of the other, unless it is a case of rape, so-called seductions of the young and physically vulnerable, physical violence or intimidation, and abusive language or verbal violence. We know when another's anger shatters us, almost as though the sound barrier we inferred earlier is a real thing, something vulnerable to aggressive tonalities, especially when they are repeated, as well as to physical trauma. These, strictly speaking, are the mechanisms of dumping pure and simple, as distinct from the hook provided by projective identification, for good or ill.

17. It is a force that can displace that other I who holds sway with more discernment. But the fact of this movable force does not explain those moments when energy and insight are in lockstep. As we shall see, the energy that

bats around fretfully in boredom or follows in frustration the opinionated directions of the judgments is energy that has lost some of its links with the logos. But it can remake those links when it is once more aligned with consciousness. In such a case, Schopenhauer's will, at the human level, is no longer blinded. "The soul has achieved its dearest aim of union with the body," as Augustine put it.

18. Bion, *Experiences in Groups*, 149.

19. Even passions in Kant's restricted, obsessional sense—perversions of the reasoning process—can be explained by the distortions effected by positioning. These positions are not the affects, but they produce the affects. The idea that they operate without the redeeming fuel of human emotions (which at least leaves us capable of compassion) feels evil because the connection with flesh and blood is so tenuous, the body a simple means to an end at odds with its purpose. The ambiguity in Kant's treatment of the passions and affects, as with his apparently shifting allegiance between animism and mechanism, is consistent with the notion that feelings regulate the just relation between the inside and the outside—for example, how much of grief should be retained, how much should be released? This is a mechanical relation related to pressure; however, the build up of affects is different from the feelings that sense those buildups and find pleasure in their release. The affects can either overwhelm the feelings (negative affects, unpleasure) or be regulated by them, but they are not the same as them. Nor need they only come from within.

20. Freud, "Recommendations to Physicians Practicing Psycho-Analysis" *Standard Edition*, vol. 12, 111–20. In discussing how an analyst can possibly remember all that is expected by several patients at once, Freud recommended a "very simple" technique. "It consists simply in not directing one's notice and in maintaining the same 'evenly-suspended attention' (as I have called it) in the face of all that one hears. In this way we spare ourselves a strain on our attention which could not in any case be kept up for several hours daily, and we avoid a danger which is inseparable from the exercise of deliberate attention. For as soon as anyone deliberately concentrates his attention to a certain degree, he begins to select from the material before him; one point will be fixed in his mind with particular clearness and some other will be correspondingly disregarded, and in making this selection he will be following his expectations or inclinations. This, however, is precisely what must not be done" (Ibid., 111–12). It must not be done if one is to remember and to understand and learn, rather than confirming what one already knows. But perhaps it must also be done if one is to discern the origin of affects and, as suggested above, to enter into another's vision of the world in the most literal sense.

21. Just as the life drive is organized, this agency must be organized as well to work with it.

22. Freud, "Remembering, Repeating, and Working-through (Further Recommendations of the Technique of Psycho-Analysis)," *Standard Edition*, vol. 12, 147–56.

23. But this courage is only really courage if what it does is socially difficult; that is to say, if it risks the loss of the love of friends and family at one extreme, or even the general good approval of others, intellectually or financially. Atheism in the nineteenth century was socially difficult, but that is no longer the case.

24. See C. S. Lewis, *Mere Christianity*.

25. Freud made the same point when he said that those who are well have the ability to love and work.

26. Gillian Rose, *Love's Work* (London: Chatto and Windus, 1995).

27. W. B. Cannon, *Bodily Changes in Pain, Hunger, Fear, and Rage* (New York: Evanston, 1963).

28. The act of resistance is loving, intelligent, never neutral, and always historically based, whether it is exercised in an isolated or a social context.

29. Form was always intelligence in that it organized matter into intentional patterns that gave each pattern its distinct being or aim. That is the point of the logos as proportionate matter, a point that is obscured the more the ego gets things out of proportion, as is its wont.

30. See Freud's account of the perceptual apparatus in chapter 7 of *The Interpretation of Dreams, Standard Edition*, vol. 5.

31. The experience of rival interpreters in one's head is probably less common than the experience of rival interpretations, but I would hazard that inner dialogues are as recognizable an experience as throwing one's reason to the winds when gripped by passing affects.

32. See Abramson, "Like Water," 16. As Abramson notes, the arousal from below has been connected by respected Cabalists with the immediate communication between hearts, which is connected by Abramson with the sense of smell.

7. Interpreting the Flesh

1. The ego is slower in its calculations and its ability to reach a conclusion, slower than what is commonly called intuition. I have argued that it is slower because it almost always removes itself, to a greater or lesser extent, from the present. (See *Exhausting Modernity*, chapter 3.) The ego—as the reflecting part of the mind—exists in past and future time, either calculating, anticipating, desiring, regretting, remembering, or in reverie. Occasionally, the mind is occupied by concentrated attention following a path aligned with the living logic, in which case reverie functions to redirect. I am not saying that anticipation and reflection can be avoided. The idea rather is that their exercise has a living cost. Really, all I am doing here is making Hegel's old point that reflection and naming kill the very thing they name, "like capturing the fly in aspic," as Lacan later put the same point. See Lucio Colletti, *Marxism and Hegel*, trans. Lawrence Garner (London: New Left Books, 1973), 52–67, and Jacques Lacan, *Le Seminaire livre 20: Encore* (Paris: Seuil, 1975). For Augustine, a similar contradiction between awareness and

consciousness is evident when he observes that until he is asked the time he knows the time, but when he says the time he no longer knows the time. Augustine, *Confessions*, trans. R. Warner (New York: New American Library, 1963), 1:17.

2. Before proceeding, I note that there are two forms of reflection. In addition to calculation, there is the reflection that unblocks energy, the time-out that enables feeling and energy to return as the knots of anxiety are undone and the slowdown in logic caused by the affects—which register visually and aurally as fantasies and judgments—is reversed.

3. Brennan, *Exhausting Modernity*, chapter 9.

4. For a comprehensive account of the influence of notions of systems and structures on twentieth-century thought, see Anthony Wilden, *System and Structure: Essays in Communication and Exchange* (London: Tavistock, 1972). Wilden traces systemic and structural thinkers from Saussure to Bateson and Lacan, arguing, rightly, that thinking in terms of systems and structures with their own logic is the specific contribution of the twentieth century to knowledge.

5. Ferdinand Saussure, *Course in General Linguistics* (New York: McGraw-Hill, 1959).

6. Claude Lévi-Strauss, *Structural Anthropology*, trans. Claire Jacobson and Brooke Grundfest Schoepf (New York: Basic Books, 1963).

7. "The human being's development is in no way directly deducible from the construction of, from the interferences between, from the composition of . . . meanings (*significations*), that is, instincts (*instincts*)." Lacan is clear that more is at stake here than subject/object perception, noting that dealing with the "bodily, excremental, pregenital exchanges are quite enough for structuring a world of objects, a world . . . in which there are subjectivities." Jacques Lacan, *Le Seminaire livre 3: Les Psychoses* (Paris: Seuil, 1973), 189.

8. Ibid., 190.

9. Ibid., 189–91.

10. Ibid., 190. What is also interesting about this discussion is that Lacan defines meanings (*signification*) in terms of death and being toward death; these terms are, he stresses, antithetical to the endless chain of signification (which has no beginning and no end).

11. See the discussion of Derrida in Richard Rorty, *Philosophy and the Mirror of Nature* (Princeton: Princeton University Press, 1979), for the clearest exposition of the contradiction.

12. Lacan, *Les Psychoses*, 187.

13. Ibid., 187–89.

14. Ibid.

15. One speaks one's truths to the extent that one speaks from one's place in a logical chain rather than from one's place as a subject.

16. Not that these perspectives are necessarily opposed, anymore than are free will and determinism, or in Nietzsche's terms, will and necessity. For instance, if ceasing to exploit the planet beyond its capacity and human necessity is also necessary to the continuation of life on that planet, then

human exploitation will be brought to an end, one way or another. But how that end is achieved is open. What I am proposing is that humans have a limited free will. They are not limited in the means, but there are limits placed on the ends, insofar as the continuity of all striving or will, free and unfree, depends on the continuity of life as such. In the same way, it can be ordained either by my genes, my soul, my consciousness, my just or logical place in the scheme of things, or God (or all five) that I will end up in this or that place or occupation. But whether I reach that end by studying either medicine or philosophy in the first instance is within the scope of my free will, the choices I make, although the reasons I give myself at the time may not have the logic I perceive only in retrospect. Experience, as Kierkegaard noted, only reveals the logic that guides it with hindsight, and it is not the logic of the conscious mind, although consciousness determines the choices made in acquiring that experience (See Kierkegaard, *Fear and Trembling and The Sickness unto Death*, trans. Walter Lowrie (Garden City, New York: Doubleday, 1954). Experience that yields fruit is evidently guided by the intentionality of the life drive, even though the long-term intention is represented by short-term ambitions whose relation to the life drive is obscure to the subject.

17. In this connection, it is worth recalling that trauma cannot be symbolized. No one is clear on what this means, since traumas can evidently be described in words, words that somehow fail to work the release effected by the talking cure. There is something in trauma that defeats the means whereby analysis draws out thorns from the flesh. In a trauma, words do not free you; they reiterate the trauma by recalling what the body must forget if it is to live. Yet the body's forgetfulness comes about by paths that are different from those of personal consciousness. It forgets only when what is alien to it is dissolved. It can only be dissolved when the pathways set up in response to that trauma are activated again. Herein lies the healthy side of the trend to repetition that marks trauma. As Freud observed of hysterical symptoms, traumatic symptoms are forged through a union of two forces: one is the life drive (including the libido), seeking release from what constrains it; the other is the death drive, meaning the direction energy takes when it immobilizes the body by paralyzing repressions, keeping much of the body's energy illicitly locked up. The life drive is evident in the body's attempt to release the trauma by repeating it in the right way. It is the death drive that diverts the repetition away from its true purpose, which is to seek release by a means that permits it to symbolize even though it cannot speak. The tendency to self-blame and related shame (survivor guilt) that marks all trauma, in the theory offered here, is another mark of the death drive, insofar as it is (I suggest) the mark of what the body experiences as an alien deposit, often literally in cases of rape and incest. But the body knows that the freedom from trauma only comes when it is repeated in such a way that its affective direction is reversed (by love for instance), by which energy the direction or disposition the trauma establishes is cancelled out. Personal consciousness can learn from trauma and expand itself. But it cannot release it-

self without the intervention of one of the strange tongues of the body. As Proust put it, "Unhappiness is good for the mind, but not for the body"—the body insists on joy sufficient to its suffering before it can negate that suffering.

18. As discussed, the gateway between linguistic consciousness and the codes of bodily sensation is manned by visual images. To make itself conscious, a bodily process has to be imagined—given an image. The images it can be given are determined by signification—words and concepts deploying words. The use of visualization in some cancer experiments suggests that the direction of bodily processes can benefit from an image imposed by consciousness, but for the main part, the image obstructs the admission of the best word to consciousness.

19. Once this is appreciated, an old paradox about life and death can be understood, if not resolved. The problem with the life drive as Freud conceived it is that it is charged with preserving both the subject and the race. The life drive, I am arguing, is forged by the logical and self-referential chains of the flesh in context, chains that extend beyond the boundaries of individual subjects and which, when asked to choose between an individual and a species, will choose a species. This is why the ego is opposed to the life drive and should properly be conceived of as an amalgam of life and death drives, or energy and affects. (The death drive is a "drive" in that it has captured the energy of the life drive and diverted it back against itself, but it can only do this by keeping that energy ignorant of its direction, as the life drive may also do.) The task of the critical intellect is to trace out and reveal that direction. As long as it is split from the ability to understand the logic of its own flesh in relation to the chains of life with which it intersects, the critical intellect will have to rely on its reason in the face of its sensory perception. But I hazard that the more the intellect understands, the more it will feel.

20. This negotiation is effected by what we may term loving intelligence, which is a derivative of the life drive together with affection, as distinct from sensuality or sexuality. It is a derivative insofar as it is a conscious means for reconnecting the subjective perspective with the things from which it has been split.

21. Proust's fascination with and sense of the historicity of olfaction is a linguistic turn of its own. Malcolm Bowie, *Proust among the Stars* (New York: Columbia University Press, 1998).

22. Arlie Hochschild, *The Managed Heart: Commercialization of Human Feeling* (Berkeley: University of California Press, 1983), 29.

23. St. Bernard of Clairvaux, *The Works of Bernard of Clairvaux* (Shannon: Irish University Press, 1970).

24. By "distorts," I mean makes of its substance objects that interrupt the flow of life; toxic waste is paradigmatic here, as is violent persecutory anger at the affective level.

25. This elevation and eventual disembodiment of form embodies an identification with the masculine principle as a prior principle, rather than the principle of distinct identity (which it is). As with the phallus or the *nom du*

père, this principle has always effected separation, but because of this it also allows for the pleasures of distinctness.

26. There is no reason why an experiment on the discernment of affect could not be done. For instance, the technique of screening in experiments, where an observer or observers are invisible, could be utilized. If a small group of clinicians in the same room as a clinician in session independently recorded experiencing the same affect, that would at least indicate strongly that the phenomenon exists, even if we are still no wiser as to the nature of the faculty for discernment.

27. For a discussion of the question of mysticism, see Teresa Brennan, Drucilla Cornell, and Jacques Derrida, "Exchange on Time" in *Is Feminist Philosophy Philosophy?*, ed. Emmanuella Bianchi (Evanston, Ill.: Northwestern University Press, 1999).

28. See the discussion of St. Bernard in Julia Kristeva, *Histoires d'amour* (Paris: Denoël, 1983).

29. Quentin Skinner, *Reason and Rhetoric in the Philosophy of Thomas Hobbes* (Cambridge: Cambridge University Press, 1996), 260.

30. Ibid., 269–70.

31. If Michele Le Doueff is correct in assuming that Hobbes and Shakespeare were the first men of genius to deny the transmission of affect, this gives Hobbes an additional responsibility in relation to the direction of individualist thought. See Michele Le Doueff, *Vénus et Adonis suivi de genèse d'une catastrophe* (Paris: Alidades, 1986).

Works Cited

Aaron, Leslie A., Laurence A. Bradley, Graciela S. Alarcon, Mireya Triana-Alexander, Ronald W. Alexander, Michelle Y. Martin, and Kristin R. Alberts. "Perceived Physical and Emotional Trauma as Precipitating Elements in Fibromyalgia." *Arthritis and Rheumatism* 40 (1997): 453–60.

Abrahamson, Henry. "Like the Water, the Face to the Face: Transmission of Affect in Rabbinic Literature." Unpublished paper, 2000.

Ackerman, Diane. *A Natural History of the Senses*. New York: Vintage, 1991.

Allport, Floyd H. "The Influence of the Group upon Associative Thought." *Journal of Experimental Psychology* 3 (1920): 159–82.

——. "The Group Fallacy in Relation to Social Science," *Journal of Abnormal and Social Psychology* 19 (1920).

——. *Social Psychology*. Boston: Houghton Mifflin, 1924.

Amoore, John. *The Molecular Basis of Odor*. Springfield, Ill.: Thomas, 1970.

Aquinas, Thomas. *Summa Theologica: A Concise Translation*. Edited by Timothy McDermott. London: Eyre and Spottiswoode, 1989.

Aristotle. *De Anima*. Translated by Hugh Lawson-Tancred. London: Penguin Books, 1986.

——. *On Rhetoric*. Translated by George A. Kennedy. New York: Oxford University Press, 1991.

Augustine. *Confessions*. Translated by Rex Warner. New York: New American Library, 1963.

——. *The City of God*. Translated by Marcus Dods, introduction by Thomas Merton. New York: Modern Library, 1993.

Averill, James R. "Emotion and Anxiety: Determinants." In *Explaining Emotions*, edited by Amélie Oksenberg Rorty, 50. Berkeley: University of California Press, 1980.

Barkley, Russell A., Arthur D. Anastopoulos, David C. Guevremont, and

Kenneth E. Fletcher. "Adolescents with Attention Deficit Hyperactivity Disorder: Mother-Adolescent Interactions, Family Beliefs, and Conflicts and Maternal Psychopathology." *Journal of Abnormal Child Psychology* 20 (1992): 263–88.

Bedate, Carlos A., and Robert C. Cefalo. "The Zygote: To Be or Not to Be a Person." *Journal of Medicine and Philosophy* 14 (1989): 641–45.

Benton, Ted. "Social Causes and Natural Relations." In *Alas, Poor Darwin: Arguments against Evolutionary Psychology*, ed. Hilary Rose, Steven Rose, and Charles Jencks, 249–71 (New York: Harmony Books, 2000).

Bergson, Henri. *Creative Evolution*. Translated by Arthur Mitchell. New York: Modern Library, 1944.

Bernard of Clairvaux. *The Works of Bernard of Clairvaux*. Shannon: Irish University Press, 1970.

Bernheim, Hippolyte. *De la suggestion et de ses applications à la therapeutic.* (Paris, 1887).

Biederman, Joseph, Sharon Milberger, Stephen V. Faraone, Kathleen Kiely, Jessica Guite, Eric Mick, Ablon J. Stuart, Rebecca Warburton, Ellen Reed, and Sharmon G. Davis. "Impact of Adversity on Functioning and Comorbidity in Children with Attention-Deficit Hyperactivity Disorder." *Journal of the American Academy of Child and Adolescent Psychiatry* 34 (1995): 1495–503.

Bion, Wilfred R. *Experiences in Groups and Other Papers*. Basic Books: New York, 1961. Reprint, London: Tavistock/Routledge, 1989.

Birdwhistell, Ray L. *Kinesics and Context: Essays on Body Motion Communication*. Philadelphia: University of Pennsylvania Press, 1970.

Black, Perry, ed. *The Physiological Correlates of Emotion*. New York: Academic Press, 1970.

Blakemore, Colin. "How the Environment Helps to Build the Brain." In *Mind, Brain, and Environment: The Linacre Lectures*, edited by Bryan Cartledge. Oxford: Oxford University Press, 1998.

Bloomfield, Morton W. *The Seven Deadly Sins*. East Lansing: Michigan State College Press, 1952.

Blumer, Herbert George. "Collective Behavior." In *An Outline of the Principles of Sociology*, edited by Robert E. Park. New York: Barnes & Noble, 1939.

——. *Symbolic Interaction*. Englewood Cliffs, N.J.: Prentice-Hall, 1969.

——. "Social Unrest and Collective Protest." In *Studies in Symbolic Interaction*, vol. 1, edited by Norman K. Denzin. Greenwich, Conn.: JAI Press, 1978.

Bollas, Christopher. *The Shadow of the Object: The Psychoanalysis of the Unthought Known*. New York: Columbia University Press, 1989.

Boucat, A. J. *Evolutionary Paleobiology of Behavior and Coevolution*. Amsterdam: Elsevier, 1990.

Bowie, Malcolm. *Proust among the Stars*. New York: Columbia University Press, 1998.

Brennan, Teresa. *The Interpretation of the Flesh: Freud and Femininity*. London: Routledge, 1992.

——. "Social Pressure." *American Imago* (September 1997): 210–34.

——. *Exhausting Modernity: Grounds for a New Economy*. London: Routledge, 2000.

——. *Globalization and Its Terrors: Everyday Life in the West*. London: Routledge, 2002.

Brennan, Teresa, Drucilla Cornell, and Jacques Derrida. "Exchange on Time." In *Is Feminist Philosophy Philosophy?*, edited by Emmanuella Bianchi. Evanston, Ill.: Northwestern University Press, 1999.

Brien, J. F., and G. N. Smith. "Effects of Alcohol (Ethanol) on the Fetus." *Journal of Developmental Physiology* 15 (1991): 21–32.

Brody, Cindy L., David A. Haaga, Lindsey Kirk, and Ari Solomon. "Experiences of Anger in People Who Have Recovered from Depression and Never-Depressed People." *Journal of Nervous and Mental Disease* 187 (1999): 400–5.

Bronson, F. H., and Bruce Macmillan. "Hormonal Responses to Primer Pheromones." In *Pheromones and Reproduction in Mammals*, edited by John G. Vandenbergh. New York: Academic Press, 1983.

Bryant, Jennings, and Dolf Zillman. "Sports Violence and the Media." In *Sports Violence*, edited by Jeffrey H. Goldstein. New York: Springer-Verlag, 1983.

Canetti, Elias. *Crowds and Power*. New York: Continuum, 1960.

Cannon, W. *Bodily Changes in Pain, Hunger, Fear, and Rage*. New York: Evanston, 1963.

Caputi, Jane. " 'Take Back What Doesn't Belong to Me': Sexual Violence, Resistance, and the 'Transmission of Affect.' " In *Women's Studies International Forum* 929, no. 1 (2002): 1–14.

Cautin, R. L., J. C. Overholser, and P. Goetz. "Assessment of Mode of Anger Expression in Adolescent Psychiatric Inpatients." *Adolescence* 36 (2001): 163–70.

Chalmers, David. *The Conscious Mind: In Search of a Fundamental Theory*. New York: Oxford University Press, 1996.

Churchland, Paul. *Matter and Consciousness: A Contemporary Introduction to the Philosophy of Mind*. Cambridge: MIT Press, 1988.

——. *The Engine of Reason, the Seat of the Soul: A Philosophical Journey into the Brain*. Cambridge: MIT Press, 1995.

Clark, Andy. *Being There: Putting Brain, Body, and World Together Again*. Cambridge: MIT Press, 1997.

Clarke, Adele. *Disciplining Reproduction: Modernity, American Life Sciences, and "the Problems of Sex"*. Berkeley: University of California Press, 1998.

Cohen, Mabel Blake. *Advances in Psychiatry: Recent Developments in Interpersonal Relations*. New York: Norton, 1959.

Cohn, Norman. *The Pursuit of the Millennium*. Fairlawn, N.J.: Central Books, 1957.

——. *Warrant for Genocide*. New York: Harper and Row, 1967. Quoted in Bruce Mazlish, "Group Psychology and Problems of Contemporary History." In *Psycho/History: Readings in the Method of Psychology, Psychoanalysis, and History,* edited by Geoffrey Cocks and Travis L. Crosby. New Haven: Yale University Press, 1987.

Colletti, Lucio. *Marxism and Hegel*. Translated by Lawrence Garner. London: New Left Books, 1973.

Copjec, Joan. *Read My Desire: Lacan against the Historicists*. Cambridge: MIT Press, 1994.

Cromie, William J. "Of Hugs and Hormones: Lack of Touch Puts Kids Out of Touch." *Harvard University Gazette,* June 11, 1998, 1.

Cutler, Winnifred B., et al. "Human Axillary Secretions Influence Women's Menstrual Cycles: The Role of Donor Extract from Men." *Hormones and Behavior* 20 (1986): 463–73.

Dawkins, Richard. *The Selfish Gene*. New York: Oxford University Press, 1976.

Deleuze, Gilles, and Felix Guattari. *Anti-Oedipus: Capitalism and Schizophrenia*. Translated by Robert Hurley, Mark Seem, and Helen R. Lane. London: Athlone Press, 1984.

Delumeau, Jean. *Sin and Fear: The Emergence of a Western Guilt Culture, 13th–18th Centuries*. New York: St. Martin's Press, 1990.

Diener, Edward. "Deindividuation: Causes and Consequences." *Social Behavior and Personality* 5 (1977): 143–55.

DiStasi, Lawrence. *Mal Occhio, the Underside of Vision*. San Francisco: North Point Press, 1981.

Dobbins, J. G., B. H. Natelson, and I. Brassloff, et al. "Physical, Behavioral, and Psychological Factors for Chronic Fatigue Syndrome: A Central Role for Stress?" *Journal of Chronic Fatigue* 1 (1995): 43–58.

Dollard, John, Leonard Doob, Neal Miller, Herbert Mowrer, and Robert Sears. *Frustration and Aggression*. New Haven: Yale University Press, 1939.

Donzelot, Jacques. *L'Invention du social: Essai sur le déclin des passions politiques*. Paris: Fayard, 1984.

Dorokovova, M., R. Kvetnansky, Z. Oprasalova, and D. Jezova, "Specificity of the Effect of Repeated Handling on Sympathetic-Adrenomedullary and Pituitary-Adrenocortical Activity in Rats," *Psychoneuroendocrinology* 18, no. 3 (1993): 163–74.

Doty, R. L. "Odor-Guided Behavior in Mammals." *Experientia* 42 (1986): 257–71.

Drury, John. *Painting the Word: Christian Pictures and Their Meanings*. New Haven: Yale University Press, 1999.

Durkheim, Émile. *The Elementary Forms of Religious Life*. Translated by Karen E. Fields. New York: Free Press, 1995.

Edgerton, Robert B. *Alone Together: Social Order on an Urban Beach*. Berkeley: University of California Press, 1979.

Ehrenberg, Darlene Bregman. *The Intimate Edge: Extending the Reach of Psychoanalytic Interaction*. New York: Norton, 1992.

Ehrenberg, John. *The Dictatorship of the Proletariat: Marxism's Theory of Socialist Democracy*. New York: Routledge, 1992.

Elias, Norbert. *The Civilizing Process*. Translated by Edmund Jephcott. Oxford: Blackwell, 1994.

Emerton, Norma. *The Scientific Reinterpretation of Form*. Ithaca: Cornell University Press, 1984.

Farmer, A., I. Jones, J. Hillier, and M. Llewelyn. "Neuraesthenia Revisited: ICD-10 and DSM-III-R Psychiatric Syndromes in Chronic Fatigue Patients and Comparison Subjects." *British Journal of Psychiatry* 167 (1995): 503–6.

Fausto-Sterling, Anne. "Beyond Difference." In *Alas, Poor Darwin*, edited by Hilary Rose, Steven Rose, and Charles Jencks. New York: Harmony Books, 2000.

Festinger, Leon, Anthony Pepitone, and Theodore Newcomb. "Some Consequences of Deindividualization in a Group." *Journal of Abnormal and Social Psychology* 47 (1952): 382–89.

Fink, B. Raymond. "Bioenergetic Foundations of Consciousness." In *Toward a Science of Consciousness: The First Tucson Discussions and Debates*, edited by Stuart R. Hameroff, A. W. Kaszniak, and A. C. Scott, 649–57. Cambridge: MIT Press, 1996.

Flores, Kate. *Relativity and Consciousness: A New Approach to Evolution*. New York: Gordian Press, 1985.

Free, John B. *Pheromones of Social Bees*. Ithaca, N.Y.: Comstock, 1987.

Freeman, Walter J. *Societies of Brains: A Study in the Neuroscience of Love and Hate*. Mahwah, N.J.: Lawrence Erlbaum, 1995.

Freud, Anna. *The Ego and Mechanisms of Defense*. New York: International Universities Press, 1964.

Freud, Sigmund. "Recommendations to Physicians Practicing Psycho-Analysis." In *The Standard Edition of the Complete Psychological Works of Sigmund Freud*, edited by James Strachey and translated from the German under the general editorship of James Strachey in collaboration with Anna Freud, assisted by Alix Strachey and Alan Tyson, vol. 12, 109–20. London: Hogarth Press, 1912.

——. "On Beginning the Treatment: Further Recommendations on the Technique of Psycho-Analysis I." In *The Standard Edition*, vol. 12, 121–44. London: Hogarth Press, 1912.

——. *Group Psychology and the Analysis of the Ego*. In *The Standard Edition*, vol. 18. London: Hogarth Press, 1921.

——. "The Ego and the Id." In *The Standard Edition*, vol. 19, 19–27. London: Hogarth Press, 1923.

———. "Civilization and Its Discontents." In *The Standard Edition*, vol. 21, 109–20. London: Hogarth Press, 1930.

———. "An Outline of Psychoanalysis" In *The Standard Edition*, vol. 23, 141–207. London: Hogarth Press, 1940.

Frisch, Karl von. *Bees: Their Vision, Chemical Senses, and Language*. Ithaca: Cornell University Press, 1987.

Fuster, J. M. *The Prefrontal Cortex: Anatomy, Physiology, and Neuropsychology of the Frontal Lobe*. Philadelphia: Lippincott-Raven, 1997.

Gadamer, Hans-Georg. *Warheit und Method: Grundzüge einer Philosophischen Hermeneutik*. Tübingen: Mohr, 1975.

Gilligan, James. *Violence: Our Deadly Epidemic and Its Causes*. New York: G. P. Putnam, 1996.

Goffman, Erving. *Behavior in Public Places: Notes on the Organization of Social Gatherings*. New York: Free Press, 1963.

Goldie, Peter. Review of *What Emotions Really Are* by Paul Griffiths. *British Journal of the Philosophy of Science* 49 (1998): 642–48.

Griffiths, Paul E. *What Emotions Really Are: The Problem of Psychological Categories*. Chicago: University of Chicago Press, 1997.

Grinberg, León, Dario Sar, and Elizabeth Tabak de Bianchedi. *Introduction to the Work of Bion: Groups, Knowledge, Psychosis, Thought, Transformations, Psychoanalytic Practice*. Translated by Alberto Hahn. New York: J. Aronson, 1977.

Grosser, B. I., L. Monti-Block, C. Jennings-White, and D. L. Berliner. "Behavioral and Electrophysiological Effects of Androstedienone, a Human Pheromone," *Psychoneuroendocrinology* 25, no. 3 (April 200): 289–99.

Grosskurth, Phyllis. *Melanie Klein: Her World and Her Work*. New York: Knopf, 1986.

Gurdon, J. B., and P. Y. Bourillot. "Morphogen Gradient Interpretation." *Nature* 413 (2001): 797–803.

Habermas, Jurgen. *Legitimation Crisis*. Translated by Thomas McCarthy. Cambridge: Polity, 1998.

Hameroff, Stuart, Alfred W. Kaszniak, and Alwyn Scott, eds. *Toward a Science of Consciousness: The First Tucson Discussions and Debates*. Cambridge: MIT Press, 1996.

Heimann, Paula. "On Counter-Transference." *International Journal of Psychoanalysis* 31 (1950): 81–84.

Hermes Trismegistus. *Hermetica*. Translation and notes by Walter Scott. Oxford: Clarendon Press, 1911–1912.

Herrick, Charles Luther. *The Brain of the Tiger Salamander*. Chicago: University of Chicago Press, 1948.

Hillier, Janis, and Anne J. Farmer. "Tired and Depressed or Just Tired: A Review of Psychiatric Morbidity Associated with Chronic Fatigue Syndrome." *Arab Journal of Psychiatry* 6, no. 1 (May 1995): 1–12.

Ho, Mae-wan, and Sidney Fox, eds. *Evolutionary Processes and Metaphors*. Chichester, England: John Wiley & Sons, 1988.

Ho, Mae-Wan, and Peter Saunders. "Beyond Neo-Darwinism—An Epigenetic Approach to Evolution." *Journal of Theoretical Biology* 78 (1979): 573–91.

——, eds. *Beyond Neo-Darwinism: An Introduction to the New Evolutionary Paradigm*. London: Academic Press, 1984.

Hochschild, Arlie. *The Managed Heart: Commercialization of Human Feeling*. Berkeley: University of California Press, 1983.

Ingold, Tim. "An Anthropologist Looks at Biology." *Man* 25 (1989): 208–29.

James, Susan. *Passion and Action: The Emotions in Seventeenth-Century Philosophy*. Oxford: Clarendon Press, 1997.

Jaynes, Julian. *The Origin of Consciousness in the Breakdown of the Bicameral Mind*. Boston: Houghton Mifflin, 1976.

Jenkins, J. Craig. "Resource Mobilization Theory and the Study of Social Movements." *Annual Review of Sociology* 9 (1983): 527–53.

Kierkegaard, Søren. *Fear and Trembling, and The Sickness unto Death*. Translated with introductions and notes by Walter Lowrie. Garden City, N.Y.: Doubleday, 1954.

Kirchner, M. "Embryonal Alcohol Syndrome" (in German). *Kinderarztl. Prax.* 47 (1979): 574–84.

Klein, David Ballin. *The Concept of Consciousness: A Survey*. Lincoln: University of Nebraska Press, 1984.

Klein, Melanie. "Notes on Some Schizoid Mechanisms." In *Collected Writings*, vol. 3, 1–25. London: Hogarth Press and the Institute of Psycho-Analysis, 1980.

Koestler, Arthur. *The Ghost in the Machine*. London: Picador, 1967.

Koestler, Arthur, and J. R. Smythies, eds. *Beyond Reductionism: New Perspectives in the Life Sciences*. New York: Macmillan, 1969.

Kraepelin, Emil. *Memoirs*. Edited by Hans Hippius, G. Peters, and Detlev Ploog; translated by Cheryl Wooding-Deane. Berlin: Springer-Verlag, 1987.

Kristeva, Julia. *Histoires d'amour*. Paris: Denoël, 1983.

——. *New Maladies of the Soul*. Translated by Ross Guberman. New York: Columbia University Press, 1995.

Lacan, Jacques. "Form and Function of Speech and Language in Psychoanalysis." In *Écrits: A Selection*, translated by Alan Sheridan, 30–113. London: Tavistock, 1953.

——. *Le Seminaire livre 3: Les Psychoses*. Paris: Seuil, 1973.

——. *Le Seminaire livre 20: Encore*. Paris: Seuil, 1975.

Laing, R. D. *Self and Others*. New York: Pantheon, 1969.

Le Bon, Gustave. *The Crowd: A Study of the Popular Mind*. London: Ernest Benn, 1952.

Le Doeff, Michele. *Vénus et Adonis suivi de génese d'une catastrophe*. Paris: Alidades, 1986.

Lee, Sing, Hong Yu, Yungwok Wing, Cynthia Chan, Antoinette M. Lee, Dominic T. S. Lee, Char-mie Chen, Kehming Lin, Mitchell G. Weiss. "Psychiatric Morbidity: Illness Experience of Primary Care Patients in Hong Kong." *American Journal of Psychiatry* 157 (2000): 380–84.

Levinas, Emmanuel. *Basic Philosophical Writings.* Edited by Adriaan T. Peperzak, Simon Critchley, and Robert Bernasconi. Bloomington: Indiana University Press, 1996.

Lévi-Strauss, Claude. *Structural Anthropology.* Translated by Claire Jacobson and Brooke Grundfest Schoepf. New York: Basic Books, 1963.

Lieberson, Stanley, and Arnold R. Silverman. "The Precipitants and Underlying Conditions of Race Riots." *American Sociological Review* 30 (1965): 887–98.

Lings, Martin. "The Seven Deadly Sins in the Light of the Symbolism of Numbers." In *The Sword of Gnosis: Metaphysics, Cosmology, Tradition, Symbolism*, edited by Jacob Needleman. Baltimore: Penguin Books, 1974.

Liu, D., J. Diorio, J. C. Day, D. D. Francis, and M. J. Meaney. "Maternal Care, Hippocampal Synaptogenesis, and Cognitive Development in Rats." *Nature Neuroscience* 3, no. 8 (August 2000): 799–806.

Lloyd, G. E. R. *Demystifying Mentalities.* Cambridge: Cambridge University Press, 1990.

Lofland, John. "Collective Behavior: The Elementary Forms." In *Social Psychology*, edited by Morris Rosenberg and Ralph H. Turner. New York: Basic Books, 1981.

——. *Symbolic Sit-ins: Protest Occupations at the California Capitol.* Washington, D.C.: University Press of America, 1982.

——. *Protest: Studies of Collective Behavior and Social Movements.* New Brunswick, N.J.: Transaction, 1985.

Loser, H. "Alcohol and Pregnancy: Embryopathy and Alcohol Effects" (in German). *Ther. Umsch.* 57 (2000): 246–62.

MacIntyre, Alisdair. *After Virtue: A Study in Moral Theory.* Notre Dame, Ind.: University of Notre Dame Press, 1981.

Mackay, Charles. "Extraordinary Popular Delusions and the Madness of Crowds." London: Office of the National Illustrated Library, 1852. Reprint, New York: Farrar, Straus and Giroux, 1980.

Margot-Duclos, J. "Les phenomenes des foules." *Bulletin de Psychologie* 14 (1961): 856–62.

Marx, Gary. "Conceptual Problems of the Field of Collective Behavior." In *Sociological Theory and Research*, edited by Hubert M. Blalock, 258–74. New York: Free Press, 1980.

Mayer, A. "Über Einzel und Gesamtleistung des Shulkindes." *Arch. ges. Psychol.* 1 (1903): 276–416.

McClintock, Martha K. "Menstrual Synchrony and Suppression." *Nature* 229 (1971): 244–45.

——. "Pheromonal Regulation of the Ovarian Cycle." In *Pheromones and Reproduction in Mammals*, edited by John G. Vandenbergh, 113–49. New York: Academic Press, 1983.

McDougall, William. *The Group Mind: A Sketch of the Principles of Collective Psychology with Some Attempt to Apply Them to the Interpretation of National Life and Character*. New York: G. P. Putnam's Sons, 1920.

McGuire, Gregory R. "Pathological Subconscious and Irrational Determinism in the Social Psychology of the Crowd: The Legacy of Gustave Le Bon." In *Current Issues in Theoretical Psychology*, edited by William J. Baker, M. E. Hyland, H. Van Rappard, and A. W. Staats, 201–17. Amsterdam: Elsevier, 1987.

McPhail, Clark. *The Myth of the Maddening Crowd*. New York: Aldine de Gruyter, 1991.

Mead, George Herbert. *The Philosophy of the Act*. Chicago: University of Chicago Press, 1938.

Michael, R. P., and Eric B. Keverne. "Pheromones in the Communication of Status in Primates." *Nature* 218 (1968): 746–49.

Miller, Neal, and John Dollard. *Social Learning and Imitation*. New Haven: Yale University Press, 1941.

Milner, Marion. *On Not Being Able to Paint*. New York: International Universities Press, 1958.

Mintz, Alexander. "A Re-Examination of Correlations between Lynchings and Economic Indices." *Journal of Abnormal and Social Psychology* 41 (1946): 154–60.

Montaigne, Michel de. *Essays*. Translated by J. M. Cohen. London: Penguin, 1958.

Monti-Bloch, L., V. Diaz-Sanchez, C. Jennings-White, D. L. Berliner. "Modulation of Serum Testosterone and Autonomic Function through Stimulation of the Male Human Vomeronasal Organ (VNO) with Pregna-4, 20-diene-3, 6-dione." *Journal of Steroid Biochemistry and Molecular Biology* 65 (April 1998): 237–42.

Moreno, J. K., M. J. Selby, A. Fuhriman, and G. D. Laver. "Hostility in Depression." *Psychological Reports* 75 (1994): 1391–401.

Moscovici, Serge. *The Age of the Crowd*. Translated by J. C. Whitehouse. Cambridge: Cambridge University Press, 1985.

National Center for Environmental Health. "Attention-Deficit/Hyperactivity Disorder: A Public Health Perspective," NCEH Pub. No. 99-0362, Sept. 1999. Atlanta, Ga.: Centers for Disease Control.

National Institute of Mental Health. "The Numbers Count." Bethesda, Md.: NIMH, Jan. 2001.

Needleman, Jacob. *The Sword of Gnosis*. London: Routledge & Kegan Paul, 1986.

Neumann, Erich. *The Great Mother: An Analysis of the Archetype*. Translated by Ralph Manheim. Princeton: Princeton University Press, 1963.

Offidani, C., F. Pomini, A. Caruso, S. Ferrazzani, M. Chiaroti, and A. Fiori.

"Cocaine during Pregnancy: A Critical Review of the Literature." *Minerva Ginecologica* 47 (1995): 381–90.

Park, Robert E. *Principles of Sociology*. New York: Barnes & Noble, 1939.

———. *The Crowd and the Public*. Translated by Charlotte Elsner and edited by Henry Elsner. Chicago: University of Chicago Press, 1972.

Parker, G., K. Roy, K. Wilhelm, and P. Mitchell. " 'Acting out' and 'Acting in' as Behavioral Responses to Stress: A Qualitative and Quantitative Study." *Journal of Personality Disorders* 12 (1998): 338–50.

Pinard, Maurice, Jerome Kirk, and Donald von Eschen. "Processes of Recruitment in the Sit-in Movement." *Public Opinion Quarterly* 33 (1969): 355–69.

Plotkin, H. C., ed. *Learning, Development, and Culture: Essays in Evolutionary Epistemology*. Chichester, England: John Wiley & Sons, 1982.

Pope, H. G., Jr., E. M. Kouri, and J. I. Hudson. "Effects of Supraphysiologic Doses of Testosterone on Mood and Aggression in Normal Men: A Randomized Controlled Trial." *Archives of General Psychiatry* 58, no. 4 (April 2001): 403–4.

Powers, William. *Behavior: The Control of Perception*. Chicago: Aldine de Gruyter, 1973.

Relier, J. P. "Importance of Fetal Sensorial Capacity in the Establishment of Mother-Child Exchange during Pregnancy" (in French). *Archives de Pédiatrie* 31 (1996): 272–82.

———. "Influence of Maternal Stress on Fetal Behavior and Brain Development." *Biology of the Neonate* 79 (2001): 168–71.

Restak, Richard M. "Possible Neurophysiological Correlates of Empathy." In *Empathy*, vol. 1, edited by Joseph Lichtenberg, M. Bornstein, and Donald Silver, 63–75. New Jersey: Analytic Press, 1984.

Reynolds, Vernon. *The Biology of Human Action*. Reading, England: W. H. Freeman, 1976.

Roizen, N. J., T. A. Blondis, and M. Irwin, et al. "Psychiatric and Developmental Disorders in Families of Children with Attention-Deficit Hyperactivity Disorder." *Archives of Pediatrics and Adolescent Medicine* 150 (1996): 203–8.

Rorty, Amélie Oksenberg. "Explaining Emotions." In *Explaining Emotions*, edited by Amélie Oksenberg Rorty, 104–126. Berkeley: University of California Press, 1980.

Rorty, Richard. *Philosophy and the Mirror of Nature*. Princeton: Princeton University Press, 1979.

Rose, Gillian. *Love's Work*. London: Chatto and Windus, 1995.

Rousseau, Jean-Jacques. *Émile, or On Education*. Translated by Allan Bloom. New York: Basic Books, 1979.

Sacco, W. P., S. Milana, and V. K. Dunn. "Effect of Depression Level and Length of Acquaintance on Reactions of Others to a Request for Help." *Journal Of Personal Social Psychology* 49 (1985): 1728–37.

Sapolsky, Robert M. *Why Zebras Don't Get Ulcers*. New York: W. H. Freeman, 1994.

Saussure, Ferdinand. *Course in General Linguistics*. New York: McGraw-Hill, 1959.

Schmid, F. "Alcohol Embryo-Fetopathies" (in German). *Fortschr. Med.* 95 (1977): 2003–5.

Searles, Harold. *Coutertransference and Related Subjects: Selected Papers*. Madison, Conn.: Psychosocial Press, 1999.

Servius. *Servii Grammatici qui feruntur in Vergilii carmina commentarii; recensuerunt* [Commentaries on Vergil]. Edited by George Thilo and Herman Hagaan. Leipzig, 1881; reprint, Hildesheim: Olms, 1896.

Shorey, H. H. *Animal Communication by Pheromones*. New York: Academic Press, 1976.

Simmel, E. C., R. A. Hoppe, and G. A. Milton. *Social Facilitation and Imitative Behavior*. Boston: Allyn and Bacon, 1968.

Skapinskis, P., G. Lewis, and H. Meltzer. "Clarifying the Relationship between Unexplained Chronic Fatigue and Psychiatric Morbidity: Results from a Community Survey in Great Britain." *American Journal of Psychiatry* 157 (2000): 1492–98.

Skinner, Quentin. *Reason and Rhetoric in the Philosophy of Thomas Hobbes*. Cambridge: Cambridge University Press, 1996.

Smelser, Neil J. *Theory of Collective Behavior*. London: Routledge & Kegan Paul, 1962.

———. "Mechanisms of Change and Adjustment to Change." In *Industrialization and Society*, edited by Bert F. Hoselitz and Wilbert E. Moore. Paris: Mouton, 1966.

Smith, Anthony. *The Body*. London: George Allen and Unwin, 1970.

Smith, Blake. "Great Vision? Think Again." *Arizona Daily Wildcat*, April 11, 2000.

Smith-Lovin, Lynn. "The Sociology of Affect and Emotion." In *Sociological Perspectives on Social Psychology*, edited by Karen Cook, Gary Alan Fine, and James S. House. Boston: Allyn and Bacon, 1995.

Snyder, David, and Charles Tilly. "Hardship and Collective Violence in France, 1830–1960." *American Sociological Review* 37 (1972): 520–32.

Solomon, R. C. "Some Notes on Emotion, 'East and West.'" *Philosophy East and West* (1995): 171–202.

Spinoza, Benedictus de. *Ethics*. In *Collected Works of Spinoza*, vol. 1, translated by Edwin Curley. Princeton: Princeton University Press, 1985.

Stern, Daniel. *The Motherhood Constellation*. New York: Basic Books, 1995.

Stern, Kathleen, and Martha McClintock. "Regulation of Ovulation by Human Pheromones." *Nature* 392 (1998): 177.

Stoddart, D. Michael. "Human Odour Culture: A Zoological Perspective." In *Perfumery: The Psychology and Biology of Fragrance*, edited by Steve van Toller and George H. Dodd. London: Chapman and Hall, 1988.

———. *The Scented Ape: The Biology and Culture of Human Odour*. Cambridge: Cambridge University Press, 1990.

Storey, A. E., C. J. Walsh, R. L. Quinton, and K. E. Wynne-Edwards. "Hormonal Correlates of Paternal Responsiveness in New and Expectant Fathers." *Evolution and Human Behavior* 21, no. 2 (March 2000): 70–95.

Sturner, W. Q., K. G. Sweeney, R. Callery, and Nancy Haley. "Cocaine Babies: The Scourge of the '90s." *Journal of Forensic Science* 36 (1991): 34–39.

Suarez, Antoine. "Hydatidiform Moles and Teratomas Confirm the Human Identity of the Preimplantation Embryo." *Journal of Medicine and Philosophy* 15 (1990): 627–35.

Tarde, Gabriel. *On Communication and Social Influence*. Edited by Terry Clark. Chicago: University of Chicago Press, 1969.

Thompson, D'Arcy. *On Growth and Form*. Cambridge: Cambridge University Press, 1969.

Tilly, Charles. *From Mobilization to Revolution*. Reading, Mass.: Addison-Wesley, 1978.

Tilly, Charles, Louise Tilly, and Richard Tilly. *The Rebellious Century: 1830–1930*. Cambridge: Harvard University Press, 1975.

Triplett, Norman. "The Dynomogenic Factors in Peacemaking and Competition." *American Journal of Psychology* 9 (1898): 507–33.

Trotter, Wilfred. *Instincts of the Herd in War and Peace*. New York: Macmillan Company, 1916.

Turner, Ralph. "Collective Behavior." In *Handbook of Modern Sociology*, edited by Robert E. L. Faris. Chicago: Rand-McNally, 1964.

Turner, Ralph H., and Lewis M. Killian. *Collective Behavior*. New Jersey: Prentice-Hall, 1987.

Tye, Michael. *Ten Problems of Consciousness: A Representational Theory of the Phenomenal Mind*. Cambridge: MIT Press, 1995.

Veith, Jane L., et al. "Exposure to Men Influences the Occurrence of Ovulation in Women." *Physiology and Behavior* 31, no. 3 (1983): 313–15.

Vroon, Piet. *Smell: The Secret Seducer*. Translated by Paul Vincent. New York: Farrar, Straus and Giroux, 1997.

Walker, Edward A., David Keegan, Gregory Gardner, et al. "Psychosocial Factors in Fibromyalgia Compared with Rheumatoid Arthritis: II. Sexual, Physical, and Emotional Abuse and Neglect." *Psychosomatic Medicine* 59 (1997): 572–77.

Warner, Marina. *Alone of Her Sex: The Myth and Cult of the Virgin Mary*. New York: Knopf, 1976.

Weiss, Paul A. "The Living System: Determinism Stratified." In *Beyond Reductionism: New Perspectives in the Life Sciences*, edited by Arthur Koestler and J. R. Smythies. New York: Macmillan, 1969.

Wenzel, Siegfried. *The Sin of Sloth: Acedia in Medieval Thought and Literature*. Chapel Hill: University of North Carolina Press, 1967.

Wilden, Anthony. *System and Structure: Essays in Communication and Exchange*. London: Tavistock, 1972.

Wilson, E. O., and William H. Bossert. "Chemical Communication among Animals." In *Recent Progress in Hormone Research*, edited by Gregory Pincus. New York: Academic Press, 1963.

Wright, Sam. *Crowds and Riots: A Study in Social Organization*. Beverly Hills, Calif.: Sage Publications, 1978.

Yates, Frances. *Giordano Bruno and the Hermetic Tradition*. Chicago: University of Chicago Press, 1964.

Zajonc, Robert. "Social Facilitation." *Science* 149 (1965): 269–74.

Zillmann, Dolf. *Hostility and Aggression*. Hillsdale, N.J.: Lawrence Erlbaum, 1979.

Zimbardo, Phillip. "Individuation, Reason, and Order vs. Deindividuation, Impulse, and Chaos." In *Nebraska Symposium on Motivation* 17, edited by W. J. Arnold and D. Levine. Lincoln: University of Nebraska Press, 1969.

Zuckerman, Miron, et al. "Verbal and Nonverbal Communication of Deception." *Advances in Experimental Social Psychology* 14 (1981): 1–59.

Index

Abramson, Henry, 114–15, 188 n. 2
Acedia, 101, 188 n. 3, 192 n. 19. *See also* Sloth
Active/passive dichotomy, 14, 93, 101–2
Adorno, Theodor, 106
Adrenalin (epinephrine), 80–81, 86, 185 n. 17
Agency, 21, 76–77. *See also* Free will
Aggression: and anxiety, 40, 44, 119–20, 133, 135; and death drive, 36, 64, 110; and depression, 44, 67, 110, 112, 167 n. 10; and hormones, 68, 85; and the image, 71, 73; increase in prevalence of, 48; and individuality, 67–68; inverted, 112; and life drive, 58, 110; as masculine affect, 43; modulations of, 110; object of, 15; and the other, 42, 67, 111–12; and repression, 49; in short-lived group, 58; and stress on recipient, 48–49
Allport, Floyd, 59–60
Amour propre, 105
Anger: and depression, 6, 43–44; and the imaginary, 111; and projection, 185–86 n. 18; power of, 196 n. 16; restraint of, 124; and testosterone, 77
Animal magnetism, 17–18, 53
Antidepressants, 44, 170 n. 33
Anxiety: and absence of life drive, 58; and aggression, 40, 44, 119–20, 133, 135; and basic assumptions, 63; Bion

on, 32; and death drive, 36, 64; versus discernment, 133; and environment, 6; and ethics, 133; and the feminine other, 42; and health, 157; and imaginary threat, 111; maternal, 90; and the object, 15; and pain, 167–68 n. 13; and smell, 68, 70, 95–96; and thoughts, 7
Apathy, 129–31
Aquinas, St. Thomas, 103, 105, 189 n. 5, 191 n. 13
Aristotle: on action, 103; on emotion, 4, 105; on the evildoer, 118; and foundational fantasy, 14; on generation, 89; on judgments, 103; on the maternal organism, 89, 91, 193 n. 24; and the self-contained individual, 77
Arousal from below, 138, 151, 198 n. 32
Atmospheric affects, 1, 6–7, 9, 20, 46, 65–68, 97, 113. *See also* Environment
Attention: for Bion, 31, 36; and discernment, 128–30; evenly suspended, 128, 131, 197 n. 20; and love, 131–32, 135; and reflection, 183 n. 5; and thought, 49–50, 140; withdrawal of, 50; and words, 140. *See also* Living attention
Attention deficit/hyperactivity disorder (ADHD), 3, 45–46, 112, 175 n. 44
Augustine, St., 41, 98, 100, 110, 117, 198–99 n. 1
Autonomic nervous system, 80–83, 183 n. 5

Basic assumptions, 63–68, 113, 179 nn. 36–37
Bedate, Carlos, 91
Benjamin, Jessica, 41
Benjamin, Walter, 145
Berk, Richard, 61
Bernard of Clairvaux, St., 155
Bernheim, Hippolyte, 76
Biological, the: in Bion, 41–42; and entrainment, 49; and hormones, 10; primacy given to, 23; and the social, 1–3, 5, 7, 19, 21, 23, 74–75. *See also* Codes, biological
Bion, Wilfred: on attention, 31, 36; on basic assumptions, 113; and container and contained, 30, 41; and countertransference, 127; and "fight" assumption, 67; and mother/infant relationship, 20, 30–32; and predecessors, 65; and psychosis, 52, 64–65; on rage and anxiety, 32; and taxonomy, 41–42; on valency, 66
Bioregulation, 128, 146, 155–59, 161–62
Blakemore, Colin, 78–79, 88
Blame: of individuals, 46; of mother, 12–15, 33, 37–38, 46; of other, 30, 38; and repression, 38. *See also* Dumping
Blood: and affect, 139; circulation of, 75; and the heart, 114; and intelligence, 136; menstrual, 188 n. 2; mother's, 79, 91–92, 187 n. 42; and rhythm, 187 nn. 42–43; and smell, 114
Bloomfield, Morton, 188–89 n. 5, 190 nn. 7–8
Blumer, Hans, 58–59, 69
Body without organs, 14, 170 n. 30
Bollas, Christopher, 28
Boundaries: and the "borderline" patient, 26–29, 63; cultural specificity of, 25; and dead matter, 116–17; and depression, 15; and the ego, 123, 134; establishment of, 24; and the feminine party, 174 n. 36; health of, 11; historical dimension of, 15–16; Klein on, 30; Kristeva on, 170 n. 32; and projection, 11–12, 26, 134; and the psychotic patient, 33; and sight, 10, 17
Bowlby, John, 33
Breast, 37–40, 65

Cannon, W. B., 80
Caputi, Jane, 47
Carlson, Mary, 35

Cefalo, Robert, 91
Chain, living, 146–47, 152, 156–58
Child-rearing, 123–24, 196 n. 14
Chronic fatigue syndrome (CFS), 3, 6, 45–47, 101, 112, 175 n. 49
Codes, biological, 141, 144–49, 153, 156–58, 161–62, 201 n. 18
Codes of conduct, 118–19, 125, 134, 139
Codes of courtesy, 12, 51, 118, 122–23, 132
Cohen, Mabel, 27
Comparison, 102, 109–11, 121–22, 126–28, 130, 157
Concentration: and life drive, 153; and living logic, 198 n. 1; and meditation, 195 n. 5; and words, 122
Contagion, 49, 53, 57, 68–70
Corpus Hermeticum, 189 n. 5, 190 n. 10
Cortex, formation of, 87–88
Couch, Carl, 61
Countertransference, 26–29, 31, 127
Coyne, James, 43
Crowd: and affective transmission, 3, 20, 49, 178–79 n. 33; defined, 178 n. 32; ethical capabilities of, 54; versus group, 55; pathology of, 18, 53–54, 61–62, 177 n. 27; and taxonomy, 181 n. 62. *See also* Gathering; Group

Dante Alighieri, 101
Darwin, Charles, 4–5. *See also* Neo-Darwinism
Dawkins, Richard, 74–75, 77
Death, 116–17, 151–53, 163, 187–88 n. 44, 199 n. 10
Death drive: and affects, 40; and anxiety, 36, 64; derivatives of, 34; and disorganization, 58; and hate and envy, 64; and Klein, 33; and the life drive, 36, 200 n. 17; and trauma, 200–201 n. 17
Deleuze, Gilles, 14
Demons: and birth of the ego, 100; and history of affect, 21–22; and hours of the day, 190–91 n. 10; in Jesuit tradition, 120–21; and living energy, 164; noonday, 99, 192 n. 19; and passifying affects, 113; possession by, 115; and repression, 99–100; sense of term, 191 n. 10; and smell, 97–98
Depression: and aggression, 44, 67, 110, 112, 167 n. 10; and anger, 6, 43–44; and the feminine other, 42–43; and glucocorticoids, 81, 83–84; and individual-

ity, 6–7; and inertia, 22, 34, 100–101; interpersonal, 43–44, 82, 185 n. 28; and negative judgment, 22; prevalence of, 15, 48, 170 n. 31; and rejection, 43–44; secondary, 44; and steroids, 80; and stress, 82; and transmission by sight, 10

Descartes, René, 4, 103, 117, 120–21, 126

Detachment, 11, 68, 122, 125, 125–31

Diener, Edward, 59

Differentiation, cell, 78–79, 88–91

Directionality, 15, 75, 112, 170 n. 33, 185 n. 19, 201n. 19

Discernment: and anxiety, 133; and attention, 128–30; and civil codes, 123–24; and classical virtues, 125–26; and comparison of memories, 120–21; and disproportion, 127; and the ego, 118, 120, 163; and ethics, 119–20, 132–33; experiments on, 202 n. 26; and feeling, 23, 120, 139; habits of, 126; identity based on, 134; and intentions, 94; and language, 121; and love, 129; and modernity, 117; and resistance, 11, 23, 129; and sealing, 113–14; and self-possession, 128; and the senses, 120; and smell, 94, 136–37, 188 n. 2; and social context, 134–35; and subject/object dichotomy, 150; and the virtues, 132

DNA codes, 141, 154, 158

Dollard, John, 60, 67, 73

Dreams, 39, 107, 150

Drive: affect and, 40, 112; and the crowd, 57, 60, 72; diversion of, 38; and environment, 192 n. 21; and fantasies, 36, 40; and the individual psyche, 12; and living attention, 48; and the object-relations school, 33–34, 40; and observation, 4; striving of, 152; structuring of, 106; theory of, 40; turned inward, 112. See also Death drive; Life drive

Dumping: in affective dyads, 196 n. 16; and codes of conduct, 125–26; defined, 6; and energy, 34; and the mother, 13, 169 n. 25; and projective identification, 30; by psychological literature, 46; and race and sex, 15; and self-containment, 119; and victimization, 47

Dyads, affective, 13, 42, 49, 84, 173 n. 17, 196 n. 16

Ego: affect as, 98; and attentiveness, 128–29; and basic assumptions, 68; and belief in self-containment, 95; birth of, 100; and boundaries, 123, 134; and censorship, 137–38, 150; and comparison, 109–11, 122, 130, 157; constellation of, 118; and the deadly sins, 99; and discernment, 118, 120, 162–63; and distinctiveness, 167 n. 13; era of, 106; and grandeur, 105–6; versus intuition, 198 n. 1; and judgments, 111, 113, 130; as lack, 103; and life drive, 116, 132–33, 152–53; logic of, 116; maintenance of identity and, 130; and meditative tradition, 118; and musculature, 48; narcissistic diversion by, 131; and pain, 167–68 n. 13; passions as, 105; and passivity, 103; and repression, 106; sloughing off of, 163; and time, 198 n. 1

Ego-ideal, 57–58

Ehrenberg, Darlene, 27–28

Émile, or On Education (Rousseau), 119

Emotions, 3–6, 61, 165–66 nn. 4–7, 168 n. 14

Empathy, 44–45

Endocrinology, 79, 81, 187 n. 42

Endogenous affect, 7–8, 10, 43

Energetics, 42, 106, 110

Energy: and affect, 6, 34, 41, 108; and attention, 129; binding of, 38; and the biodegradable, 152; blockage of, 40; and concentration, 195 n. 5; and contagion, 56; depletion of, 40, 112; derived from life drive, 108; direction of, 36; and discernment, 121; and disconnection from logos, 196–97 n. 17; and drives, 34; enhancement of, 36–37, 40, 112; and feelings, 23; and femininity, 42; and the group, 8; and group psychology, 51; and interlocking relationships, 196 n. 16; and judgment, 126–27; love as, 34, 151; modulation of, 48; Montaigne on, 16; and new diagnostic disorders, 45; and nonseparation, 14; and position, 195 n. 8; and primary repression, 109; of the real, 36; release of, 107, 113, 140, 150, 199 n. 2; and self-containment, 6; and social interaction, 40; and subjective standpoint, 36, 148, 157; and suggestibility, 56; and thought, 49–50; and unconscious repression, 12; unimpeded, 149

Entrainment: in aggression, 68; chemical, 20, 52, 69–70, 79; and conscious attention, 162; defined, 9; and demons,
97–98, 115; electrical, 70–71; and gender, 83–84; and the group, 20; and
hypnosis, 184 n. 9; means of, 49, 112;
and pain, 167–68 n. 13; rhythmic, 70;
and sight, 10–11; in utero, 16, 79
Environment: and bodily health, 157;
and changes in human biology, 73–75;
chemosignals from, 84; and drives,
192 n. 21; and energy, 8; and free will,
93; and genes, 88; and the individual,
6–8; and the senses, 92–93; and smell,
169 n. 22; and shaping of brain, 77–79,
88; toxic, 22, 114, 210 n. 24; understanding of, 95. See also Atmospheric
affects; Social, the
Environmental sciences, 152
Envy: and countertransference, 27; and
the death drive, 36, 64; and the foundational fantasy, 21; and the imaginary, 111; and projection, 6, 30; restraint of, 124
Ethics, 104–5, 132–33. See also Codes of
conduct
Evagrius, 99, 190 nn. 7–8
Exhausting Modernity (Brennan), 12, 21,
98
Experiences in Groups (Bion), 63

Faith, 131–32
Fall, the, 21, 98, 189 n. 5, 191 n. 16
Fantasy: and affects, 122; and comparison, 110; defined, 12; and drives, 38,
40; and fleshly codes, 149; of imaginary, 109; and intellectual history, 184 n.
12; and living attention, 40; and nega-
tivity of affect, 38; and the oral 39, 40;
as passionate judgment, 111; and positioning, 22; and science's bias, 76; and
self-containment, 171 n. 39; unconscious as parents', 32; for Winnicott
and Klein, 33. See also Foundational
fantasy
Fear, 63, 70, 111, 115, 183 n. 5
Feelings: versus affect, 5, 122, 129, 139,
183 n. 5, 195 n. 4, 197 n. 19; and consciousness, 95; defined, 19; and discernment, 23, 120, 139; and energetic
release, 140; as information, 116; as
material process, 94; the other's, 123;
and resistance, 23; terminology of,

105; trust of, 155, and the uncon-
scious, 183 nn. 5 and 7; and words, 5,
120, 140, 183 n. 5
Femininity, 12, 15, 42–44, 84, 119, 174 n.
36
Festinger, Leon, 59
Fetal alcohol syndrome, 89, 186 n. 38
Fetal development, 20–21, 35, 37, 78–80,
88–92, 187 n. 42. See also Maternal environment
Fibromyalgia, 45–47, 167 n. 11
Finiteness, 144–47
Fixity, 34–38, 42, 130
Forgiveness, 133–34
Form, 89–92, 102–4, 198 n. 29
Foucault, Michel, 2, 18, 106
Foundational fantasy: and bias against
smell, 136; and bodily intelligence,
158; defined, 12–13; dislodgement of,
140; and intellectual work, 184 n. 12;
and maternal agency, 20–21; and passification of self, 111; and reversal of
positions, 37; and science, 73; and self-
containment, 13–14; and the seven
deadly sins, 21; and slowing of communication, 141, 147–48; and sub-
ject/object distinction, 20
Free will, 21, 93, 104–5, 156, 159, 187–88 n.
44, 199–200 n. 16
Freedom, 118, 124, 134
Freeman, Walter, 75
Freud, Sigmund: on attention, 128; and
containment, 12; and the drives,
34–36, 57, 107, 116, 201 n. 18; on evenly
suspended attention, 128, 131, 197 n.
20; and the group, 54, 56, 58; on infant's hallucination, 37; and Klein, 33;
on language and affect, 145; metapsychology of, 13; on murder of the father, 196 n. 16; on obsessional neurosis, 192 n. 19; on repression, 38–39,
112; on thoughts, 7; on trauma, 200 n.
17; and visual identification, 72

Galen, 184–85 n. 17
Gathering, 61, 178 n. 32
General will, 124, 196 n. 15
Genes, 1, 74–77, 88–92, 187 n. 42
Global destruction, 106, 161–62, 187–88 n.
44, 199–200 n. 16
Globalization, 22, 65
Globalization and Its Terrors (Brennan),
159

Glucocorticoids, 80–84, 87
Gnosticism, 99, 151, 188–89 n. 5, 190 n. 5
God, existence of, 132, 198 n. 23
Goffman, Erving, 61
Goldberg, Steven, 187 n. 42
Grandeur, 105–6, 108, 194 n. 40
Gregory the Great, 99–101, 188 n. 3, 189n. 5
Group: and the aggressive response, 67–68; and basic assumptions, 63–64; binding ties of, 65; defined, 51, 178 n. 32; and entrainment, 20; Freud and, 54, 56, 58; gathering of, 65; irrational aspect of, 53, 66; Le Bon and, 52–54; and loss of individuality, 53; Mc-Dougall and, 55–56; and organization, 58; pathology and, 18, 52, 58, 61, 176 n. 13; and psychosis, 63, 65; ungathered, 64; work aspect of, 65–67
Group mind (âme collective), 17–18, 51–53, 58–61
Group Mind (McDougall), 55
Group psychoanalysis, 179 n. 34
Group psychology, 25, 52, 62

Hallucination: and bodily intelligence, 158; of the breast, 37; as empty hole, 100; and expenditure of energy, 40; and fixity, 38; and inertia, 147–48; physicality of, 95; as projective phenomenon, 29; and repression, 39, 106, 109; and self-containment, 171 n. 39
Harvey, William, 92
Hatred, 27, 41, 58, 63–64
Health, 142, 152, 156–57, 159
Heart, 85–86, 97, 114–15. See also Sealing of the heart
Heimann, Paula, 26–27
Herd instinct, 55, 66, 176 n. 13
History, personal, 6–7, 85–87, 121–22, 195 n. 9
Hobbes, Thomas: on action, 104; and individual thought, 202 n. 31; on meditation, 126; opponents of, 166n. 4; on reason, 160, 184 n. 10
Hochschild, Arlie, 155
Horace, 101, 190 n. 7, 191 n. 14
Hormones: and acknowledgment of communication, 144; and affect-related drives, 9–10; and aggression, 68, 85; and attractor-receptor model, 112; and the blood, 136; and the couple, 84; and demons, 115; and di-

rectionality, 112, 185 n. 19; and emotional states, 78, 184 n. 14; and the environment, 73; and the fetus, 16, 79–80; and gender, 83–84; in group aggression, 68; and human agency, 77; and images, 71; and individual differences, 11; and intentionality, 75–76; language of, 141; masculine and feminine, 185 n. 26; overproduction of, 145; and pheromones, 69, 72, 78; and positioning, 9; projection of, 83; releasing and inhibiting, 81; and resistance, 85–86; signatures of, 86–87; and smell, 10, 52, 72, 165 n. 1; and the social, 52–53; and stress, 80–82, 165 n. 1, 168–69n. 20; and unemployment, 71–72; in utero, 21
Hume, David, 104
Hunger, 39, 134–35
Hypnosis, 53–58, 76, 184 n. 9
Hypothalamus, 81, 87, 184 n. 14

Id, 145–46
Identification, 30, 49, 57–58, 73. See also Projective identification
Ignatius of Loyola, St., 117, 194 n. 40
Image: and aggression, 71, 73; and the body, 108, 150, 201 n. 18; and comparison, 110; and crowd violence, 72; and hormones, 71; as physical force, 10, 16; physiological response to, 182 n. 65; and repression, 37, 39
Imaginary, 108–11
Immortality, 149, 151
Imprint, 37–38
Individual: antecedents of, 77; and the crowd, 53–62, 177 n. 27; and the environment, 6–8; formation of, 25; and group affect, 73; history of notion of, 2; in neo-Darwinism, 74; and neglect of transmission, 17; and objectivity, 19
Inertia: and deadly sins, 98; and depression, 22, 34, 100–101; as drive turned inward, 112; and the ego, 130; and evil, 192 n. 16; and identity, 109; and obsessional neurosis, 192n. 19; as resting place for devil, 191 n. 11; and sloth, 100–101, 188 n. 3, 191 n. 11; social, 162; and subjective standpoint, 147–48
Ingold, Tim, 88
Intelligence, bodily, 136–37, 140–41, 144, 153–54, 158, 161

Passion: and affect, 5; definitions of, 4, 105, 166 n. 4; for Hobbes, 104; for Kant, 41, 130–31, 197 n. 19; and living attention, 41; modulations of, 104; as passification, 101–5; and positioning, 197 n. 19; and reason, 120–21; as site of struggle, 104; Spinoza on, 193 n. 23; taxonomy of, 193 n. 29; as true nature, 105

Passivity, 93, 102–3, 107, 109–10

Pathology: and deadly sins, 22; and emotionality, 63; of group, 18, 52, 58, 61, 176 n. 13, 177 n. 27; and maternal environment, 90; transmission of affect as, 26

Pathways, living, 153, 183 n. 5

Pausing, 141, 144–45, 148

Pepitone, Anthony, 59

Perception, human, 22, 77, 107, 153. *See also* Sight

Pheromones: and attractor-receptor model, 112; communication and, 68–69; defined, 180 n. 53; and entrainment, 9–10; and fear, 111; and formation of the fetus, 79–80; and gender, 83; and hormones, 69, 72, 78; and intentionality, 75–77, 183 n. 5; and menstrual synchrony, 168 n. 18, 180–81 n. 54; overload of, 82; overproduction of, 145; and primary repression, 186 n. 34; research on, 182–83 n. 4; and sealing of the heart, 114; and social construction of gender, 187 n. 42

Physicality: of affects, 6; of the Fall, 191 n. 16; of fantasies, 109; of feelings, 94; of good and evil, 99; of hallucination, 95; of language, 32; and object-relations theory, 41; of positioning, 22; of psychic reality, 188 n. 45; and the soul, 103; of urges, 156; of vibration, 71, 96

Planets, 189 n. 5, 190 n. 5, 191 n. 10, 191 n. 15

Pleasure, 105–6, 116

Port-Royal Logic, 118

Positioning: comparison of, 122; emotional, 9; and fantasy, 22; and hormones, 9; and human perception, 22, 107–8; and maternal environment, 91; and the passions, 197 n. 19; and subjective standpoint, 107–9, 145

Poststructuralism, 151, 158

Pregnancy. *See* Fetal development; Maternal environment

Pride, 100, 108, 124

Projection: of anger, 185–86 n. 28; benefits of, 49; and boundaries, 11–12, 26, 134; and cohesion of negative affects, 106; defined, 29; and depression, 15; and the ego, 130; and envy, 6, 30; and foreclosure, 95; and formation of the unconscious, 38; and the foundational fantasy, 14; and hormones, 83; by infant, 37; and judgments, 5, 111–13, 134; and masculinity/femininity, 42; onto mother, 13, 20; of one's position, 122; and pain, 95; resistance to, 14; and self-containment, 113–14; and self-definition, 15

Projective identification, 29–30, 172–73 n. 13

Psyche, 12, 20, 113, 156. *See also* Ego; Soul

Psychosis, 33, 52, 63–65, 107, 132, 179 n. 34

Psychotherapy: blaming the mother and, 15; and release of energy, 107, 113, 196 n. 10; success of, 13–14; transmission in, 2, 20, 24–29, 31

Race riots, 60, 67

Racism, 15, 119

Rationalization, 75–76

Reason: and the crowd, 61; and faith, 132, 153; Hobbes on, 160, 184 n. 10; and living attention, 41; and the logic of life, 150; and love, 132; and passion, 120–21; versus self-interest, 160

Reductionism, 4, 21, 23

Reich, Wilhelm, 142

Religion, 22–23, 118, 122–23, 126, 132–33, 198 n. 23

Repetition, 200 n. 17

Repression: and aggression, 49; consciousness of, 155; in dreams, 107; and the eighth sin, 100; and energy, 12, 18, 42, 106, 109; and fixity, 38; and foreclosure, 95; of hallucination, 39, 106, 109; lifting of, 113; primary, 37–39, 99–100, 109, 186 n. 34; secondary, 39, 100, 112; and sloth, 101; of testosterone-associated affects, 85–86

Resistance: collective, 65; and discernment, 11, 23, 129; and energy, 130; to the ego, 134, 138; for Freud, 57; Gandhi and, 135; of individual in group, 73; love and, 132, 138; nature

Smell (cont.)
97–98; and discernment, 94, 136–37,
188 n. 2; and entrainment, 9; and fear,
111; and the group, 52; and hormones,
10, 52, 72, 165 n. 1; and intentionality,
75, 77; and language, 154–55, 173 n.
17; as methodological tool, 19; and the
newborn, 84; and pheromones, 69,
180–81 n. 55; and sealing of the heart,
114; and sensing, 139–40; and shaping
of affect, 21; and sight, 10–11, 23, 137;
and social environment, 169 n. 22; and
subjective standpoint, 136–38
Smelser, Neil, 59
Social, the: and affects, 46, 65, 134–35;
and atmosphere, 1–2; and the biological, 1–3, 5, 7, 19, 21, 23, 74–75; and
discernment, 134–35; and entrainment, 49; and the flesh, 25; and hormones, 10, 52–53, 77, 185 n. 26; and
new maladies of the soul, 112; and
pheromones, 187 n. 42; and religious
and cultural codes, 134; and sealing of
the heart, 139; and smell, 169n. 22; in
transmission, 3; and vibration, 71
Sociology, 165 n. 2
Soul, 97, 102–5, 129, 136, 188–89 n. 5
Soul journey, 188–89 n. 5
Sound: and cognitive theory, 178 n. 33;
and deception, 181 n. 60; and entrainment, 11, 70; and groups, 57; and intensification of drives, 60; physicality
of, 71; prejudice in favor of, 27, 60
Spinoza, Baruch: and adequate causes,
101–2, 192 n. 19, 192–93, n. 21; on becoming one with God, 161; and meditation, 117; on striving, 102, 193 n. 23;
on the will, 156
Spirits, 98–99, 115, 120–21, 191 n. 10,
192n. 19. See also Demons
Spiritual Exercises (Ignatius of Loyola),
194 n. 1
Splitting, 39, 64, 108, 113, 149, 152, 154
Standpoint, subjective: and acknowledgment of communication, 144–45; and
affect, 13–14, 19; and aggression, 110;
and chains of causality, 187 n. 44; and
comparison, 109; and the ego, 118;
and energy, 36, 148, 157; and geomet-
rical positioning, 107–9, 145; irra-
tionality of, 151; and science, 94–95,
150, 152; and self-containment, 147;
and the signifier, 152; and slowing of

drive, 48; and smell, 136–38; and system, 94, 142–44; and visual perception, 109, 150
Stern, Daniel, 14, 20, 33, 41
Steroids, 80–81, 83, 35
Stoics, 190 n. 7
Stress, 80–87, 48–49, 165 n. 1, 168–69 n. 20
Striving, 75–76, 102, 93 n. 23
Structuralism, 142–43, 199 n. 4
Subject. See Standpoint, subjective
Subject/object dichotomy: and cogni-
tion, 171 n. 43; and discernment, 150;
and feeling, 93–94; history of, 77, 97;
and foundational fantasy, 20; and log-
ics of the flesh, 148; and perception,
109; and retreat of transmission, 19;
and self-containment, 2; shift in, 157;
and suppression of knowledge, 23
Suggestibility, 53–57
Symbolization, 66, 149, 178–79 n. 33
Sympathetic nervous system, 80–81,
167–68 n. 13, 176 n. 14, 183 n. 5, 184 n. 17
Systems, 94, 142–44, 151, 154, 158, 199 n.
4

Talmud, 97–98
Taxonomy: of crowds, 181 n. 62; of elements of thought, 41–42; of emotions,
3–5, 165–66 n. 4, 166 n. 4, 194 n. 34; of
passions, 193 n. 29
Teresa of Avila, St., 117
Testament of Reuben, 99, 101
Testament of the Twelve Patriarchs, 99
Testosterone: and anger, 77; and the environment, 84; and gender, 83–84; and
mania, 85–86; and odor, 182 n. 66; and
profession, 85–86, 186 n. 31; and the
social, 185 n. 26; and stress, 80; and
unemployment, 71–72
Thalidomide, 91–92
Thomson, D'Arcy, 78
Thought: and affect, 7, 113–14; and attention, 49–50, 140; of body, 145–46;
and feeling, 23, 183 n. 5; and language,
141; and the life drive, 40; and love,
131–32; and struggle, 184 n. 12
Thoughtfulness, 125, 183 n. 5
Thrive, failure to, 34–35
Tilly, Charles, 61
Time, 64, 147–48, 189 n. 5, 199 n. 1
Touch, 31–32, 59–60, 69–70, 165 n. 1,
180–81 n. 55
Transformation, symbolic, 149, 152

Trauma, 47–48, 196 n. 16, 200–201 n. 17
Trotter, Wilfred, 52, 54–55, 57, 65–66, 72

Unconscious: of analyst in patient, 33; birth of, 38; feelings and, 183 nn. 5 and 7; and the formation of symptoms, 107; in group, 54; as methodological tool, 19; and neuroendocrinology, 77; as the parents' fantasies, 32; and rationalization, 75–76; and the senses, 94–95; transmission's retreat to, 18

Valency, 66
Vices, 189–90 n. 5, 191 nn. 14–15
Violence: as catharsis, 67; causes of, 169 n. 24; group, 53, 61–62, 67–68, 72; and the image, 72; increase in, 48; and manhood, 169–70 n. 26; and restraint, 85, 124; spectator, 61, 67, 178 n. 32, 179 n. 49; and toxicity, 22. *See also* Aggression
Virtues, 13, 122–25, 131, 189–90 n. 5
Visualization, 153, 155, 201 n. 18

Wenzel, Siegfried, 190 n. 7
Will, 76, 104–5. See also Free will
Winnicott, Donald, 33
Words: censorship of, 140; and concentration, 122; and conscious consciousness, 155; and the crowd, 54; and feelings, 5, 120, 140, 183 n. 5; and release, 149; and trauma, 200 n. 17

Yates, Frances, 189 n. 5

Zimbardo, Philip, 59

The Transmission of Affect